LEARNING AT WORK

Also by the same authors:

The Dark Side of Behaviour at Work: Understanding and Avoiding Employees Leaving, Thieving and Deceiving (2004)

Learning
at WORK

Excellent practice from best theory

John Taylor

Adrian Furnham

palgrave
macmillan

First published 2005 by
PALGRAVE MACMILLAN
Houndmills, Basingstoke, Hampshire RG21 6XS and
175 Fifth Avenue, New York, N.Y. 10010
Companies and representatives throughout the world

PALGRAVE MACMILLAN is the global academic imprint of the Palgrave Macmillan division of St. Martin's Press, LLC and of Palgrave Macmillan Ltd. Macmillan® is a registered trademark in the United States, United Kingdom and other countries. Palgrave is a registered trademark in the European Union and other countries.

ISBN-13: 1–4039–4574–7
ISBN-10: 1–4039–4574–8

This book is printed on paper suitable for recycling and made from fully managed and sustained forest sources.

A catalogue record for this book is available from the British Library.

Library of Congress Cataloging-in-Publication Data

Taylor, John.
    Learning at work : excellent practice from best theory / John Taylor and Adrian Furnham.
        p. cm.
    Includes bibliographical references and index.
        ISBN 1–4039–4574–8
        1. Organizational learning. 2. Employees—Training of. I. Furnham, Adrian.
II. Title.

HD58.82.T39 2005
58.3'124—dc26   2005049832

10 9 8 7 6 5 4 3 2 1
14 13 12 11 10 09 08 07 06 05

Printed and bound in Great Britain by
Creative Print & Design (Ebbw Vale), Wales

For Memsahib and The Dauphin (AF)
For Anne, Pammie and Norah (JT)

Contents

List of Figures

List of Tables

Preface

Like so many good things in life, the idea for this book came at lunch. On this occasion, the two authors and their managing editor at Palgrave Macmillan, Stephen Rutt, thought first about a book on the blossoming world of coaching. We wanted to ask questions about the new profession of coaching and whether the theory, processes and standards are rigorous.

Both the authors have coached, mentored, counselled and delivered a wide variety of training in many countries with varied audiences and clients. It quickly became apparent that while much had been written on the subject of coaching, most of the books were light on the theory of learning.

It did not take long to recognize that this detachment from theory was true not just of coaching, but also traditional training and the other blossoming industry, learning based on technology. *Learning at Work* has one foot firmly in the academic camp of learning theory and the other in the camp of the practicing coach, trainer and designer of technology-based learning.

In the process, we not only refined our own knowledge but also explored new territory. We had both been involved in discussions about whether it was possible to assess an individual's ability to learn, sometimes described as someone's "potential to develop". Was it, for example, purely a factor of intelligence? We conclude there are a number of other factors which influence someone's ability to learn. We initially called this "learnability", a rather ugly word. As we worked on the model we adopted the phrase "Learning Quotient" – a natural progression from IQ, and EQ! More work has to be done to make the model more accessible to practitioners, but for those, particularly in the field of recruitment, who want to assess whether candidates can still learn new things, there is a methodology presented here.

There were surprises. Some of the best training happens in organizations not always associated with academia. The British army for example has long adopted practices, which could come straight out of the theory books. Their slogan of training practice: "explanation, demonstration, imitation and practice" has its roots firmly in the camp of Kolb's experiential learning. Similarly their slogan for the instructor: "tell them what you're going to tell them, tell them and tell them what you've told them" is recognizable in academic works on adult learning and memory theories.

Slightly perturbing are the serious practitioners who go about their business and write on their subjects without any reference to or concern with what theory-based research has established. The question, for example, about whether coaching should be directive or non-directive attracts strong debate, particularly among the non-directive school. They base their views on practice, which is fine except that they become dismissive of the more directive methods, which have had success over many centuries.

Similarly, consultants and some trained psychologists (who should know better) acquire an affinity for one particular psychometric test, often to the exclusion of others. They have learned how that instrument can be used and then attempt to use it in a variety of situations, many inappropriate. Some tests are better than others, but none can be applied to every situation.

One of the functions of *Learning at Work* is to open windows and alternatives to practitioners and buyers of training. Management consultants and writers have taken many ordinary words from the English language and twisted them to mean different things. Those involved in human resources are more guilty than most. Coaching, development, competences have all taken on a new meaning, which to the uninitiated are confusing. Furthermore, training and coaching are presented as difficult skills or "arts", best left to experts. Too many managers do not try to help their staff learn new skills. Coaching and training are not difficult skills.

In *Learning at Work* we have tried to put learning in the context of sound theory. We hope it is also practical and that it encourages people in the work place to become better at passing on their knowledge, skills and values.

Acknowledgements

It is hard not to learn from others. Those who have helped us with this book about learning include: Alison, Aly, Lawrence, Carole, Adrian, Pammie, David, Lindsay, Kris, Bob, Jackie, Svein, Mohammed, Roger, Clare, Simon, Ann-Marie, Ian (at least two of them), Paul, Anthony, Abstracts, Steve, Christopher, Laura, Lois, Stephen, Saleh, Marie, Micheline, Colette, Nick, the Riff Raff, all those students of training for trainers who wittingly or unwittingly contributed, as well as Simon who has to tolerate JT as a co-trainer, Roger and Chris for asking the questions which led to the creation of the Learning Quotient Model and Stephen for sowing the first seeds of this book.

Stephen and his team at Palgrave and those at Aardvark, who made the production of this book as effortless as possible, deserve, as ever, our special thanks.

Every effort has been made to trace all the copyright holders but if any have been inadvertently overlooked the publishers will be pleased to make the necessary arrangements at the first opportunity.

Introduction

"There is nothing so practical as a good theory." (*Kurt Lewin 1890–1947*)

Learning, like teaching, is a core life skill. It is commonplace; everyone does it. When there is an urgent critical need to learn we can do it. Babies and children grasp life's essentials quickly enough. But as we grow older, individuals move in different directions and at a different pace. Learning, while still essential for our happiness if not survival, is not as instinctive as it was. We need help, some would say direction, to keep up with others. Nowhere is that more apparent than in the workplace.

Employers demand skills, many of which are not taught by parents, school or university. Furthermore, in today's competitive world, employers are not just looking for people with knowledge and skills but those who have appropriate work and life values. They want staff who have commitment, who are going to win new business against the odds, who will go the extra mile.

But trainers and the professional institutions that promote and look after their concerns (ASTD in the US and CIPD in the UK) frequently lament the fact that they are not taken seriously. They believe they warrant a place on the board of directors. But do they deserve it? Are they truly professional? Do they know their job? Do they really earn their keep and deliver a high-quality product?

Training, coaching and the associated learning technologies have become big business and yet the professions are unregulated; anyone can claim to be a trainer or coach and cash in on the business needs of an ever more skill-hungry workforce.

Perhaps because learning is so commonplace, people think it is instinctive, a gift which most people share. We all know how to do it because we have

> *If money is your hope for independence, you will never have it. The only real security that a man will have in this world is a reserve of knowledge, experience, and ability.*
>
> Henry Ford 1863–1947
> American industrialist

experienced it ourselves and have taught others. Senior executives and many staff therefore believe that trainers have an easy life and do not deserve much more than a decent salary. They think this despite the fact that many cannot put together a decent presentation let alone plan, deliver or evaluate a training course.

Trainers do not always help their cause. Practitioners can go about their business and not know why they are doing something and easily become subject to fads and fashions. The world of training has plenty of those. Many new learning ideas, done in the right place and at the right moment, can help, but, in the hands of the unknowledgeable, they can, at best, be useless and at worst dangerous.

The issues are similar with technology-based training, but more complicated. The learner is distant, there is little if any human contact, there is a bigger premium on using good visual aids and the new technologies are so complex that specialists need to build the programs. The future should be bright for e-learning and other technology-based learning. But can it deliver the promises made by many on its behalf?

In the modern world of competitive global business, of ever better qualified employees and increasing labor turnover, retraining older staff and the plethora of new technologies put the learning profession under greater pressure to deliver. At present trainers and coaches rely on learners wanting to move on. The trainer often needs to do little more than put new knowledge in front of students and let them absorb it. Knowledge of the process of memory and learning will become fundamental to the professions of training and coaching.

Practice has also developed over the years through trial and error. It works, but why? What is the scientific basis for the systems that have grown in the learning environment? Too much training and coaching happens without the deliverers understanding why it works or indeed if it works.

CEOs and directors considering the training options in their organization have a wealth of choice, from the traditional prospectus offered by training departments around the world, to specialized coaching options often offered to high flyers. Exotic technologies suggest there is a quick fix.

> *It is always in season for old men to learn.*
> Aeschylus, Agamemnon

Training is experiencing some tectonic shifts as its world has to absorb the impact of new words and concepts (learning rather than training, blended learning, learning organizations as well as the remarkable increase in coaching and e-learning). Are these shifts really changing the shape of learning or will the learning crust settle back into something familiar?

Statistics provided by the leading professional bodies of learning in the US-based American Society for Training and Development (ASTD) and the UK-based Chartered Institute of Personnel and Development (CIPD) show that at the beginning of the 21st century, coaching and e-learning are increasingly popular on both sides of the Atlantic.

This has caused some excitement and both disciplines receive much coverage in their research and publications. Books on both subjects are regularly reviewed in their house magazines. But they tend to play down the fact that instructor-led classroom training still accounts for the biggest proportion of training.

According to the ASTD's *2004 State of the Industry*, over 60% of training is still done in the classroom (Sugrue and Kyung-Hyun 2004, p. 14). In the UK the CIPD found that "the emerging new orthodoxy still finds an important place for the training course. In fact on balance respondents report an increase in the level of formal classroom training offered over the past few years." (Sloman 2004, p. 31). The popularity of coaching and e-learning is, however, rising more rapidly.

Other statistics produce slightly different figures but the picture is similar: classroom learning still dominates but coaching and e-learning are increasing their share. Other concepts such as blended learning are also increasing in popularity.

Rather than trying to convince the reader that any one method, mode, mantra or mindset is best, *Learning at Work* puts the business of learning into the context of learning theory and analyses how practice matches what is known about how the mind works. There are many theories, some of which are based on scientific research and have been exposed to critical academic analysis as well as trialed in the workplace. Other "theories" have caught people's imagination; perhaps because they claim a quick fix or offer the ultimate training solution.

This book starts with the assumption that like all professions, there should be a strong knowledge base to their work. In the case of learning this means knowing about how the memory works and how people, particularly adults, learn best. The early chapters describe the theoretical underpinning of best practices in the learning business.

Learning at Work goes on to examine the options available to companies and organizations who are looking for the most effective ways of developing, teaching and training their staff. It puts the options of coaching and e-learning along with more traditional forms of learning into the context of learning in the workplace.

Managers, trainers and coaches often come across people who are reluctant to learn. This phenomenon does not apply only to those who feel they are too old, but to young people with excellent educational backgrounds and the highest IQ. Others who come with unexceptional backgrounds absorb new knowledge and learn new skills easily and with alacrity. Suggestions of slacking or lack of commitment begin to appear.

The more enlightened trainers or coaches will give such individuals more time and even call in specialists to help. However, do we really understand what is happening? Why should one individual, capable in every necessary respect, be unable to take on some new learning? Is it specific personality traits, some competence that is lacking or is it to do with self-esteem? Sports coaches know only too well that the state of mind of a sportsperson can profoundly affect the game of an individual or team. The same is true at work, although few people realize it.

People do lose confidence or fail to engage in a particular subject. They have the necessary intellectual horsepower and the determination, but somehow they fail to develop, to understand and learn. Chapter 3 analyses

> *If you think educa-*
> *tion is expensive, try*
> *ignorance.*
>
> Derek Bok, president
> Harvard University

the factors which contribute to someone's ability to learn a particular subject. New theory is developed to help to judge someone's learning quotient (their "learnability", that is, ability to learn). Conscious of why someone may be finding learning difficult, the trainer, coach or manager will be better equipped to help that person address the issues and develop properly.

There is no alternative to developing staff. It is not easy to train or coach well, although many people can do an average job. For most CEOs and budget managers, however, OK is not enough. Excellence in the learning business will come from sound knowledge of the theory and being able to put it into practice. *Learning at Work* aims to help those responsible for any aspect of learning to achieve excellence.

1 Overview

Learning is not compulsory, neither is survival. *(Demming 2000)*

Attitudes are more important than facts. (*Karl Menninger 1893–1990*)

If I had to name a driving force in my life, I'd name passion every time. (*Roddick and Miller 1991*)

Your attitude determines your altitude. *(Covey 2004)*

1.1 Introduction

The L word is spreading. People with a particular learning style work in action learning groups in a learning organization. They are encouraged to indulge in lifelong learning or blended learning, and maybe e-learning after a learning needs analysis.

But what needs to be learnt, by whom and when is not always clear. What is clear to any training manager is that the world is neatly divided into learno-phobes and learno-philes. The former strongly resist all learning initiatives, the latter embrace them all.

Naturally attention is focussed on the non-believers and non-combatants. Who are they and why do they resist? Old dogs, senior people and the uncommitted make up many of the opt-out, won't play, non-learners or at least those who don't want to be taught.

There are two antonymous proverbs: "you are never too old to learn", and "you can't teach an old dog new tricks". Which is true? Does this explain why people resist and seem unwilling to learn? Is it only a matter of age?

CEOs and directors, considering the training options in their organization, have a wealth of choice, from the traditional prospectus offered by training departments around the world, to specialized coaching options often offered to high flyers.

What are those people around the learner, coach, trainer, mentor, doing? Penny Hackett, writing in the CIPD textbook *Introduction to Training* (2000, p. 5) says: "If training is to be of any use it has to be about helping people to learn rather than trying to teach. Not all organizations recognize this as clearly as they might, but for anyone aspiring to work in the training function it must be rule number one." The concept of "helping people to learn" is one of the most common themes in the written work on these subjects, and coaches, mentors and trainers all buy into it.

For the purposes of this book, learning is defined as:

> Helping a person or persons acquire new knowledge, new or improved skills, or adopt new beliefs and values in order that they can perform more effectively at work.

Some writers draw a distinction between "education" and "learning". Joan Wright distinguished the two terms as follows:

> Education is an activity undertaken or initiated by one or more agents that is designed to effect changes in the knowledge, skills and attitudes of individuals, groups or communities. The term *education* emphasizes the educator, the agent of change who presents stimuli and reinforcement for learning and designs activities to induce change... The term *learning* in contrast, emphasizes the person in whom change occurs or is expected to occur. Learning is the act or process by which behavioural change, knowledge, skills and attitudes are acquired. Learning is not necessarily accompanied by intent, either on the part of the learner or some other actor. Much learning is acknowledged to be incidental, acquired without a conscious purpose. (Wright 1980, p. 100)

1.2 Theory and Practice

There is a fortunate coincidence between theory and some current practice. Indeed many practitioners have been able to build a successful business on the commercialization of theories. It would be nice to see a reference and some recognition of the original work in their literature, but so is the way of the business world and in any event their methods are mostly soundly based.

Of concern also, many serious writers on the subject of learning and its associated disciplines make only a passing reference to the theory. Even less effort is sometimes made to link what is known about learning and memory with their own process of helping others or vice versa.

In practice, most learning in the workplace relies on the work of David Kolb and his theories of experiential learning. Instruments such as Honey and Mumford's learning styles questionnaire are based on Kolb's work and trainers have for some time now taken their students through the various stages of the learning cycle.

Other theories have some relevance to the workplace. The CIPD recently produced a report which, having recognized Kolb's posi-

> *Education is when you read the fine print. Experience is what you get if you don't.*
>
> Pete Seeger (1919–) American folksinger and songwriter

tion in the theory of learning in the workplace, went on to describe four clusters of learning theory: behavioral, cognitive, constructional and social (Reynolds et al. 2002).

1.2.1 Learnability (learning quotient)

Recruiters of high-quality staff often challenge the psychologist or management consultant and ask for a judgement or instrument which will be able to help identify those who have stopped learning. They are looking for some kind of litmus test to show whether an individual will be able to take on not just the new skills of the organization but also the culture: the beliefs and values of their new employers.

There are plenty of pundits in the field. The evidence shows that it should be possible to make an informed judgement. There are three factors, which appear to predict willingness to take part in learning. Two are pretty immutable and they effect the third which fortunately is. The first factor is our *learning history*, specifically our experience of secondary school and beyond. Experience of exam success and failure shapes expectations of the learning process: how easy/difficult it is; how much fun it all is; and the cost–benefit analysis.

To a large extent these expectations are shaped by the whole business of social comparison. This means how well a person has done compared (as he/she sees it) to their peers. Thus the peer group is fundamentally important to the whole business. At school and university people get a sense of their ability, their preferred learning style and how good they are at learning new things.

Over the years adults develop a series of ever more elaborate stories justifying their lack of success in educational contexts. Poor teaching, undiagnosed cognitive problems, poor facilities, various types of discrimination all feature highly. On the other hand, learning success can neatly and succinctly be attributed to sheer ability, plus a little effort.

Adults at work have strong memories of learning contexts. They have clear beliefs about how right they are; what is easy to learn and what's not. And, not unnaturally, they will strongly resist being "shown up" or having to endure tedious and difficult tasks that bring little obvious benefit.

The past is a different country. It is done. But memories can be changed and they influence strongly how people approach any new learning. Indeed the great rise in cognitive behavior therapy attests to success in changing memories and beliefs. Clearly good experiences in the past predict willingness and (also probably) ability to do so in the future.

The second factor refers to a person's actual *intelligence and personality*. Bright people learn faster; they are able to learn more complicated things. People need to be bright enough to learn whatever is being taught. It is harder to learn Mandarin than Spanish. Bright people, particularly those with a good ear, do better.

The question then is roughly what level of intelligence should be the "cutoff" point for each learning exercise. And related to this is whether people have a realistic view of their own intelligence. Most do, but because of inaccurate feedback there are the problems of hubris and humility: the less bright who think they are clever, and the talented who seem unsure of their ability. Testing people thoroughly and giving them accurate, honest feedback on their performance should overcome the problem.

Three personality variables are clearly implicated in the whole learning business: *conscientiousness, neuroticism* and *openness* to experience. Conscientiousness, or whatever synonym one prefers – diligence, the work ethic, achievement striving, prudence – is a good predictor of learning success. The conscientious work harder, longer and smarter. They take learning seriously. They put in extra effort and are usually suitably rewarded. Neuroticism, on the other hand, is a poor predictor of learning willingness and success. Neurotics are anxious and easily depressed by setbacks. They worry a lot. And their anxiety is often self-handicapping. They tend to be more tense, and more prone to illness (real or imagined) and tend to go absent more. A moderate amount of worry may be good news as it may motivate people to try harder. But go above this level and one has known learning problems.

Openness to experience is about willingness to try something new, particularly to explore new ideas, emotions and experiences. It is about curiosity and creativity. It is more than a "have-a-go mentality". It is partly about exploration and the joy of the new. It is a good predictor of both ability and willingness to learn.

So to have bright, conscientious, open and stable people in the organization bodes well. But there is something else which is influenced by all the above factors, and that is *self-esteem* or *self-belief*. It's about confidence in one's ability and not being afraid to be seen as in need of help.

Indeed, the reason why senior executives often eschew training courses is not about time (the favored excuse) or even a cost–benefit analysis. It is the fear of being "shown up" as less able and knowledgeable than they like to pretend. They are usually much happier to do one-on-one learning because it is private, hence the popularity of coaching, which is often a mixture of counseling and teaching.

All clinicians will tell you that self-esteem is difficult but possible to budge. They will also tell you that it often bares little relation to reality. Just as anorexic patients see themselves as obese, so some talented, able people see themselves as "pretty average". And vice versa but these overconfident, even arrogant types are another story.

The good trainer knows that many adults are nervous about learning, particularly older people who probably did not have the educational opportunities of the young and who feel, often quite correctly, that their memory and cognitive agility is not what it used to be. The good trainer gives hesitant adult learners early experience of success without patronizing them. It also shows them the benefit, and even the joy, of learning something new that is both interesting and useful.

1.3 Choice

One of the problems facing providers of training or learning in the work-place is choice, learning venue, course approach and so on. There is a wealth of literature available and the proponents of each discipline in the learning business are strident in their beliefs that theirs is the best and most effective.

Furthermore some of the old techniques are changing. Training is now much more sophisticated and trainers are conscious of the need to be more professional and listen to their students.

One of the themes of this book is that all forms of learning have their place. An organization which provides its staff with variety is the one that is serving itself and its employees best. People learn in different ways.

It is not the intention of this book to promote any one method over that of others; each has significant advantages and some people prefer a particular style. Equally all have their disadvantages and these need to be clearly understood. The concept of *blended learning,* whereby learners use a combination of learning methods, is a clear recognition of this principle and one which this book endorses, although without the hype that goes with some of the proponents of blended learning.

The circumstances of the learner, the objectives, the nature of the learner, the subject to be learnt and perhaps in too many cases the budget will determine what kind of learning is best for each situation.

Learning for the purposes of this book is broken down into four categories:

▷ Learning in a group (traditional training)
▷ One-to-one learning (coaching, mentoring and so on)
▷ Technology-based learning (e-learning, videos, CD-ROMs and so on)
▷ Self-learning.

This section reviews each and compares the principal methods of learning used.

1.3.1 Learning in groups

The work-based classroom is no longer the place where the instructor stands up, delivers for an hour (or more) and departs. The good trainer is sensitive to the group's needs and desires. This means speaking for relatively short periods of time, giving the group the chance to interact, and providing opportunities for the group to test out what they have learnt.

Training is what everyone knows about. Many companies and virtually every public service department have a training department, some trendily renamed "learning department" or "learning suite". They publish a prospectus with a wide variety of courses: the ubiquitous IT training courses together with those on core skills and management. Within a few days of starting work, if not the first day itself, new entrants go to training department for an induction course.

There are many advantages and disadvantages of the classroom. The advantages are substantial and the method is unlikely to be eliminated from the options available to the learner. It lends itself to the more directive style of learning and is therefore often looked down on by those in the coaching profession who tend to a non-directive style. There is an irony in that many of the books and courses which train coaches adopt a very directive style in putting over their message.

Most, although not all, of the disadvantages of classroom training can be handled by experienced trainers who can design their own courses and therefore allow time for different methods to be deployed as the course continues. On average less than 15% of time on a course is spent listening to lectures. One-to-one sessions with the trainer are now regular features of training and practicing the new skills takes up more time than any other activity.

Table 1.1 Advantages and disadvantages of classroom learning

Advantages	Disadvantages
Economically more efficient (more students per trainer)	Does not cater well for people learning at different speeds
Contributions of others in the class will provide more experience than the trainer alone would	Potential distraction of having other people around
Opportunities for participation by and with others will help learning	Vulnerable to disruption from difficult or disinterested students
Contributions by others will provide variety and can therefore help the learning process	More opportunities for learners to "drift off" and lose concentration
Opportunities for group or team exercises	More difficult to handle the awkward student in a group
Opportunities for syndicate work	Non-professional speakers often dislike the experience of presenting to a group or do it badly
The principal method available for training a team	Students often feel intimidated by others when trying or wanting to contribute

1.3.2 One-to-one learning

Of all the various techniques of learning in the workplace, the past two decades has seen the greatest rise in coaching and executive coaching in particular. Not surprisingly, therefore, it is also the subject of many books, each of which has a special angle and definition. There is no single accepted definition. Furthermore, the boundaries between disciplines such as coaching and mentoring are blurred because definitions of the two (and others such as counseling, consultancy, therapy) overlap.

It is possible to discern amongst all of this some common practices and qualities required by those in the business of delivering one-to-one learning. The issue of directive and non-directive is still controversial. Writers and practitioners from outside the workplace mostly espouse a non-directive style. Managers and supervisors and indeed some learners in the workplace fear the time taken to get messages over in this non-directive manner counts against it.

Managers prefer what they see as a more efficient method, that is, to tell the coachee what to do. There is a place for directive methods, particularly where there are health and safety issues or knowledge is required at the beginning of a learning process.

Mentoring programs are becoming increasingly popular in all kinds of organizations. Mentors are generally outside the line and tend, although not exclusively, to be older, more experienced advisors. Their role is to encourage and guide their mentee.

Table 1.2 Advantages and disadvantages of one-to-one learning

Advantages	Disadvantages
Learning is designed specifically for the needs of the learner	No opportunity to hear others' views
Highly efficient for the learner	Group exercises, discussions and syndicate work are not possible
Time and place can be flexible	Expensive – the coach is only used for one person at a time
Learner will not fear peer criticism	
Can sometimes be conducted by phone or video link	When done in-house can be time-consuming for the manager/coach

1.3.3 Technology-based learning (TBL)

Technology is one of the hot topics in today's world of learning. E-learning is defined by the CIPD as "learning that is delivered, enabled or mediated by electronic technology for the explicit purpose of training in organizations. It does not include stand-alone technology-based training such as the use of CD-ROMs in isolation" (www.cipd.co.uk). Clive Shepherd (2003a) takes a broader view:

> E-learning utilizes computers and computer networks as an additional and complementary channel of communication; connecting learners with media, with other people (fellow learners sources, facilitators) with data (about learning, about media, about people) and with other processing power.

In fact all kinds of technology have been used to help learners for many decades; TV, the video/DVD and the radio have all played their part and continue to do so. The computer has added a new dimension.

But the new technologies do not suit all and it is not applicable to all types of learning; it can however be very effective and relatively cheap and it is surprising what it can achieve. For the "quick win" manager it has enormous attraction: no need for large and expensive classrooms, the work can be done at the desk; no difficult trainers to manage.

People can learn at their own pace. In a classroom all students have to move at the same speed. This inevitably means that the quickest learners become bored and the slowest are out of their depth. Trainers do their best to put people together who are at about the same level, but this streaming is not always possible. TBL provides training for the individuals

> *Technology, especially electronics, is not what you might call my strong point ... I mean all I know about computers wouldn't cover a silicon chip.*
>
> George Bush (1924–)
> 41st president of the United States

and even allows them to have a coffee when they want. Conversely it also panders to the lazy, who will adopt a pace which is gentle and not very challenging – more time away from the desk than is necessary therefore: a gift for the training junky.

Trainers, by and large, dislike speaking from a rigid script. It is dreary and if repeated to classes day after day the ensuing boredom shows in the training and its effectiveness drops. Computers famously do not get bored and do exactly what they are supposed to do.

Good computer programs will be highly interactive and allow students to explore paths of their own choosing, thus satisfying individual curiosity without frustrating others in a class who are not interested in that particular question. Tests can be put in place, which ensure that the student has fully grasped an aspect of a subject before being allowed to move on. At the end, an assessment of the students' overall performance can be made.

However, TBL is not the final solution. Many people have an aversion to computers, particularly long exposure to them. While short spells can be helpful, sitting alone in front of a screen is not only bad physically, but it also dehumanizes people and takes away much of the pleasure of work. Many come to work to interact with other people. Some welcome the fact that the computer needs them to display no social graces, but they are in the minority.

Table 1.3 Advantages and disadvantages of TBL

Advantages	Disadvantages
Efficiency	Some students are not computer literate
Consistency of training	Looking at a screen for long periods is tiring and potentially hazardous to the eyes
Students can develop at own speed	
Students can take a break when they want	Few opportunities for practicing the skills learnt unless they are IT skills
Assessing students can be done easily and fairly	No interaction with human beings
Excellent for some skills, for example IT, flight simulators	

While the potential for TBL and in particular computer training is great, it is matched by the difficulty of finding quality programs, which combine technology with learning theory. A good program requires three equally important inputs: knowledge of the subject to be trained, knowledge of how people learn and finally someone with the IT skills to put the results into an exciting program. All too often one of the skills is missing.

1.3.4 Self-learning

In the world of training and coaching, it is easy to forget that many people happily sit down, on their own initiative, and read, think, and work out many of the answers on their own. Many enjoy hobbies, which are involved with both skill and knowledge acquisition. This may happen formally after a coaching session, reading books suggested by the coach or trainer. It may happen in the bath and in a very informal way, such as watching television or during a chat with friends. Truly motivated workers will take their work home with them and want to learn more and find a solution.

Some individuals seek out like-minded people who wish to improve their knowledge in particular areas. They form, in a sense, self-help groups which meet on a regular basis to acquire knowledge and understanding of topics such as a foreign language or how the stock market works.

Table 1.4 Advantages and disadvantages of self-learning

Advantages	Disadvantages
Very cheap, there may be the occasional claim for a book or magazine subscription	No control over what is being learnt
Being self-motivated, the learner is likely to learn much more than in a classroom	Learner may pick up bad or incorrect information
Can share the knowledge gained with others in the office	

1.4 Comparison of Methods

Learning affects the individual in a variety of ways. New behaviors, ways of doing things and how to approach an issue can all be affected by learning. They are most often broken down into the following categories: knowledge, skills and beliefs and values. The greatest is knowledge. It lies at the heart of all advances in the human condition.

The methods of learning described briefly above are not equally effective for each of these categories. Table 1.5 summarizes their relative effectiveness.

Table 1.5 Comparison of the effectiveness of various learning methods

Method of learning	As applied to knowledge	As applied to skills	As applied to beliefs and values
Training in a group	**Medium to low** – listening to a presentation is one of the least effective ways of learning	**High** – there are many opportunities in a group to exercise and so practice all kinds of skills	**Medium** – trainers exercise most influence through their own example, as role models. It is possible but takes time. The potential in short courses is therefore **low**
One-to-one learning	**Low** – the coach has effectively to give a presentation, something most coaches are loath to do and it is no more effective than it is for the presenter to a large group	**Medium or high** – coaching in the business context tends to be more of a discussion but when applied to such skills as public speaking or driving a car it can be very effective	**High** – over a period of time a coach can become very important to the learner. The potential to influence their beliefs and values increases in direct proportion to the time spent together
Technology-based learning	**High** – a computer can provide the information in a written form, and can then test the student until ready to move on	**High** in IT skills and skills which lend themselves to simulators, **low** in most others, for example those relating to interpersonal skills	**Low** – a computer's influence over people's beliefs and values is relatively limited
Self-learning	**High** – reading, thinking, rationalizing, writing are good ways of accumulating knowledge	**Low** – some skills can be learnt on one's own, particularly if combined with reading, such as IT, but others such as interviewing are difficult	**Low to medium** – people can be influenced by the written word and having seen something or someone impressive will, through their own thought processes, change their attitudes

The judgements in Table 1.5 apply to the motivated high flyer. It would not apply to staff who lacked motivation and ambition and who scored low on a "potential to learn" scale. Table 1.5 is only indicative. Most people learn through a combination of methods. Wise trainers with a group will find time for the slower individuals and give them coaching. Trainers will also provide handouts and bibliographies so their students can spend time reading or thinking about the earlier lessons alone and so encourage self-learning.

On discovering a need for interviewing skills, coaches will look for others to join their sessions or perhaps identify a course. Self-learning with or without a computer may well be part of the curricula.

If the learner has to accumulate large amounts of information or data, he or she should have access to computer programs, books or other written material. If skills are involved, they will need to go on a training course or in some cases use a coach. For IT skills, a computer is very effective. To develop beliefs and values, coaches and mentors are invaluable as well as longer training courses.

1.5 Conclusion

Training is big business and properly skilled staff are essential for any enterprise. The challenge for the organization is to ensure a good return on the investment; the challenge for the provider is to stay at the cutting edge of the business.

The modern version of instructor-led classroom training relies much less on "instruction" and good trainers are conscious of the need to provide support for individuals. The emphasis is on helping people to learn. Coaching and technology are highly effective and valuable methods of learning but they are not a panacea.

Those in the business of learning would do well to learn from each others' disciplines. The trainer can learn how to ask questions and be less "directive"; coaches could be more creative in finding exercises for their learners to practice their new skills; the computer program designer could spend more time understanding the theory of learning. Training managers should be aware of the full breadth of what is available to them and be sure that they are offering staff in their organizations a variety of learning methods.

2 Memory and Learning Theory

2.1 Introduction

Learning and adaptation is fundamental to life and the success of an organization. Without it, an individual will not only fail to prosper but will have to rely entirely on others for survival. Organizations that fail to learn will eventually be engulfed by others keen to remove the competition or strip their dwindling assets.

Learning must be a continuous process. Many people see colleges and universities as places of learning but too frequently assume that, once people have graduated from these institutions, learning or at least institutional learning is complete. But the acquisition of knowledge and skills is a lifelong business.

Lifelong learning occurs in diverse settings: at work, at play and in the home; but primarily in the workplace, where it is of necessity a requirement to keep the job. The question therefore remains how best to ensure that people effectively, efficiently and happily learn in the workplace.

It is not surprising that learning has for centuries been the subject of fascination of first philosophers, then educationalists, psychologists and even politicians. The academic literature is rich with eminent people defining and plotting the process and progress of learners and learning. But a short journey into the literature and a number of surprises emerge:

▷ There is little agreement on how even to define learning
▷ Of the large number of theories on learning, most have *some* relevance to those who make their living out of helping others to learn
▷ Literature on the practical aspects of helping others to learn, coaching training, e-learning and mentoring makes few if any inroads into learning theory (and vice versa)
▷ Paradoxically, theory rarely informs practice or vice versa
▷ Perhaps faced with this complexity and uncertainty, the business world of training and learning contains both the unscrupulous and the charlatan, who peddle evidence-free, quick-fix "solutions" to learning and training problems.

This chapter attempts to bring some order and highlight what is useful for the learner and those helping the learner in the workplace to understand. It will discuss and describe the fundamental facets associated with learning.

The Concise Oxford Dictionary (COD) defines "learn" as: "acquire knowledge of, or skill in, (something) through study or experience or by being taught; commit to memory; become aware of by information or from observation." This is a useful starting point, but does not cover everything required in the modern workplace.

Acquiring knowledge and skills is uncontroversial, but the demand for high performance in organizations has added a third element to the definition – values and beliefs. Other words may occasionally be used, but by this, they mean someone's way of thinking, their approach to a problem, their attitudes; often it is about accepting and following the culture of an organization.

Knowledge is usually thought of as know-how and skills as the successful, behavioral application of know-how. However, attitudes towards learning and training are crucially important in determining whether, how and why knowledge and skills are (or are not) acquired.

The term "learning" emphasizes the person in whom the change occurs or is expected to occur. Learning is the act or process by which behavioral change, knowledge, skills, and attitudes are acquired (Knowles 1998, p. 10).

Boud and Garrick (1999, p. 52) put learning in the context of the organization as follows: "A large proportion, although not all, of an organization's knowledge resides in three human reservoirs, namely (1) the cognitive understandings, (2) the learned skills and (3) the deeply held beliefs of individuals. They go on to quote Quinn: "Bringing the three together has been the success formula for most outstanding teachers, entrepreneurs and coaches whether in education, sports, the professions or general business" (Quinn 1992, p. 254).

Breaking down the learning process into these elements – knowledge, skills, beliefs and values – is important for those in the business of helping people to learn; each demands a different approach by the learner and their trainer, coach or mentor. There may be some overlaps and dangers of oversimplification, but none that take away from the usefulness of this separation of concepts within the definition of learning.

2.1.1 Knowledge

London taxi drivers have to spend months often years learning about their capital city and then take a rigorous test. This is known by them as "doing the knowledge". They are acquiring vast amounts of information about the names of roads and the best routes from one place to another. Once qualified, the driver uses his knowledge to take passengers to their destination by the shortest or quickest route, invariably without reference to a map.

Classically, schools but also universities, put great emphasis on learning facts. In history, pupils learn the names of kings, presidents and prime ministers and the dates of their tenure. In arithmetic, tables are memorized. Law students have to remember the facts and outcomes of large numbers of legal cases as a large part of their coursework. At work, employees have to learn the format of reports, the names of the various departments and significant people in the organization if they are to function properly.

People often need knowledge before they can move to the stage of acquiring related skills. When learning a language, students need to learn the vocabulary, the rules of grammar and the intonations. This is knowledge. A computer can do this much, but translation of a great work of literature into another language requires something else – skill.

Before learning the skill of driving a car, a learner will need some information. In the UK you drive on the left side of the road, in the US and most of Europe you drive on the right. The right pedal on the floor is called an accelerator and when pressed makes the car go faster, the pedal in the middle (manual cars) slows or stops the vehicle. There is of course much more.

2.1.2 Skills

There is knowledge of facts but also knowledge of principles. Thus, doctors' knowledge of the working of a body allows them to diagnose a new case. Similarly, architects' knowledge of engineering allows them to design buildings that do not fall down. Further knowledge of Spanish may help one acquire knowledge of Italian. Knowledge can easily be forgotten, as we shall see, if it is not rehearsed.

So what are these skills? Skill is essentially about doing something. It is about expertise and dexterity: usually observable behaviors. You cannot see knowledge but you can see behavior upon which it is based. As soon as someone wants to do something with their knowledge, they need a skill.

Driving a taxi is a skill, particularly in London! Translation from one language to another is a skill. The way a lawyer interprets a precedent to further the interests of his or her client is a skill. Tiger Woods shows the ultimate skill when driving a ball down the fairway; some would claim the more important skill is when he is on the green and has to putt.

Communication is a greatly desired skill in the workplace. Writing or speaking effectively is a skill much admired by others. Everyone knows the words and how to order them to make sense. That in itself is a skill. But the great communicators do more, they inspire, they make people laugh, they make them feel sad. These too are skills but of a higher order.

Just as people cannot remember everything, not everyone can become as good a golfer as Tiger Woods. Indeed, by definition there can only be one person who can become the greatest in the world in his or her particular skill.

One of the questions learners and trainers have to confront is, can anyone learn a particular skill? The simple answer at this stage is mostly yes. The more difficult question is, how well will the learner be able to perform the skill? There is inevitably a continuum of skill from poor to excellent. Many factors determine the answer to that question.

Assessors of skills will give a finite level that people have to achieve before they can perform the skill on their own. Thus, there are driving tests, examinations and less specifically time that people have to be in a job or role gaining experience before they can move on to the next stage. Qualifications are required before acceptance into many professions.

For this and other reasons trainers place great emphasis on learning objectives. These state not only what learners will be able to do at the end of a training or coaching session but also identify the level they will have attained and the conditions under which they can achieve the objective. This is not some perverse rite which trainers devise to make the lives of students difficult, but reflects what is needed if they are to perform in the workplace (see pp. 66–9 for more on objectives).

Most skills have different levels at which they can be performed. They are judged qualitatively, whereas knowledge is quantitative. At the highest level, a skill is often described as an art. This evokes the beauty, inspiration and mystery of great works of art, unique and highly prized.

The difference between a skill and an art seems to be that the latter cannot easily be taught. People may have particular talents or indeed intuitions that make them particularly good at skilled activities like playing the violin or interviewing patients. Some people contrast art and science, suggesting somehow that the former is mysterious, immeasurable. People sometimes use the term "art" to make their skill that little bit more unattainable, difficult to learn and therefore more valuable. It is a term sometimes used by coaches to describe their skill.

Most skills in the workplace are more prosaic. They can be taken to great heights of accomplishment but most practitioners need only achieve a good or high standard. They need to be good enough.

2.1.3 Beliefs and values

Organizations are interested in more than just building up their knowledge and skill base. They seek to develop beliefs and values in their employees that encourage hard work, integrity, determination, drive or creativity. Each company will have its own version; these often appear in the company's mission and vision statements.

> ▶ Birmingham Area Chapter Vision Statement: "To be recognized as a compassionate organization setting the standard for alleviating human suffering" (http://www.redcrossbirmingham.org/Mission.htm).
>
> ▶ "BP believes in being performance driven, innovative, progressive and green in everything we do and say" (http://bp.com).
>
> ▶ "ABB expects all its employees to uphold the highest standards of ethical behavior and integrity. We believe that ethical and economic values are interdependent and that the business community must always strive to operate within the accepted norms established by national and international authorities.

High business ethics and integrity ensure our credibility. All ABB companies and employees have to conform to the laws and regulations of the countries in which they operate and must fulfill their obligations in a reliable manner. They must insist on honesty and fairness in all aspects of their business and expect the same from their partners" (http://www.abb.com).

Many trainers and writers have adopted the word "attitude" to describe this third attribute. Traditionally, attitude is thought of as having three components: emotional (affective), thinking (cognitive) and behavioral. They partly determine how the brain approaches issues or responds to situations. People respond differently when faced with a beggar on the street. Some give money; others give food, fearing the beggar will use the money on drugs; some stop and talk and try to provide comfort; some will ignore them, on the grounds that they already give money to charity and some will ignore them completely, either because they don't care or because they believe that by giving they will encourage more beggars on the street.

However, for psychologists "attitude" has other, more specific meanings. To avoid confusion, in this book "attitude" has been replaced generally with the words "beliefs and values". Occasionally the word attitude is used and where it does occur it means no more than defined in the COD: "a settled way of thinking or feeling".

People respond to stimuli that confront them based on previous experience. They may respond in that fashion because they have thought through the issues themselves or because someone else influenced them, either in an article or by something said. Whatever their action, they adopt an attitude similar to responding to beggars.

Employers want to influence their employees' approach to certain things as well. It falls to the line managers, trainers, coaches or mentors to encourage and sometimes insist on particular values. For example, employers will want those working in or visiting a building site to wear a hard hat to protect them against injury. Employers can impose a rule on their employees to do so. They can put up notices ordering all visitors to wear a hat, but they have no jurisdiction over them. Unless the employees working on that building site respond to every visitor who is hatless by approaching them and asking them to wear a hat, the rule will quickly fall into disrepute. The workers' response is conditioned by their attitude to safety and caring for others (they may of course need training in the skill of approaching someone and persuading them to do as requested).

More controversially, employers will want to develop particular values and beliefs at work. What should the response be to a call from an important client at 4:30 on a workday afternoon that requires immediate action, likely to take some time to complete? The office hours are 9 to 5 and technically nothing can prevent the worker leaving at 5 whether or not the work is done. For whatever reason, most staff will respond to the client and take whatever action is necessary. They will in effect be putting the office before their personal wishes. This is the kind of attitude to work that employers want.

There are other beliefs and values that employers will want to foster: honesty, trust between colleagues, a no-blame culture, encouraging new ideas, security of documents or property. To some extent the official or unofficial office rule book can be used to impose them but that will rarely be enough. To a large extent, corporate culture consists of unwritten, implicit ideas. The trainer, coach or mentor, amongst others, has a role to play in helping the learner to embrace these attitudes.

A final word in this section about terminology. Many trainers use the word "behavior" instead of skills or attitudes (or beliefs and values). Trainers do of course help people to change or develop behaviors and the use of the word is reasonable in a training or coaching context. There is, however, real advantage in separating out the two parts of behavior – skill and attitude – because they are developed in different ways. This is discussed in more detail in Chapter 3, but the major differences are that attitudes take longer to change or develop than skills and a worker's attitude is much more susceptible to role models than their ability to learn a skill.

A football coach need not be the best player in the world to develop excellent skills in his players. But if he wants his players to work hard in their preparations for a match, their attitude to training will be considerably affected if they discover the coach is out every night at nightclubs and only starting work at 11 am, whereas they are expected to be on the track at 7 am.

2.2 Memory

Before embarking on a journey through the various learning theories and practices, it will be helpful to look at memory. If something has to be learnt, it has to be retained and it has to be retrieved to be useful. Those involved in helping people to learn need to present knowledge, skills, beliefs and values in the most effective way to help people to remember. It is in fact a subject which, surprisingly and inappropriately, receives only scant attention, if any at all, in most books and fewer courses.

Memory as a discipline was left to philosophers until the 1880s when Hermann Ebbinghaus, a German philosopher, broke with tradition and started to analyse memory experimentally and thus brought scientific methodology to the subject. He is perhaps best known amongst trainers for the Ebbinghaus curve of learning, or more precisely a curve demonstrating how quickly people forget (see Figure 2.2, p. 31).

While significant progress has been made in understanding how memory works and there is plenty of useful research for trainers and coaches, much is still a mystery. There are, however, a number of useful concepts which are established. Understanding these will help the trainer, coach and learner.

Baddeley (2003) identifies three kinds of memory; working, short-term and long-term memory (Figure 2.1).

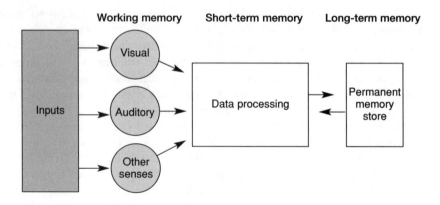

Figure 2.1 **Memory processes**

The working memory allows us to perceive what is happening in the world through the memorization of stimuli from our eyes, ears and sense of touch. Thus when someone hears a click in a room, they know where the noise has come from because the sound reaches our ears at slightly different times. The brain has to remember when the first sound came so that it can calculate the time difference and thus the direction of the sound.

Similarly, vision is not a continuous flow of light, as far as the brain is concerned it is a series of images, which the brain retains for a very short period of time.

Trainers use this memory system to ensure that their messages get through. They have to be clear and not confusing. Too many signals, and the message is likely to be lost in the disorder. John Townsend has experimented over the years and found that when tested after 24 hours, participants' recall of a visual message (80% correct answers) and a "feeling" message (79% correct answers) is almost twice as good as messages from auditory sources (45%) (Townsend 1996, p. 16).

The working memory processes information as it comes into the brain and makes sense of it. Learners listening to a presentation have to remember what was said at the beginning of a sentence and connect it to the rest of the sentence in order to understand what the presenter was saying. It is for this reason that presenters are urged to use short sentences to aid understanding.

Some facts about the brain and memory:

► The brain only weighs 1.4 kilograms

► About 90% of the brain's mass is water

► It burns 25% of the calories we consume

▶ It uses up to 20% of the body's oxygen

▶ The brain has up to 100 billion brain cells (neurons)

▶ Intelligence is related to the number of connections between neurons

▶ There are up to 10 trillion connections

▶ Proper amounts of protein, carbohydrates, the lipid (fat) lecithin and vitamin B1 are essential

▶ Some research suggests that vitamins C and E have an important role in keeping the memory sharp

▶ If the brain is stimulated, it creates more cell branches and therefore boosts intelligence

Sources: Townsend 1996; Malone 2003

2.2.1 Distribution of practice

Ebbinghaus discovered early on that there was an almost linear relationship between the quantity of information learnt and the time devoted to learning. However, there are ways of developing this principle; as Baddeley described it: "The generalization that 'you get what you pay for' is a reasonable rule of thumb, but within this broad framework there are good buys and bad ones, bargains and items that are not worth the asking price" (Baddeley 2003).

Trainers and educationalists usually have to work to a tight timetable. Once they have their students in the training room and away from the desk, they often feel that they have to make the most of that time and deliver their training. Courses are usually a single unit of a day or a number of consecutive days. But is this the best way of learning?

Research shows that it is more efficient to distribute learning packages over a period of time rather than pack them into one marathon effort. This widespread phenomenon is known as the "distribution of practice effect" (Baddeley 2003).

The question of how long a gap between practices is also significant (and what, if anything, should be done in those gaps). When, for example, learning vocabulary for a new language, the sessions are more efficient when there are small gaps, which gradually extend in time. Baddeley uses the example of learning four French words:

stable	l'écurie
horse	le cheval
grass	l'herbe
church	l'église

Working with a teacher, a good routine would look like this:

Teacher	Learner
Stable = l'écurie	
Stable?	l'écurie
Horse = le cheval	
Horse?	le cheval
Stable?	l'écurie
Horse?	le cheval
Grass = l'herbe	
Grass?	l'herbe
Stable?	l'écurie
Horse?	le cheval
Grass?	l'herbe
Church = l'église	
Church?	l'église
Grass?	l'herbe
Church?	l'église
Stable?	l'écurie
Grass?	l'herbe
Horse?	le cheval

When learning a word for the first time, the gap is short but each time the word is recalled correctly, the gap before having to repeat it is increased. If a word is recalled incorrectly, it should be presented after a shorter delay; whenever the learner is correct, the delay should be increased (Baddeley 2003, p. 75).

Each discrete learning session might last, say, 45 minutes and then be repeated the next day. In this way there is a "micro-distribution of practice", combined with a longer distribution effect.

The same principles work for skills. Baddeley worked with the British Post Office and advised on how to train postmen and women to type (this was in support of the Post Office's introduction of postcodes).

Four schedules were offered:

1 two sessions a day each of two hours
2 one session of two hours a day
3 two sessions of one hour a day
4 one session of one hour a day.

The results were clear. Those on the one-hour-a-day schedule learnt much more rapidly, in terms of hours spent in training, than those on more intense daily schedules. Indeed the one-hour-per-day group learnt as much in 55 hours as the four-hours-a-day group learnt in 80 hours. When tested after several months, the one-hour group had retained their skill better than the four-hour group.

The implications of this are clear for the trainer or coach, but there are a couple of qualifications:

▷ the one-hour group took 55 days to learn, while the four-hour group needed only 20 days
▷ the one-hour group were less content with their progress than the four-hour group, because they felt as if they were not achieving results so quickly (Baddeley 2003, pp. 73–5).

A balance needs to be made and there are practical considerations for many trainers. Persuading managers to let their staff get away at regular intervals over a few weeks is probably more difficult than letting them go for a few days at a time. Learners probably feel the same.

E-learning comes into its own when considering how best to distribute training packages. An hour or two a day at the desk is not going to make much impact on an individual's output, but it does require considerable self-discipline.

Knowledge of this effect also reinforces the desirability of reviewing the previous day's work each morning of a course. Going through the previous day's learning will help the learner (as well of course of letting the trainers know whether they need to repeat lessons forgotten or not understood).

> "You can get a good deal from rehearsal
> If it just has the proper dispersal.
> You would just be an ass
> to do it en masse;
> Your remembering would turn out much worsal"
>
> Ulrich Neisser

Adopting new beliefs or values presents the scientist and psychologist with a different problem and there is little research available on the subject. As discussed earlier, establishing new attitudes at work requires different processes. Thus we may have to separate knowledge and skill acquisition from changing beliefs and values. People at work are conditioned by the rules and existing authority establishing compliance, which is gradually replaced by an inner motivation not only to follow the practices but to pursue them actively and encourage others to do the same. The subject is closely associated with motivation to learn and is explored later under that subheading.

2.2.2 Timing

There are a number of considerations which the trainer has to consider associated with the timing of learning. On the micro-scale, when, for example, is a learner most attentive in a presentation? Attention is usually high at the beginning of a session and, depending on the quality of trainer or coach, will diminish thereafter. The length of attention is, for the trainer, depressingly short; perhaps only 7–10 minutes – and that is when everything is in the trainer's favor!

Similarly, attention will return towards the end of a session when learners recognize that they will soon be free and their mind no longer wanders. The lessons from this are:

▷ ensure that important information is included in the first and last few minutes of a presentation
▷ ensure that the presentation is sufficiently varied to maintain maximum levels of attention throughout the presentation.

Trainers and presenters are well aware of the "graveyard slot" – that period in the afternoon after lunch when learners traditionally find it hard to stay awake. There is little doubt that the body has too much to do after a heavy lunch and would rather devote its energies to digestion than brain activity. This suggests that lunches should be light and time given to digest. Alcohol does little if anything to aid attention and memory.

However the whole afternoon need not be written off. Indeed, researchers at the University of Sussex discovered that school children had better long-term recall of lessons learnt in the afternoon than in the morning (Folkard et al. 1977).

2.2.3 Association and mnemonics

The book market is cluttered with authors who make impressive claims about how they will help people to remember. Almost all base their claims, and their own sometimes phenomenal ability to remember, on association systems. Writers such as Tony Buzan and Dominic O'Brien (six times world memory champion) provide many examples of how to develop association systems that will help the learner (although these are more about rote learning than understanding principles).

Even without such sophisticated systems, everyone uses some form of memory aid, be it shopping lists, mind maps, computer software programs such as "tasks" in Microsoft's Outlook or perhaps the most common of all – the diary.

Good trainers recognize that they can help learners by providing mnemonics: systems for improving and aiding the memory. These can be rhymes, alliterative headings or more typically the using the first letter of words to make a more memorable single word. There are some examples of these later in this chapter and also Chapter 4 has an example concerning good feedback in training – "BOOSTS", the feedback should be balanced, owned, objective, specific, timely and provide solutions. Everyone who has attended a management seminar which included how to set objectives will have come across the mnemonic SMARTS, objectives which should be specific, measurable, achievable, relevant, time-bound and stretching.

Remembering how many days in the month has been set for centuries by the following verse:

> 30 days hath September
> April, June and November.
> All the rest have 31
> Save February which has 28.
> Leap year coming once in four,
> February then has one day more.

There are variations but without some such aid, many would struggle to remember. Association or linking the object to be remembered with some fixed list is more sophisticated and requires practice and discipline. It is the method most frequently used by "memory entertainers".

The principle is simple enough; the learner establishes a constant list of items or objects, perhaps those seen along a journey to work (front door, hedge, bus shelter, bus, tunnel). The item to be remembered is then associated with the first subject on the fixed list. Suppose a business executive going to a meeting wants to remember to ask about other clients, the price, delivery time and quality controls. He or she would then associate client with front door, price with hedge, delivery time with bus shelter and quality control with bus.

The secret is to use associations that are very funny, bizarre, rude (as in crude!) or extraordinary in some other way. The image of a client walking through the front door is not enough. As the executive opens the front door, the whole drive is full of potential clients all desperately trying to talk to him. As she comes to the hedge, she notices that someone has put a price tag on the hedge which is exactly that of the Ferrari the husband has been going on about for the last few weeks; at the bus shelter a new timetable has just been posted saying that the next bus is not expected until next week and that depends on the delivery of spare parts for the bus on that route. When the bus eventually does arrive, the interior has the same quality finish as a Rolls-Royce, even the front has a Rolls radiator design.

The memory likes to have something outstanding to remember; the ordinary, the mundane or the plain are only logged in the short-term memory and are therefore easily forgotten.

2.2.4 Chunking

The trainer and the psychologist researching memory, when asked to explain the word "chunking" will approach the subject in slightly different ways but base their work on the same theories or practical experience of what works.

The psychologist may recall the feats of Professor A.C. Aitken of Edinburgh University and Ian Hunter a psychologist who studied his remarkable talents. Aitken himself was a mathematician who was able, for example, to recall the value of pi to the first thousand places. One of the techniques he used was to "parcel" several digits into "chunks" (Baddeley 2003, p. 25).

For those not blessed with a natural memory of such enormity, when faced with a list of digits (for example the 10 or 11 figures in a telephone number), tend to group the numbers into smaller groups of three or four: 79357211754 is impossibly long for most to remember as a single string of numbers, but it becomes much easier when broken down to 7935 7211 754. It would be even easier if the series in any of the groups were familiar because of a birth date or an already known number (a credit card pin or house number).

Companies and advertising agencies go to great lengths to find telephone numbers that are easily remembered. Deregulation of British Telecom's virtual monopoly of "directory enquiries" led to a spate of advertisements, each trying to outdo the other with their uniquely wonderful service, identified by their catchy, repetitious phone numbers.

Just as writers attempt to break down their work into chapters and paragraphs, a trainer will seek to break down a complex subject into "digestible chunks". Imagine teaching someone who has never driven before how to drive a car. The wise instructor would explain each of the functions separately (brakes, accelerator, gears, clutch and so on). They would not attempt to tell the learner everything about driving the car in one session and expect them to remember it all.

A training program on interviewing skills might be broken down into the following elements:

▷ Purposes of interviewing
▷ Objective setting
▷ Setting the scene – room and chair layout
▷ Building rapport
▷ Active listening
▷ Elicitation techniques
▷ Questioning techniques – probing and challenging
▷ Influencing techniques
▷ Checking results against objectives
▷ Summarizing
▷ Write up methodology
▷ Follow-up.

Depending on the course objectives, the list may be shorter or longer, but each element will be discussed separately before moving onto the next. As each element is learnt, it will be combined with others, so that by the end the learner has become accomplished in each and can achieve the overall objectives of the course. What the good trainer does is present the context (the whole picture), chunk it (take the subject apart) and then put it back together.

2.2.5 Meaning

In 1932, Frederic Bartlett published his book *Remembering* in which he produced evidence that people remembered the same material in different ways. Bartlett went on to claim that memory is a *process of reconstruction*, and that this construction is in important ways a social act. Asked to read a story and recall it afterwards from memory, people invariably remembered a shorter version, which was more coherent and tended to fit more closely with the subject's own viewpoint (Bartlett 1932).

Ask two people who have been arguing to explain their side of the story and this phenomenon is easily observed. Facts become adjusted, changed, conveniently left out – "forgotten"; inconsistencies become reconciled.

For those involved in helping people to remember and remember in a way that is common to the whole group, this finding has a warning and provides a clue to helping people to remember. The warning is fairly obvious: people will adjust what is said by their trainer, coach or mentor to their own experience and social values. They are in effect attempting to remember by "linking" (see above under Association) the new information or skill to something they already know about.

In a debate about a proposed new nuclear reactor to provide electricity, participants will recall different parts of the history of nuclear energy. This is in part deliberate, to advance their own argument, but also happens in fact. Those against nuclear reactors will remember in much more detail the horrors of the Chernobyl or Long Island disasters. Those in favor will not remember so much detail of those events but are likely to have a lot of data to explain how nuclear energy is much cleaner than coal and that climate change can only be reversed by replacing traditional energy methods with nuclear power stations. They may have looked particularly for that evidence, but they are also more likely to remember it.

Learners and those delivering coaching or training should also see what is needed in this to help the learner. To help people to remember, links have to be provided, usually through the medium of stories. The Bible, and the New Testament in particular, is rich with such stories or parables that allow for multiple interpretation. By telling stories that are relevant to the learner, he or she will be better able to recall the lessons.

For those learning new skills, the problems are just as big. A squash player taken to a tennis court is likely to hit the ball into the net or out of the court entirely as they struggle to adjust their swing and racquet control to the less "wristy" techniques necessary in tennis. Having learnt to type on a PC keyboard in the UK, try doing it in France or the Middle East where they have moved the letters and symbols to different places on the keyboard. A and Q, @ and " are in entirely different places and the writer has to concentrate much harder to produce something that is readable.

Adjusting to new cultures when people change jobs can be very trying, both for the individual concerned and the new employer and colleagues. Unlearning deeply embedded attitudes to work from an earlier employer is sometimes impossible. At interview the candidate will rarely recognize this and say he or she is very flexible.

Organizations such as the army and the police have strong cultures. When soldiers or policemen move on to another career, some find it hard to adjust to the new culture.

As well as providing meaning to help the learner, the wise trainer will also provide some kind of meaningful order to the new information or skill. It would not, for example, be very helpful for the driving instructor, having learnt to chunk the information, to teach in the following order:

▷ Driving on the motorway
▷ Brakes
▷ Adjusting the driving chair and mirrors
▷ Reversing into a parking place
▷ Hill start
▷ Turning right
▷ Starting the engine
▷ Selecting and engaging gears.

Order can be introduced through chronological significance or some other system of categorization. Many people like to do this visually, some will use sounds and others use cognitive logic.

Needing to remember a list of possible visual aids, a trainer of trainers will be confronted by a list in alphabetic order that would look like this:

DVDs
Electronic whiteboard
Flip chart
Handouts
Objects
Overhead projector
PowerPoint
Videos
Visualizer
Whiteboard

The instructor could group them logically into two groups: those requiring technology, that is, electricity, and those that do not.

A learner might however find it easier to group them according to colour – those such as the flip chart, the whiteboard, handouts, overhead projector and electronic whiteboard which are predominantly white or use a white background as opposed to the rest which could be remembered by association with gray.

Another learner might remember them according to the level of personal involvement, touch and interaction he or she might have with them as they are used. Thus at the top of the list might be objects, followed by flip charts. This order of things might then end with PowerPoint and DVDs.

Learners need to find their own way of remembering and the trainer or coach should be sensitive to this, by giving time to remember or a variety of orders for the information.

2.2.6 Forgetting

So far this section has been concerned with how people learn and how the trainer or coach can best help them to store information efficiently that can be retrieved later. But for the learner forgetting is a fact of life. Not only do they have to use a number of ploys to help the memory but they have to avoid the pitfalls which encourage forgetfulness.

Forgetting is discussed here to help those responsible for learning avoid doing things which will encourage forgetfulness. By understanding the causes of forgetting, trainers can do things which will prevent or retard memory loss.

That memory fails is dramatically demonstrated by Ebinhaus's forgetting curve (Figure 2.2).

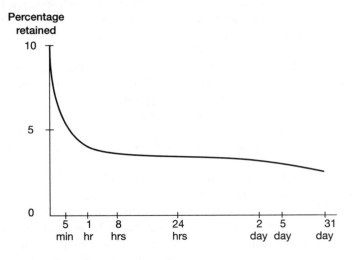

Figure 2.2 **Ebbinghaus's forgetting curve**

This is a thoroughly depressing picture for trainers. Potentially an hour after a presentation nearly 60% of the information is lost. Trainers counter this in a number of ways, some already discussed, such as providing associations and some methods to organize the information. Another frequently deployed tactic is repetition or, in trainer jargon, "reinforcement". Thus, programs will include review times when participants are asked to go over the previous day's work and recall lessons learnt and to identify areas of confusion or that have been forgotten. They also provide written material or tapes to reinforce.

Baddeley identifies two theories of forgetting (Baddeley 2003, p. 119). One suggests that memory simply fades away; the second suggests that forgetting happens because the original memory is overwritten or disrupted by other information or events. There is evidence that both occur, although psychologists continue to discuss which might be the most significant.

For the learner and those helping the learner, the messages are clear enough. The first is readily recognized; learners do need help through reinforcement.

But all too often those involved in learning processes forget that too much information or information of the wrong kind can produce overload or interfere with earlier attempts to remember.

Interference comes in two forms, *retroactive*, when new information or skills overshadows or replaces old information. This is sometimes desirable. It equates in computer terms to an upgrade; the new information is in some way superior to the old.

More often learners want to remember the old information as well. At a basic level an individual may well remember the land line telephone number of a friend but a new mobile number may be too much and the memory of the first number may be superseded by the mobile.

A computer hardware engineer may have learnt his trade in early 1990s; some of that hardware will not be found in new computers. He or she will have learnt about the new technology, but when faced with an old computer may well have forgotten how the old technology worked.

Learners may also have to contend with *proactive* inhibitions, when old information or responses break through. A diplomat may, for example, learn a number of languages over a career. Having learnt French, he or she might then take up Russian. Some words sound the same, floor = étage, or take their word from a proper name such as pencil in Russian is *karrandash*, taken from the French Carron d'Ache, who made pencils in the last century and sold them to Russia.

With French still dominant in the learner's mind and subconsciously aware that French words are relatively common in Russian, he might well remember a French word instead of Russian when speaking the latter.

There are some differences that scientists have observed in memorizing knowledge and skills. Some skills once learnt are not forgotten, for example riding a bicycle or swimming, but others such as typing are more easily forgotten. Baddeley (2003) quotes a study when airline pilots were trained in a flight simulator and tested 9–24 months later. Their level of performance was virtually unchanged:

> Unfortunately however, this lack of forgetting is not true of all skills. Flying a plane or riding a bicycle involves a continuous or *closed-loop skill*, in which each action provides the cue for the next action, in contrast to a discrete or *open-loop skill* such as typing, where each key press involves a separate response to a discrete stimulus. (Baddeley 2003, p. 113)

Most skills are a complex combination of closed and open loops, requiring regular practice if they are to be maintained. We can observe some of these: scuba diving needs regular practice, whereas skiing needs less; cooking an elaborate Christmas lunch needs the help of a recipe book, for all but the professional cook.

Baddeley acknowledges that at present our understanding is inadequate: "Understanding the principles of maintenance of skill and knowledge offers a challenge that has been largely neglected in the past. Fortunately ... more extensive research in this area is now beginning to emerge" (Baddeley 2003, p. 114).

2.2.7 Age

There is no doubt that age affects the brain just as it affects the physical body. Not only do people forget more (some might argue, erroneously, that they have more to forget) they also find it harder to learn – "you can't teach an old dog new tricks".

Too often, older people (that is, over 60 years old and some much younger) use this as an excuse to avoid learning new skills – as if their learning skills have completely deserted them. How many companies have suffered from older executives refusing or not bothering to learn the new computer technologies? It is a matter of degree and not of absolutes.

The subject of aging and its effect on learning and memory is complex. An individual's ability to respond rapidly and flexibly gradually diminishes with age. To compensate there is more in the memory banks and this together with experience will help the older person predict potential problems and therefore find the solutions as quickly as the younger, more agile brain: "in general, memory deteriorates, but is to some extent compensated by the increased use of knowledge, memory aids, and strategies" (Baddeley 2003, p. 272).

For those helping older people to learn, this underlines the importance of providing aids, links and ensuring the learner is motivated and understands the need to learn.

Older workers:

1. Are older workers less effective than younger ones? Across jobs in general there is no evidence of age differences. Older workers are thought of as more careful, reliable, loyal, knowledgeable and socially skilled but less willing to change. Further, absenteeism, accidents and turnover are higher with younger staff.

2. Why might one expect older workers to be less efficient? Older workers do less well on fluid intelligence tests (solving new problems); have poorer working memories; poorer information-processing strategies; indeed slower mental processes overall. These deficits are naturally apparent with job tasks which are complex and new. Of course systems can be established to help older workers.

3. Does not experience help the older worker? Older workers do, almost inevitably, have greater experience and expertise and, since these are related to work performance, may make excellent workers. Age is positively related to crystallized intelligence, particularly vocabulary and verbal ability. Older people often have automatized work processes. Expertise is often domain-specific and there are areas like computer technology, where younger workers outperform older workers.

4. Under what conditions are young-old similarities/differences expected? Warr noted that the simple assertion that younger people do better than older people in complex mental activities with no environmental support needs to be qualified with other factors like a person's pattern of relevant expertise. Younger people do much better on complex information tasks where they already have expertise but worse on simple tasks (with simple routines, relaxed pace).

5. Are there age differences in learning? Older people tend to have lower educational qualifications, less confidence in their ability and therefore less motivation to take part in training. But when they do undertake training, older people are slower and have more difficulty remembering. However, training can be adapted to an older person's limitations and expertise.

Source: Warr 2000

2.3 Adult Learning

Theories of adult learning borrow, wittingly or not, from the above principles. In his book *The Adult Learner* (1998), Malcolm Knowles uses the word "andragogy", first coined by a German grammar school teacher, Alexander Kapp in 1833, to describe adult learning and to differentiate it from youth learning, pedagogy. Knowles' andragogical model is based on six assumptions:

1 *Needing to know relevance:* If adults are to begin learning some new skill or knowledge, they need to know why it is important or useful. Those involved in training or coaching make an effort at the beginning of any new learning experience to explain why it is relevant to the individual
2 *Learners' self-concept:* Adults respond better when they feel they have some control over events, when they are responsible for their own decisions
3 *The role of learners' experiences:* Adults have relevant experiences which should be utilized in the learning
4 *Readiness to learn:* In short, the learning is happening at the right time
5 *Orientation to learning:* The learning has to be related to work
6 *Motivation:* There are the external drivers such as promotion, better jobs, improved pay. There are also demotivators which have to be removed if learning is to take place. Lack of confidence, self-doubt, inappropriate resources, and insufficient time can produce barriers to learning. Violation of the principles of andragogy are also demotivators.

These principles suggest that the trainer, coach or designer of technology-based learning packages should consider the processes as much as the content of learning. Trainers (hopefully) become facilitators and responsive to their clients. The business of learning becomes a partnership rather than a one-way street of information.

2.4 Learning Theories

A number of theories have been developed which attempt to help understand how people learn. This relates to how the memory works but takes it a step towards the practical.

2.4.1 Kolb's theory of experiential learning

Of all the theories used by trainers, Kolb's is the best known, although few training institutions outside the academic world of universities teach much theory. Kolb's work has spawned a number of hybrid theories, often dressed up as some new advance. A closer examination shows how much they have relied on Kolb's work.

Kolb identified four stages in learning: concrete experience, reflective experience, abstract conceptualization and active experimentation. His learning styles inventory associated various words with these four stages, for example (in the same order): feeling, watching, thinking and doing. He proposed that learning originated with experience. Children, for example, learn about heat from the sensation of touching hot water or a hot radiator pipe. Similarly, how would a blind person who is about to receive sight for the first time understand the color blue other than experiencing it through sight? It is impossible to describe color to a blind person. Equally, it would be impossible to describe the concept of freezing temperatures to a tribesman living in an equatorial rain forest, who had never come across a refrigerator or air conditioning unit.

In his book *Experiential Learning* (1984), Kolb refers throughout to "knowledge", although he does refer to some skills when giving examples. The inference is that all learning concerns knowledge. Kolb's learning cycle looks like Figure 2.3 (simplified version).

Honey and Mumford (H&M) (1992) based their work on Kolb and tried to make it more accessible to the general public through their learning styles questionnaire. They created four learning styles: pragmatist, reflector, theorist and activist, roughly equivalent to Kolb's four learning stages. H&M suggested that individuals have a preferred learning style, although for a subject to be fully learnt, individuals have to go through each stage. Some however would start as an activist, others as a theorist. This can be demonstrated, for example, by observing how individuals react when presented with a new electronic gadget (for example mobile phone). Do they immediately start playing with the gadget and try to make it work (activist/pragmatist) or do they read the instructions first (reflector/theorist)?

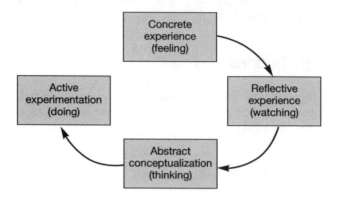

Figure 2.3 **Kolb's learning cycle**

H&M do not seem to insist on an order of learning experience, that is, pragmatist first, activist last. Their learning process might look like Figure 2.4.

Trainers are taught about Kolb (in the better courses) and most include H&M in their curriculum. Kolb gives some academic credence to the subject and H&M provide practical help in understanding what might be happening in the learner's mind.

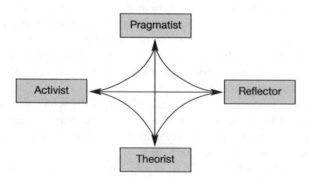

Figure 2.4 **Honey and Mumford learning styles**

Trainers, however, are taught to deliver their training in a different sequence from that suggested by Kolb: first, they describe the principles of the subject, give a demonstration, then help the student to do it and finally ask the student to do it on their own. Thus the regimental sergeant major explains the workings of the rifle and then demonstrates how to strip it down and reassemble it. He asks the soldiers to do it by walking between the ranks and barking helpful (or not so helpful) comments at them until finally they can do it on their own. The British army summarize the process in a typically succinct but easily remembered way:

"Explanation, Demonstration, Imitation and Repetition"

The trainers' learning circle looks like Figure 2.5.

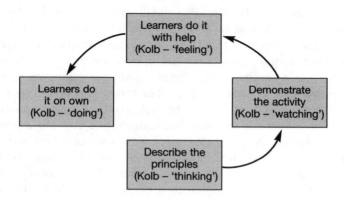

Figure 2.5 **The trainers' learning cycle**

Both Kolb and trainers end with the same concept: doing. But they start at opposite ends of the spectrum. The trainers approach seems the sensible one when dealing with, for example, dangerous weapons or learning how to drive a car. But it seems to work for all skills. Leaving someone in front of a keyboard and expecting them to learn the intricacies of a spreadsheet, word processing or PowerPoint purely by experience does not seem a very efficient way of progressing.

The above examples refer to skills, the use of knowledge to do things. Does the same apply to knowledge and attitudes, the third of the three aspects of learning?

There are two kinds of knowledge in this context: totally new knowledge to the learner and those around him and, secondly, knowledge that is known by others but not by the learner. The first is original creative knowledge; the same in many ways to that sought by the inventor, the original thinker. This kind of knowledge falls much more neatly into Kolb's learning circle. New knowledge (that not known by anyone in the immediate circle of the learner) comes from experience. Someone coming into contact with snow for the first time and without some outside advice will need to feel it to know that it is cold. Similarly, scientists experiment with materials and once a new phenomenon is experienced, they will then reflect and theorize before designing new medicines or machines.

Where knowledge is known by others and "passed on", the learning process is different and reflects the trainers' model. Thus when we learn something new, for example that by mixing yellow and blue paints we will produce green, we usually reflect on the idea, then experiment with it before actually using it to paint the living room. The watching and feeling stages are often conflated. It is perhaps worth noting that Kolb also describes the "abstract conceptualization" stage as "grasping via comprehension" which is very much what happens when learning new information.

The proponents of Kolb might argue that reading or listening is in itself an experience. But this is a different process from the one described by Kolb, although easily confused. Both reading and listening are intellectual processes.

The process of learning or adopting a belief or value is perhaps more complex. Trainers recognize that they are helping learners to change in one way or another: acquire more knowledge, skills or attitude. Changing an attitude amounts in common language to molding or influencing a person's mental approach to a job, another person or group of people, a sport, learning, project or organization. It is about such words as loyalty, commitment, will, drive, determination, achievement, honesty, integrity and caring.

In the workplace, new entrants arrive with a set of values and ways of thinking. Their loyalties may be towards others: old employer, school, university, friends, family and so on. They may not have a "good" work ethic or they may lack the determination to do a job as quickly as possible with maximum success. Sportspeople at the highest level suffer all sorts of mental demons which distract them even though they may well want to be the best or win.

Do Kolb or the trainers' approach help people to change their attitudes? Take the new entrant at work. He or she is given a set of rules and procedures to follow, some in the form of a formal contract, some in written regulations, some in a psychological contract and some by word of mouth which are passed on by fellow workers. These are passed on with varying degrees of effectiveness during the induction process. This equates to the trainers' first phase "describe in principle".

The new entrant then enters the workplace and sees people around him working in a new (for him) way. These become the role models and in the trainers' model represent the "demonstration" of what should be.

The individual then experiments and tries the new attitudes (determination, integrity, caring, commitment, loyalty). Others around him will be supportive and helpful at this stage. Finally he steps out and adopts the new attitudes and himself becomes a role model for those who follow.

Chapter 3 describes our theory of the "learning quotient", in which the various factors which affect someone's ability to learn are discussed. These factors (education, intelligence, family background, previous experience, personality, gender and, perhaps most significantly in this context, self-esteem and motivation to learn) are significant when calculating how to influence someone's attitude. If their learnability score is low, changing an attitude will be close to impossible.

What of attitude changes required after a merger and acquisition? The same process will be involved, but instead of an induction course, the wise new managers will "communicate" what they want, set the example and the rest will follow.

Many modern business coaches adopt a different approach, much closer to Kolb. Those who follow such ideas as expressed in *The Inner Game of Work* (Gallwey 2000) encourage their coachee to change through their own experiences and self-confidence in their abilities. The coach does very little "instructing" or "telling". In effect, they experience, reflect, theorize and then act, although as explained earlier the middle two phases are often conflated; but this is only for people who are at the top of their professions – more therapy than skill.

Sportspeople know what they have to achieve (their coaches will have told them: focus, see yourself winning, you are the best, believe in yourself), thus satisfying the first of the trainers' stages. They will see others achieving, the second stage. But however much others may help, the mind still plays tricks and frustrates the best performance at the crunch time, even if achieved a thousand times before in practice.

Sportsmen who have achieved greatness and then go through a fallow period can be said to have gone through Kolb's experiential phase; they can reflect and think as much as they like but they can't do it. Indeed, some coaches argue that it is the process of thinking which is the cause of the problem. For these coaches the issue comes back to that sometimes elusive quality mentioned above in the learnability matrix: self-esteem.

2.4.1.1 Learning styles and personality

Kolb has provided the basis for most learning theory as it is applied in the classroom and various theories of learning styles have been spawned as a result. There has been some interesting work done on the connection between learning styles and personality.

Much research has examined differences between extraverts and introverts. Eysenck (1981, pp. 203–4) summarized the findings as follows. In spite of the relatively small volume of research on the effects of introversion/extraversion on learning and memory, there appear to be some fairly robust findings:

▷ Reward enhances the performance of extraverts more than introverts, whereas punishment impairs the performance of introverts more than extraverts.
▷ Introverts are more susceptible than extraverts to distraction.
▷ Introverts are more affected than extraverts by response competition.
▷ Introverts take longer than extraverts to retrieve information from long-term or permanent storage, especially non-dominant information.
▷ Introverts have higher response criteria than extraverts.
▷ Extraverts show better retention test performance than introverts at short retention intervals, but the opposite happens at long retention intervals.

While it is probably premature to attempt any theoretical integration of these various findings, it is nevertheless tempting to argue that introverts are characteristically better motivated on performance tasks than extraverts, with the consequence that their normal expenditure of effort and utilization of working memory capacity is closer to the maximum. Since introverts, as it were, start from a high motivation baseline, it follows that they are less able than extraverts to utilize extra processing resources to handle increasing processing demands (for example from distracting stimulation, response competition or difficult retrieval tasks).

On the basis of personality and styles of learning, it is possible to hypothesize on what kind of training certain types are likely to prefer. Figure 2.6 uses period of learning and nature of learning as its axes.

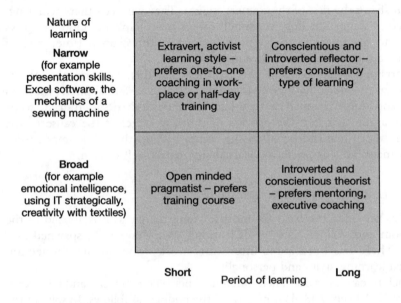

Figure 2.6 **Some learning preferences**

2.4.2 Behaviorist theory of learning

Three basic assumptions underlie the behaviorist theory of learning:

▷ Learning is manifested by a change in behavior. The focus of study should therefore be observable behavior rather than internal thought processes, and the learner's perceptions and motivation are not considered.
▷ The environment shapes behavior.
▷ The principle of contiguity and reinforcement are central to the learning process. The principle of contiguity is that two things are easily remem-

bered if they occur together. If behavior is reinforced or rewarded, it is more likely to occur again in similar conditions. Reinforcement can thus be used to shape behavior.

The behaviorist theory has four key principles for learning. These can be recalled by means of the acronym ROAR – repetition, objectives, activity, and reinforcement.

▷ *Repetition* – Practice makes perfect, and practice makes permanent. If you want to learn a skill, you must practice frequently. Repetition is also needed to memorize key learning points.
▷ *Objectives* – As trainers we are taught to formulate our objectives in behavioural terms, for example "By the end of this training session participants will be able to ...".
▷ *Activity* – Learning is more effective when the learner is active rather than passive: learning by doing is best.
▷ *Reinforcement* – Positive reinforcers like praise, rewards, and success are better than negative ones like punishments and failure. Feedback is an important part of the process.

Systematic training design, training objectives, programed learning, computer-based training, and competences are grounded in behaviorist learning theory. This approach is suitable where objectives are unambiguous, performance criteria can be clearly defined, and the learner has little knowledge. Examples include computer programing, studying accountancy procedures or learning to operate a sophisticated machine. Behaviorist principles have thus been applied extensively to the development of low-level psychomotor skills.

Today the environment is constantly changing so that we must be flexible and adaptable. In such cases different approaches to learning are more appropriate. In addition, behaviorist theories of learning still do not allow for the relevance of thoughts, feelings or motives in the learning process, regarding learning as merely a series of conditioned responses with an emphasis on inputs and outputs (Malone 2003).

2.4.3 Cognitivist theory of learning

Cognitivists are interested in how the mind makes sense of the environment. Perception, insight, imagination, meaning, and how information is processed, stored and retrieved, and the importance of language to our thinking process are key elements in the contribution of cognitive theory to learning. Rather than being passive, the human mind interprets information and gives meaning to events based on prior knowledge, experience and expectations.

Gestalt theory, which is part of cognitive theory, proposed looking at the whole rather than its parts, at patterns and conceptual frameworks rather than isolated events. For gestaltists, the locus of control (the mind's "authority figure") lies with the individual, while for behaviorists it lies with the environment.

Modern developments in cognitive theory include models of the memory system and comprehension, computer simulations and artificial intelligence. Cognitivist principles are being applied to screen design in computers, for example, in the use of icons and hypertext.

Cognitive psychology offers several key principles to learning that can be recalled via the acronym PROFIT:

▷ *Prior knowledge* – To facilitate learning it is important that new information is linked to prior knowledge and experience.
▷ *Relationships* – The whole is greater than the sum of its parts. Subjects have an inherent structure. Learners should try to see the links between key ideas and concepts. An important aspect of cognitive learning is insight, which arises when a person suddenly sees the link between concepts, understands an issue or perceives a solution to a problem. Learning maps can facilitate this process.
▷ *Organization* – Organized materials are easier to learn and remember.
▷ *Feedback* – Learners need to know about their success or failure at the learning task as soon after the event as possible. Knowledge of results is a motivator and a type of reinforcement.
▷ *Individual differences* – Different learning styles can influence the outcome of learning. Learning should be designed to cater for the different learning styles of learners.
▷ *Task perception* – Learners have different perceptions and pick out different aspects of the environment. Learning should be designed and presented to engage as many of the senses as possible.

2.4.4 Constructivist theory of learning

The constructivist theory suggests that learners construct their own knowledge from their experience, mental models and beliefs. This implies that what is learnt depends on the way you look at things. The theory was put forward by John Dewey and other innovators. They maintained that meaningful learning relies on active engagement in planning, problem solving, communicating, and creating, rather than on rote memorization and repetition. Learning is a process by which people make sense of their environment and personal history. The acquisition of new knowledge is affected and shaped by prior knowledge, interaction with others, experience, and inherited predispositions. Our ability to learn is also influenced by logic, emotion, intuition, and motivation.

According to the constructivist view, knowledge is relative rather than absolute. New paradigms replace old ones as new theories and discoveries are made. The basic philosophy underlying this view is that knowledge must be presented in a meaningful context to facilitate effective learning.

The trainers' role is thus to act as a learning facilitator, to engage the interest of learners and get them actively to seek out and discover knowledge. In the decontextualized setting of the training room, the responsibility of the trainer is to relate the learning to the practical work situations to which the learners will return. Learners are primarily responsible for their own learning.

The constructivist theory of learning has been applied to experiential learning, self-directed learning, discovery learning, and notions of the role of reflection in learning. Life experience is seen as a resource and stimulus to learning. Practical activities supported by group discussion form the core of many training and development programs. Adult training is a process of negotiation, involving the construction and exchange of relevant information. We must talk and debate with others to test our understanding (Malone 2003).

2.4.5 Humanist theory of learning

The humanist theory considers learning from the viewpoint of the human potential for growth. Unlike behaviorists, humanists do not accept that either the environment or the subconscious determines behavior. People have free will and can determine their own destiny. People have (it is supposed) unlimited potential for growth and development. Learning occurs primarily through reflection on personal experience. Reflection leads to insights and understanding of others and ourselves.

Humanism facilitates collaborative learning in which trainers and learners jointly agree methods of identifying training needs, learning objectives, training methods and evaluation approaches. The approaches used include asking stimulating questions, project work, debriefing sessions, action planning, self-assessment, visualization and guided reflection. We learn more effectively if we feel secure, respected, esteemed and empowered. Learning is undermined if we feel threatened, anxious, hostile, demeaned.

In summary, the assumptions underlying the humanist approach to learning are:

▷ People are inherently good.
▷ People are free and autonomous and capable of making decisions.
▷ The motivation for learning is primarily from within.
▷ The potential for personal growth and development is virtually unlimited.
▷ Self-concept plays an important part in personal development.
▷ People move towards becoming self-actualized.
▷ People are responsible to themselves and others. They are capable of evaluating their own learning.
▷ The whole person should be involved in learning. Feelings and emotions as well as thinking are part of the learning process (Malone 2003).

2.4.6 Social theory of learning

The social learning theory centers on the fact that people learn from observing and modeling themselves on others and that, by definition, such observations take place in a social setting. But the social learning theory also includes the concept of self-regulation, which suggests that people can regulate their own behavior by visualizing the consequences of it. Some models of behavior are more likely to be imitated than others, notably people who are regarded as attractive, competent, powerful or famous. Your self-efficacy, that is, the competence you know you have and the confidence you have in knowing it, will determine your effectiveness or otherwise in dealing with others and the environment. There is a reciprocal aspect, in that people influence their environment which in turn influences the way they behave.

The social theory of learning has three important connotations for trainers:

▷ Learning centers on the relationships between people. Dialogue is an important aspect of collaborative learning.
▷ A key role for trainers is to help people become more socially effective in the workplace.
▷ Learning is an active process. Learning is part of daily living. Problem solving and learning from experience are a central part of the process (Malone 2003).

2.5 Grouping the Theories

In 2002 the CIPD commissioned the Cambridge Programme for Industry to produce a report *How do People Learn?* (Reynolds et al. 2002). This report suggested that learning theories could be grouped into four clusters. Martyn Sloman summarized these as follows.

Learning as behavior

The first cluster is concentrated around the theory of behaviorism and the work of B.F. Skinner. These theories originate from the natural sciences. Behaviorism asserts that any change in an individual's behavior is the result of events, known as stimuli, and the consequences of these events. Reinforcing responses through reward is the behaviorist's way of encouraging the desired behaviors. By rewarding the desired behavior, the behaviorist conditions the individual to perform the action again and again (Sloman 2003, p. 38).

Learning as understanding

Unlike behaviorism, which focuses on the conditioning of behavior, cognitive learning theories view learning as a process of understanding and internalizing the principles, connections and facts about the world around us. Seen this way, the learner is like a powerful machine that processes information and internalizes it as knowledge. Theorists such as Robert Gagné, Jean Piaget and Benjamin Bloom have all written about cognitive development.

Piaget's notions of assimilation and accommodation offer an interesting perspective on how learning takes place. Assimilation refers to the integration of perceptions into existing mental models, whereas accommodation involves the alteration of mental models to explain perceptions that could not otherwise be understood. Equilibrium is achieved when a coherent mixture of strategies and rules can comfortably explain the world.

Strategies for cognitive development frequently deploy facilitation to assist understanding. By exposure to learning materials and guidance, the learner can pass through developmental stages more quickly than if left to their own devices. Clearly, the facilitator needs to have a good understanding of where the learner is starting from in order to guide them effectively (Sloman 2003, p. 38).

Learning as knowledge construction

Constructivist theories view the individual as an active agent in their own learning. Constructivists believe that all knowledge is personal knowledge, in other words, knowledge is not something "out there" ready to be grasped. This means that knowledge is subjective, tacit and highly dependent on context. Constructivists would argue that knowledge management systems in fact manage information rather than knowledge, since the latter only exists inside people's heads.

Individuals assign meaning to knowledge that they have obtained through their own experience and only then does it become usable. This focus on the learner contrasts with behaviorism where the "expert" is the source of learning and with the cognitive approach where "content" is emphasized. In constructivist theories it is the learner who is at the center of the learning experience. Interaction and dialogue (with other learners or with a facilitator) are used by the learner to enhance his or her own personal experiences and understanding (Sloman 2003, p. 38).

Learning as social practice

Social theories of learning do not contradict the behavioral, cognitive or constructivist theories. Instead, they simply argue that learning is more effective when it arises and is applied in a social setting. This idea goes back to the work of L.S. Vygotsky, who observed children interacting with older individuals. He discovered that they could perform well above their age if given the chance to interact with someone older. This led him to conclude that social interaction was crucial to some forms of learning.

Anthropologists, sociologists, social psychologists and cognitive theo-

rists have all contributed to this cluster of theories. There are several different forms of social learning theories. Cognitive social theories, as exempli-
fied by Albert Bandura, regard learning as the outcome of social
interactions that foster shared standards of behavior. Activity theories
regard established patterns of social interaction as the source of learning, for
example problem resolution within established work processes and patterns.
Lastly, theories of social practice, made famous by Jean Lave and Etienne
Wenger, point to the importance of participation in communities of practice as the source of learning. Here individuals don't so much learn facts
and principles about the world; instead they learn how to "be" (Sloman
2003, p. 38).

Psychologists have developed various theories to explain how, when and
why people learn. Many of these theories are based on specific principles.
Furnham (1999) summarized these as follows:

▷ *Goal setting:* people learn best when they have clear goals that are difficult enough to challenge rather than discourage them.
▷ *Reinforcement:* people learn best when given prompt, continuous and
  positive reward for having learnt new skills.
▷ *Feedback:* learning is virtually impossible without clear and accurate feedback on results.
▷ *Modeling:* people can learn efficiently and effectively by copying others
  who have the required skills.
▷ *Distributed practice:* most people prefer to learn complex tasks at various
  "sittings", rather than on one occasion.
▷ *Whole versus part:* for many complex tasks, people prefer and do better
  with part learning (each part separately) rather than whole training (the
  complete entity).
▷ *Transfer of learning:* the more similar the place, tools and conditions of
  learning to the circumstances under which the learnt behavior is to be
  exercised, the better the transfer of learning.

2.6 Conclusion

Knowledge and understanding of how the memory works and how we can
best exploit the memory through learning is central to those in the
business of learning. Most conduct their work without much idea about
how they work. People have helped others learn since they started to
procreate. Much of it is instinctive and where it is not it has developed on
a trial and error basis.

This book argues that much of today's practice works, but that as the
demands for greater efficiency increase and new techniques and technologies are promoted at a speed which is at times literally bewildering, the
understanding of learning theory is now an essential element of the learning profession.

Currently, not much is made of the theories which underpin our under-standing, no doubt suiting the more "activist" learners amongst the trainers who write about the subject. Few books include any reference to research in the subject, be they books on training, coaching, mentoring, e-learning or any other subjects related to helping people learn.

There is nothing so practical as *good* theory, which should guide the whole process of designing and delivering training courses.

3 Learning Quotient

3.1 Introduction

That people have a quantifiable amount of intelligence has been established for some time. Methods of how to measure it and what exactly is being measured have fascinated psychologists, educationalists and laypeople for some time. It is also now accepted that social skills/emotional intelligence can be assessed, although probably not with the same kind of precision that observers have expected when measuring intelligence. But what about the ability to learn effectively and efficiently. Is it possible to measure in a quantifiable way an individual's learning potential: their ability to learn new things, their "learnability", their learning quotient?

For most people it is enough to establish that someone has sufficient intelligence for the job they are required to do. Enlightened recruiters will recognize that a university degree is not necessarily the only or the best way to judge someone's intelligence or their ability to learn how the workplace operates, appropriate business knowledge or the skills required. But some people seem to resist learning for no good reason. Myths develop around the "you can't teach old dogs new tricks" syndrome. The wave of IT that engulfs virtually every office is seen as a threat and many are overwhelmed by the changes that are forced upon them. Why do some embrace learning and others avoid it? Whence learno-phobes and learno-philes; have they always been like this or do they change? Do things get worse as people get older? Does it depend on *what* they are expected to learn?

3.2 Learning quotient

There are three factors, which appear to predict willingness to take part in learning:

▷ Learning history, social and family factors and age
▷ Intelligence and personality
▷ Self-esteem and motivation.

The first two are pretty immutable and they affect the third which fortunately is not.

Other factors such as the quality of training play their part and that is the concern of many books, including this one. Few have attempted to analyse an individual's ability to learn, dubbed for this chapter a person's *learning quotient* (LQ).

3.2.1 Learning history

The first factor is our learning history, specifically our experience of secondary school and beyond. Personal experience of exam success and failure from primary school onwards shapes expectations of the learning process: how easy/difficult it is; how much fun it all is to learn knowledge or skills; and the cost–benefit analysis.

To a large extent these expectations are shaped by the whole business of social comparison. This means how well a person has done compared (as he/she sees it) to their peers. Thus the peer group, past as well as present, is fundamentally important to the whole business. At school and university people get a sense of their ability, their preferred learning style and how good they are at learning new things – albeit sometimes an unrealistic view.

Over the years adults develop a series of ever more elaborate stories justifying their lack of success in educational contexts. Poor teaching, undiagnosed cognitive problems, poor facilities, various types of discrimination all feature highly. On the other hand, learning success can and often is neatly and succinctly attributed to ability, plus a little effort – "I succeed because of my ability; I fail because of my teacher".

Adults at work have strong memories of learning contexts. They have clear beliefs about how right they are; what is easy to learn and what's not. And, not unnaturally, they will strongly resist being "shown up" or having to endure tedious and difficult tasks that bring little obvious benefit to them or their organization.

Families, friends and peer groups influence young and old people's attitude to learning in obvious ways. A young person growing up in an atmosphere where reading and learning more generally is encouraged is more likely to have good learning experiences than someone where school is derided, truancy is rife and sitting in coffee shops, bars and ball parks is the norm. The latter are likely to find learning something new, intimidating and will associate the idea with bad and unfamiliar experiences.

The past is a different country. It was done differently there. But memories can be changed and they influence strongly how people approach any new learning. Clearly, good experiences in the past predict willingness and ability to do so in the future.

Age was discussed in section 2.2.7 where we said that the subject of aging and its effect on learning and memory is complex. An individual's ability to respond rapidly and flexibly gradually diminishes with age. To compensate there is more in the memory banks and this together with experience will help the older person predict potential problems and therefore find the solutions as quickly as the younger, more agile brain: "in general, memory dete-

riorates, but is to some extent compensated by the increased use of knowledge, memory aids, and strategies" (Baddeley 2003, p. 272).

3.2.2 Intelligence and personality

The second factor refers to a person's actual intelligence and personality.
Bright people learn faster; they are able to learn more complicated things.
People need to be bright enough to learn whatever is being taught. It is
harder to learn Mandarin than Spanish. Bright people, particularly those
with a good ear, do better.

The question then is roughly what level of intelligence should be the
"cutoff" point for each learning exercise. And related to this is whether
people have a realistic view of their own intelligence. Most do, but because
of inaccurate feedback there are the problems of hubris and humility: the less
bright who think they are clever, and the talented, who seem unsure of their
ability. Testing people thoroughly and giving them accurate, honest feedback on their performance should overcome the problem.

Where the subject to be learnt has a physical element, say a plasterer or
surgeon, manual dexterity has also to be measured.

Three personality variables are clearly implicated in the whole learning
business: conscientiousness, neuroticism and openness to experience.
Conscientiousness or whatever synonym one prefers – diligence, the work
ethic, achievement striving, prudence – are all good predictors of learning
success. The conscientious work harder, longer and smarter. They take learning seriously. They put in extra effort and are usually suitably rewarded.

Neuroticism, on the other hand, is a poor predictor of learning willingness and success. Neurotics are anxious and easily depressed by setbacks.
They worry a lot. And their anxiety is often self-handicapping. They tend to
be tenser and more prone to illness (real or imagined) and tend to go absent
more. A moderate amount of worry may be good news as it may motivate
people to try harder. But go above and beyond this level and one has known
learning problems.

Openness to experience is about willingness to try something new, particularly to explore new ideas, emotions and experiences. It is about curiosity
and creativity. It's more than a "have-a-go mentality". It's partly about
exploration and the joy of the new. It is a good predictor of both ability and
willingness to learn.

3.2.3 Self-esteem

So to have bright, conscientious, open and stable people in the organization
bodes well. But there is something else which is influenced by all the above
factors. And that is *self-esteem* or *self-belief*. It is about confidence in one's
ability and not being afraid to be seen as in need of help.

Self-esteem at work as a motivating variable has attracted some attention since the work of Korman (1970). The idea is relatively simple: people with self-confidence outperform those without confidence (Furnham 1999).

One of the reasons why senior executives often eschew training courses is not about time (the favored excuse) or even a cost–benefit analysis. It is the fear of being shown up as less able and knowledgeable than they like to pretend. They are usually much happier to do one-to-one learning because it is private; hence the popularity of coaching which is often a mixture of counseling and teaching.

All clinicians will tell you that self-esteem is difficult but possible to budge. They will also tell you that it often bares little relation to reality. Just as anorexic patients see themselves as obese, so some talented, able people see themselves as "pretty average". And vice versa but these overconfident, even arrogant types are another story.

The good trainer knows that adults are nervous about learning, particularly older people who probably did not have the educational opportunities of the young and who feel, often quite correctly, that their memory and cognitive agility is not what is used to be. The good trainer gives hesitant adult learners a safe environment and early experience of success without patronizing them; and shows them the benefit, and even joy, of learning something new that is both interesting and useful.

Self-esteem stems from a perception of ability and probability of success. Many things, already identified, can affect this: previous educational experience, age, and the desire not to be shown up in front of colleagues. If someone is overconfident, the coach or trainer has a problem because that individual will think that they already know everything and will probably be there under sufferance. The coach has to find a way of showing him or her that they will benefit from learning.

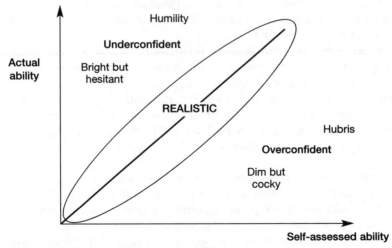

Figure 3.1 **Actual and self-assessed ability**

Similarly, where the individual is underconfident, the trainer has to encourage and persuade the learner that they have the ability and potential to learn.

3.2.3.1 Motivation

As well as self-esteem, most adults have to have a reason to learn. Many will avoid it if they possibly can for the reasons described above. Organizations introducing new software often find that some of the most senior or older members of staff resist the new technology, hoping that it will pass them by or that their secretary will carry the burden. Only when they realize that the secretary is being taken away (staff cuts often being the rationale behind the introduction of IT) do they realize that they have to learn the new technology or be left out of the prime information circle.

But if any of those individuals, say a journalist, had to go to a dangerous part of the world (Iraq or Afghanistan in 2004), they would not need much encouragement to go on a personal protection course before they went. They would be highly motivated for reasons of survival to go on such a course and learn.

Motivation for learning

> may be *intrinsic*, coming from within, or *extrinsic*, coming from without. Intrinsic motivation is the stronger because it corresponds to the desire to learn to meet your own goals and needs rather than the expectations or goals of others such as parents or peers. Sources of external motivation include promotion prospects, fear of redundancy, managerial pressure and peer competition. (Malone 2003, p. 198)

The journalist going to Afghanistan would have strong intrinsic motives to go on a personal protection course.

In other words, there is learning for learning's sake and learning for some other benefit. Intrinsic motivation to learn refers to the experience of learning being in, and of itself, sufficient. Extrinsic motivation means people are prepared to learn and practice new skills but that they do so for some reason like promotion or regrading.

Coaches who use non-directive methods of instruction are relying on tapping into people's intrinsic motivations (see, for example, Gallwey 2000; Downey 2003; Whitmore 2002).

Many writers on the subject of learning motivation refer to Maslow's hierarchy of human needs as a useful model (Maslow 1970). In particular they emphasize the concept of self-actualization. Hardingham (1998, pp. 158–9) describes its significance as follows:

> Where our participants see that the change or development being offered by our programmes really fits with their own primary purpose in life, with their values and the realization of their personal; potential, they will commit to it with considerable force. One of the reasons why participants often appreciate our including personality questionnaires in the programmes we run is that they offer people an opportunity to understand and explore their own potential above and beyond the constraints their employing organization has placed on the programme objectives.

Two of Knowles' six principles of adult learning relate to motivation. The first states that "adults need to know why they need to learn something before undertaking to learn it" (Knowles 1998, p. 149). The sixth specifically identifies motivation: "While adults are responsive to some external motivators (better jobs, promotions, higher salaries, and the like), the most potent motivators are internal pressures (the desire for increased job satisfaction, self esteem, quality of life, and the like)" (Knowles 1998, p. 68).

Perhaps the most relevant theories in helping to assess a learner's motivation come from "need" theories. Murray (1938) produced one of the most sophisticated theories and listed 20 needs (Table 3.1). His theory was

Table 3.1 Murray's original taxonomy of needs

Need	Description	Relevance to learning
Abasement	To submit passively to external force; to accept blame, surrender, admit inferiority or error	Not considered a useful source of motivation, although some instructors may still use such methods
Achievement	To accomplish something difficult; to master, manipulate, surpass others	A potentially strong motivator, it is about ambition
Affiliation	To draw near and enjoyably cooperate or reciprocate with liked others; to win their affection, loyalty	A potentially strong motivator, both in its own right and as a spin-off from attending a course
Aggression	To overcome opposition forcefully to fight, revenge an injury, oppose or attack others	An unlikely motivator to learn
Autonomy	To get free of confinement or restraint; to resist coercion, be independent	A potentially strong motivator
Counteraction	To master or make up for a failure by restriving; to overcome weakness	A potentially strong motivator
Defendance	To defend oneself against assault, criticism, blame; to vindicate the ego	A potentially strong motivator
Deference	To admire and support a superior; to praise, be subordinate, conform	Not a strong or frequently observed motivator to learn
Dominance	To control one's human environment; to influence, persuade, command others	A potentially strong motivator
Exhibition	To make an impression, be seen and heard; to excite, amaze, fascinate, shock others	A potentially strong motivator
Harm avoidance	To avoid pain, physical injury, illness, and death; to escape danger, take precautions	For some specific courses, a potentially strong motivator
Infavoidance	To avoid humiliation; to quit or avoid embarrassing situations, refrain from acting because of the fear of failure	A potentially strong motivator
Nurturance	To give sympathy and gratify the needs of someone helpless; to console, support others	For some specific learning, such as counseling, a potentially strong motivator

Table 3.1 cont'd

Need	Description	Relevance to learning
Order	To put things in order, to achieve nearness, organization, cleanliness	For some people a potentially strong motivator
Play	To act funny without further purpose; to like to laugh, make jokes	Not a very strong motivator
Rejection	To separate oneself from disliked others; to exclude, expel, snub others	Not a strong motivator
Sentience	To seek and enjoy sensuous impressions	Perhaps for some courses but generally not a frequently observed motivation
Sex	To form and further an erotic relationship; to have sexual intercourse	For some individuals perhaps but not a frequently observed motivator
Succorance	To have one's needs gratified by someone sympathetic; to be nursed, supported, protected, consoled	Perhaps a strong motivator for those seeking one-to-one help
Understanding	To ask or answer general questions. An interest in theory, analysing events, logic, reason	Potentially a strong motivator

Source: Adapted from Murray 1938.

designed to answer more general questions concerning what energizes and organizes perceptions, thoughts and actions, thereby transforming an existing unsatisfying situation in the direction of a particular goal (Furnham and Taylor 2004, p. 28).

Murray's list of needs for the purposes of learning can be reduced to 13 motivators that are regularly found in the learner:

Achievement
Affiliation
Autonomy
Counteraction
Defendance
Dominance
Exhibition
Harm avoidance
Infavoidance
Nurturance
Order
Succorance
Understanding

These will be considered in more detail later to discover how they might be measured.

Finally in this section it is interesting to combine confidence and motivation. The best kind of learners are those who are realistic about their own

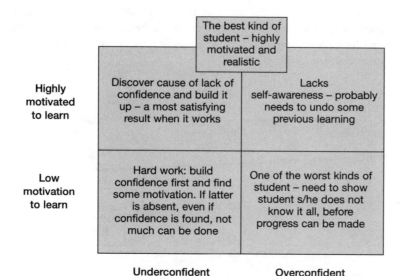

	Underconfident	Overconfident
	The best kind of student – highly motivated and realistic	
Highly motivated to learn	Discover cause of lack of confidence and build it up – a most satisfying result when it works	Lacks self-awareness – probably needs to undo some previous learning
Low motivation to learn	Hard work: build confidence first and find some motivation. If latter is absent, even if confidence is found, not much can be done	One of the worst kinds of student – need to show student s/he does not know it all, before progress can be made

Figure 3.2 **Motivation to learn and confidence**

abilites and are highly motivated to learn. Figure 3.2 identifies the more common learners and how they might be handled.

Pick up any book by a sportsperson or their coaches and the subject quickly comes round to synonyms or metaphors for self-esteem or confidence. Skill in the particular sport is of course essential and there will be tips and advice on how to swing a golf club or hold a racquet, but what marks out the top athletes is their "will" to win or how they handle the mental demons that plague them when facing a crucial shot. Many people associated with the sports world try to transfer what they have learnt in their profession to business management and some have been very successful. So success is not seen simply in terms of ability. Fitness and technical skill are prerequisites but it is thought that the mental determination to win (at all costs), to be the best, is essential.

What they would have us believe is that the qualities of determination, will and drive can be learnt and they identify self-confidence or self-esteem as their target area. *The Inner Game of Work* (Gallwey 2000), which followed *The Inner Game of Golf* and its sister book on tennis, is almost wholly about such qualities and attitudes.

Consider also the following quotes:

On every putt see the ball going into the hole with your mind's eye. (Gary Player in Rotella 2001, p. 28)

You have to feel that you are a great putter to be one. If you start to tell yourself that you can't putt, you can bet your bottom peso that you won't be able to get it in the hole from three feet. (Lee Trevino in Rotella 2001, p. 16)

I have seen numerous matches where the weaker team on paper beat the other team because of greater self-belief and team spirit. And the same is true for individual players: self-confidence and inner strength can be decisive in duels on the field, even when, objectively speaking, an opponent is the more skilled footballer. (Sven Goran Eriksson 2003, p. 43)

All these factors are represented in Figure 3.3.

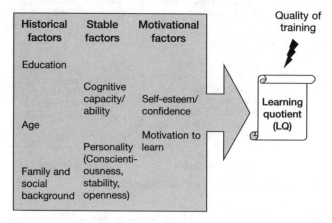

Figure 3.3 **Assessing the learning quotient**

One of the features of this model is that each of the seven factors that contribute to LQ are both direct and mediating variables. What that means is essentially this: each factor has itself a direct effect on LQ but also the factors work through each other. Thus age effects cognitive ability (as people age they are slower, more forgetful) which effects LQ. There may also be feedback loops such that education effects cognitive ability and vice versa.

3.3 Measuring Learning Quotient

Although all the factors discussed above influence an individual's ability to learn, some have more significance than others and some such as family and peers may have been counteracted by wiser (or more pernicious) counsel subsequently. It is also clear that some factors can be measured more scientifically (reliably and validly) than others.

As LQ is made up of a number of factors, some with more significance than others, together with problems of measuring some of the factors, providing a mathematical formula is not feasible. It is however possible to indicate on a chart a pattern of learnability which is instructive.

There are seven factors to assess:

Social background
Age
Education

Cognitive ability
Personality (conscientiousness, stability, openness)
Self-esteem
Motivation

A separate assessment needs to be made for each subject to be learnt.

The subject to be learnt is also relevant. Someone can feel quite confident as, say, a linguist but be a failure with anything to do with numeric skills; another will take to the sports field but take on pottery with great reluctance; new IT skills may hold no fear for some but seem a black art to others. In some questions it is important to identify the nature of the topic to be learnt. This is particularly so when considering the last two factors on the above list.

3.3.1 Measuring social background

Exploring someone's early educational experience is essentially general. The atmosphere at home or amongst friends can be assessed by asking a variety of questions. The questions can be put orally and the response recorded on a bar graph, such as the one below, or the individual can be asked to place a mark on the bar where they think it is appropriate. To what extent were you encouraged to read and/or set aside time for homework by your parents and family?

Encouraged to read   No encouragement
and work   at all

Other questions which might be asked include: What is the top qualification of your both your parents? Roughly how many books did you have in your house while a child? How high were the educational ambitions of your parents for you?

3.3.2 Measuring educational background

Measuring educational experience is important not so much because of the nature, excellence or otherwise of the various institutions attended, but how the individual felt they did compared to their peers. The questions to be asked therefore are along the lines of: To what extent did your friends at college consider you to be successful on the academic side (for a job or post which requires a major intellectual level)?

Highly successful   Very poor

Other questions might include: To what extent did you feel intellectually or educationally successful compared to your peers when influencing others (for posts where influence is an important element)? What sort of school did you go to?

3.3.3 Measuring age

Of all the factors age is the easiest to measure but some people choose to believe that age has a bigger influence on learning ability than it actually does. It is therefore worth asking the question: To what extent do you believe age seriously affects your ability to learn new skills (knowledge, values or beliefs depending what is being considered)?

A lot   Very little

3.3.4 Measuring cognitive ability

Cognitive ability is easy enough to measure well; the question is which test to use as each measures a slightly different aspect of intellect. These are explored in more detail in Chapter 7. Learning makes more demands on the ability to remember new things rather than analyse existing facts, so tests such as Raven's Progressive Matrices are therefore in general more relevant, but others may have more relevance depending on the subject concerned.

Where the skill requires some manual dexterity or physical ability, it might also be important to make a judgement on their natural physiological ability. Cognitive ability will probably still be important as the individual will have to understand the basic concepts and rules.

3.3.5 Measuring personality

Like cognitive ability there are a number of different methods of measuring personality, in particular stability, conscientiousness and openness. The NEO five-factor inventory provides one of the best validated, simplest and easiest to do this (see Chapter 7).

Cognitive ability and personality can be shown on a bar graph relatively easily as both instruments give a numeric result. They need to be adjusted for age, nationality and gender but otherwise can be represented on a graph.

3.3.6 Measuring self-esteem

Much work has been done on self-esteem and measuring it. Carole Dweck

(2000) provides two examples of how she measured confidence in people's intelligence and personality. Both have applicability in learning.

To measure confidence in intelligence, she poses the following questions (Dweck 2000, p. 181):

Check the sentence that is most true for you.
I usually think I am intelligent
I wonder if I'm intelligent

Now show how true the statement you chose is for you

Very true	True	Sort of true
for me	for me	for me

▶────────────────────────▶◀────────────────◀

Check the sentence that is most true for you.
I'm not very confident about my intellectual ability
I feel pretty confident about my intellectual ability

Now show how true the statement you chose is for you

Very true	True	Sort of true
for me	for me	for me

▶────────────────────────▶◀────────────────◀

Such questions help identify the self-esteem of someone who is faced with learning new intellectual skills, analysis or simply acquiring new knowledge.

It is also possible to measure people's self-esteem when developing rapport; a skill which is required for those appointed to chief executive posts or who are entering a job which requires other strong interpersonal skills. Many have these skills already but some have to learn how to acquire them. Again Dweck provides some examples:

1. Check the sentence that is most true for you:
   When I meet new people I am not sure if they will like me
   When I meet new people I am sure they will like me

   Now show how true the statement you chose is for you

Very true	True	Sort of true
for me	for me	for me

▶────────────────────────▶◀────────────────◀

2. Check the sentence that is most true for you
   If I was another person choosing a friend, I am not sure I would choose me

If I was another person choosing a friend, I am sure I would choose me

Very true   True   Sort of true
for me   for me   for me
▶────────────────────────────────▶◀────────────────────────────◀

3. Check the sentence that is most true for you
   I'm pretty sure people like my personality
   I'm not sure people like my personality

Very true   True   Sort of true
for me   for me   for me
▶────────────────────────────────▶◀────────────────────────────◀

Questions about self-esteem need to be closely allied to the subject to be learnt. In the examples above, they are about intellectual ability, useful for assessing someone's self-esteem when it comes to learning something with a strong intellectual element such as analysis. Personality issues might need to be assessed when considering people for sales jobs or counseling skills. For someone who wants to learn how to swim or give presentations, the questions would have to be modified.

3.3.7 Measuring motivation

Motivation is a more complex subject to measure, often because people cannot, rather than will not, report accurately on what drives them. The Freudians argue that much of the force that drives us is unconscious and that we have little real insight into where the springs of motivation come from and how they work. There are many possible motivations and these will vary from subject to subject, from place to place and with the method of learning on offer. Many, for example, look forward to training courses for the social opportunities they afford. Others prefer the solitude and minimal risk of embarrassment offered by technology-based learning. Furthermore, people are likely to be motivated for more than one reason, but there is no doubt that motivation to learn is an important factor and an attempt to measure it is important for completeness.

Earlier in this chapter, the following motivations to learn were identified from Murray's original list. More common words are provided where appropriate:

Achievement (ambition)
Affiliation (need for affection)
Autonomy (need for independence)
Counteraction (need to overcome potential failure)
Defendance (to defend against criticism or blame)

Dominance (to influence others)
Exhibition (to make an impression, be seen and heard)
Harm avoidance (to avoid pain, to take precautions)
Infavoidance (to avoid embarrassing situations, humiliation)
Nurturance (to help or support others)
Order (to achieve organization, order)
Succorance (to be with someone or people who are sympathetic, supportive)
Understanding (an interest in analysing, a liking for thinking)

When trying to assess someone's degree of motivation, it is necessary first to establish which of the above elements are part of the motivation. The question could be posed in the following way: Please indicate which of the following motivations to learn apply to you for this particular course. Please also indicate their relative importance by identifying the most important with a number 1, the second most important with a 2 and so on:

Desire to achieve
Desire to meet people
Desire for independence
Desire to overcome potential failure*
Desire to defend self against blame*
Desire to influence others
Desire to make an impression, be seen and heard
Desire to avoid pain, to take precautions*
Desire to avoid embarrassing situations, humiliation*
Desire to help or support others
Desire to achieve organization, order
Desire to be with someone or people who are sympathetic, supportive
Desire to understand, analyse, a liking for thinking)
Other, please specify . . . .
None of the above

Largely extrinsic motivations

The actual motivation is interesting but is not relevant when measuring motivation. The purpose of this question is to identify what motivations the individual has for learning a particular subject. The follow-up questions identify the relative strength of motivation.

If, for example, someone had identified "Desire to achieve" as their first priority, the follow-up question would be along the following lines: Please indicate how relevant you think this course will be in helping you achieve your aims within the organization.

Highly relevant   Little relevance
▶━━━◀

Other questions can be posed to elicit the level of motivation, both in the first priority subjects as well as in the lower ones. An interview would help when making a final judgement on what the overall level of motivation should be.

3.4 The Learning Quotient in Practice

Some of the above is based on clear statistical evidence and some on informed judgements. The results can be shown on bar graphs using the template in Figure 3.4.

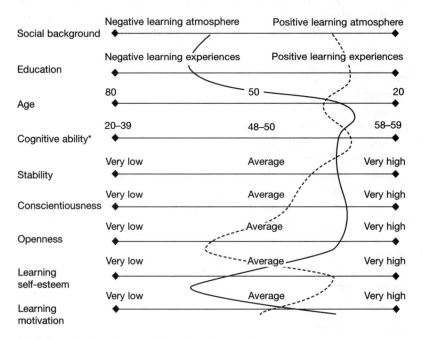

* Scale based on Raven's progressive matrices (see p. 155)

Figure 3.4 **Measuring the learning quotient**

Profiles can then be built up of individuals. For example, a profile of a socially and educationally deprived person with low self-esteem in the particular subject to be learnt but positive in all other respects is shown by the solid line in Figure 3.4. In this particular instance, the trainer or coach would need to encourage the individual so that they came to recognize that they have ability despite earlier experiences and show how he or she can learn the subject concerned.

The profile of a highly educated and socially privileged person, who is bright and confident but is closed to new thoughts on this particular subject and does not have a great deal of motive to learn much more is represented by the dotted line in Figure 3.4. On the face of it, this person might well be considered to be a high flyer and highly suited for most jobs. In fact, their low openness score and relatively modest motivation score make them unlikely to be adaptable. Some might even consider such a person to be arrogant.

3.5 Quality of Training

The final factor in someone's learning potential is the quality of training offered. If the subject can be self-taught, this is not relevant, but learning how to cope with a chemical weapon attack or some of the more obscure computer software needs the help of a trainer or coach. If the quality of training is poor, then learners are significantly hampered in their learning. But that has nothing to do with the learners' intrinsic potential to learn, their LQ.

The following chapters discuss how learning can be made most efficient and how to assess both the learner and the provider.

3.6 Conclusion

LQ is about people's learning potential. Coming into a new job or following a merger, how well will the individual concerned be able to learn the new cultures or skills required? To some, measuring an individual's learning quotient may seem more akin to searching for the Holy Grail than scientific endeavor and undoubtedly more work needs to be done. This chapter attempts to identify the main factors which combine to influence someone's ability to learn. It also attempts to demonstrate how those factors might be measured.

Whatever the merits and demerits of the above, there is insufficient understanding of why some people appear more able to learn something. Intelligence has some influence but there are many examples of people coming from an underprivileged background learning quickly in the workplace and vice versa. Other factors clearly influence people's ability to learn. This chapter is a starting place.

4 Learning in Groups

4.1 Introduction

Professional adult trainers are often a curious bunch of people. Managing them has, not unkindly, been compared to herding cats. They combine a mix of the theatre, a way with words and a confidence which comes from standing in front of a group of people and holding their attention for significant periods. But the best are nervous before their training session and their position in a company or organization is not always held in the highest regard. Too often they are tarred by the George Bernard Shaw quote:

> "Those that can – do; those that can't – teach."

And as someone added:

> "And those who can't teach, train
> And those who can't train, train trainers."

And yet trainers see top management coming into the training room and give a presentation that is poorly structured, badly delivered and which has a negative impact on the group. Furthermore, their cousins in the coaching, mentoring and e-learning industries often look down on them as lesser brethren. Coaching and e-learning are frequently trumpeted as the modern and most effective methods of learning, so where does that leave the "trainer"?

Training has moved on in recent decades. Rarely in the UK or the US do trainers in a business context lecture an hour at a time, standing behind a hefty lectern, barking questions at some poor individual, usually in the back row, who he has just seen nodding off. The students would sit in a large group in rows of desks, suffering a few hard-to-read visuals.

Trainers in the past few decades have become more conscious of the need to put the emphasis on learning as opposed to teaching. In the early 1990s, accredited courses by the CIPD entitled Training the Trainers were already defining training as "helping people learn more effectively and quickly".

> *Lecture – a process by which the notes of the professor become the notes of the students without passing through the minds of either.*
>
> R.K. Rathbun

Martyn Sloman, advisor, learning, training and development at the London-based CIPD writes:

> interventions and activities that are intended to improve knowledge and skills in organizations will increasingly focus on the learner. Emphasis will shift to the individual learner (or the team), and he or she will be encouraged to take more responsibility for his or her learning. Efforts will be made to develop a climate that supports effective and appropriate learning. Such interventions and activities will form part of an integrated approach to creating competitive advantage through people in the organization. (Sloman 2003)

Trainers and managers of training have felt this for some time; the trick is to persuade others in organizations, leaders, managers and staff, to think the same. Senior executives might recognize training is necessary, but it costs money and they will want to see a return on the investment (ROI). Replacing the word "training" with "learning" in organizational jargon is seen by some as a typical HR ruse, akin to dancing on a pin head. Learning is a better word, but it is more important to show results.

This chapter goes on to analyse learning in the classroom, provides some guidance on what works well in the classroom and how trainers can best deliver what an organization needs.

4.2 The Advantages of the Classroom

The advantages to classroom training are not just about the economics of putting a relatively large number of people in a room with one trainer. People tend to think that one-to-one training is bound to be better because the learner has the undivided attention of the deliverer. This is only partly true. There are some things that can happen in a classroom which it is not possible to replicate in a coaching session.

Having a group of people means that the trainer can write exercises which involve the group working in teams or with each other role playing so that they can actively practice the skills they are learning. This of course works particularly well with the kind of interpersonal skills required for those who have "emotional intelligence". Interviewing skills, presentation skills, negotiating can all be experienced in the classroom; it is much more limited in one-to-one coaching.

It is possible to reinforce learning through discussion either in the classroom or in syndicates. People will produce ideas and questions which will stimulate others to see the issues in a slightly different way or put the problem in a new context which will help them to remember.

The trainer is not the only person with relevant knowledge and experience. The best trainers know that others can contribute significantly to the learning of the class and will encourage people to come with views. He or she may have to moderate some contributions and correct mistakes or bad habits that may be introduced, but the plusses of student participation usually outweigh the minuses many times over.

Discussion, questions and even argument are particularly useful in helping people to acquire new knowledge, beliefs and values. The role of the trainer then becomes something closer to a facilitator. Skilfully done, this can be the equivalent of the non-directive approach of the coach (see p. 98). The learners come to the conclusions themselves and are therefore much more likely to buy into the new ideas.

Finally, some people are more comfortable in a group than one to one. A coach can be quite threatening and not the best method of learning. The work of learning is not so intense and this suits some approaches, of both the learner and the subject. It is also the case that people enjoy social interaction and meeting others is all part of the fun – and let no one deny that, to be good, training ought to have some moments of fun and light relief.

The task of controlling, facilitating and processing a group of people rather than one individual is, for some, daunting. For this reason, many trainers resort to the authoritarian styles of the traditional classroom teacher. Those brought up in a classroom disciplined by rules and punishment some-times find it hard to believe that the truly strong do not need the paraphernalia of the lectern and pointing stick. A group has some inbuilt advantages. Trainers can easily exploit these to the benefit of all.

4.3 Learning Objectives

The training or learning cycle is the foundation of many textbooks on training. It takes on various forms. Bits are added and some are subtracted but the basic cycle is shown in Figure 4.1.

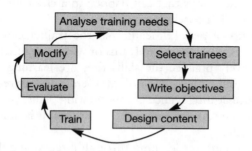

Figure 4.1 **The training cycle**

It provides a useful model and, where relevant, various parts are discussed in detail in this book. Learners, however, only see a training program and they will usually see the first level of evaluation, the so-called "happy sheet".

Much depends on whether learners are *volunteers or conscripts*, that is, whether they choose to go on a particular course or are forced to do so. Much also depends on the *purpose*, *level* and *length* of the course in determining how much of the cycle they see or understand.

A learner's first brush with a course usually comes when discussing or confronted with the objectives, if indeed they exist or are even shown to the candidate. They are at the core of all learning events. They provide trainers and learners with direction and they serve an important role in satisfying some of the theory of adult learning. For trainers, these objectives come from a training needs analysis (TNA), which itself often starts with the competency framework of the organization or department. Coaches and mentors rarely look so far back, they concern themselves with the learner and identify their goals or objectives jointly.

The best trainers take a robust attitude to objectives. Much of the groundwork was established by Robert Mager. His book *Preparing Instructional Objectives* was published in 1962 and despite its rather old-fashioned title, it contains some remarkable modern thinking and language. In it he defines an objective as:

> an *intent* communicated by a statement describing a proposed change in a learner – a statement of what the learner is to be like when he has successfully completed a learning experience. Without clearly defined goals "it is impossible to evaluate a course or program effectively, and there is no sound basis for selecting appropriate materials, content, or the instructional methods. (Mager 1962, p. 3)

He goes on to describe the additional advantage is that the student can evaluate his or her own performance and knows from the beginning what is expected of him or her. Furthermore, when there is more than one trainer, it ensures a degree of consistency.

What then are the essential qualities of a good objective? Training is about changing people: they will have more knowledge, new or improved skills or they will have adjusted their values and beliefs. Learners, trainers and other stakeholders in the process need to know how they will have changed. According to Mager and now accepted by most as best practice, this means making a statement about what learners will be able to do at the end of the session or course which is unambiguous, removing all possible alternatives to a learner's interpretation. Mager provides two lists of verbs which might be used to describe how a learner will change (Table 4.1).

Words such as "understand" and "appreciate" can be used as long as it is clear how the understanding and appreciation will be measured. In general, however, it is not helpful to use such words in objectives. "Describe", "identify", and "explain" are better.

Table 4.1 Words for objective setting

Words open to many interpretations	Words open to fewer interpretations
To know	To write
To understand	To recite
To really understand	To identify
To appreciate	To differentiate
To fully appreciate	To solve
To grasp the significance of	To construct
To enjoy	To list
To believe	To compare
To have faith in	To contrast

Source: Mager 1962, p. 11.

▶ "By the end of this session students will understand the different styles of learning." A better objective would be:

▷ By the end of this session students will be able to describe the four styles of
learning identified by David Kolb.

▶ "By the end of this session participants will understand how to repair a puncture
in a bicycle tire." A better objective would be:

▷ By the end of this session students will be able to repair a puncture in a
bicycle tire using a patch and glue so that no air escapes after the repair.

▶ "By the end of this induction course participants will appreciate the company's
corporate values." A better objective would be:

▷ By the end of this induction course participants will be able to describe the
company's corporate ideals and will follow them in their corporate life.

Figure 4.2 **Examples of good and bad objectives**

The final point about objectives is to recognize whose they are. The
objective has to be owned by both parties, with the deliverer accepting the
greater responsibility. Indeed there are three levels of ownership, shown in
Figure 4.3.

If someone fails to achieve the standard set in the objective, the failure is,
to a significant extent, that of the deliverer: he or she has not succeeded in
helping the person to learn. Perhaps this is why some trainers and coaches
like the less rigorous style involving words such as "understand"! It follows
from the above that the objectives should be given to the learners and if
possible some time before the course begins.

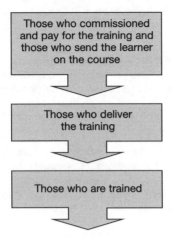

Figure 4.3 **Ownership of objectives**

Naughty typologies – trainers

More out of fun than scientific enquiry, Furnham (1996) proposed two different typologies: those of trainers and those of trainees. Both are unfair and leave out the most common in each category, namely the well-prepared, dedicated, professional trainer and the serious student. Nevertheless, there are those in training who perhaps have various ulterior motives or rather unusual styles which might be recognized.

The evangelist game show host: These trainers are often vacuously extrovert show-offs. They believe the course is about having fun, winning prizes and "believing". The programs are all about the showing and sharing of emotions. The evangelist in them feels the need to convert the delegates to their way of thinking, their models and their methods. They are often exhausting to be around, and definitely not the choice of the quiet, serious-minded participant.

The academic guru: He or she is the talking head of the training business. Often they have a touch of arrogance and let you feel that all this is slightly beneath them. Some patronize the audience, others drone on, ignoring the perplexed and puzzled looks of the delegates. The guru in them is often the dangerous element because they may genuinely believe they have found the Holy Grail of management.

The therapeutic doctor: Some trainers like to give the message "Trust me, I am a doctor" or "Put your faith in me, I am experienced". They try to cultivate the air of the wise Dr Findlay of the marketplace who has seen it all before and knows how people behave. This front can, of course, always serve as a way of diverting attention from the fact that he or she really has no data or research evidence upon which to base the theories expounded.

The belittling assassin: Some trainers revel in their power to expose and humiliate the powerful and the great-and-good, whatever their personal ability, skill or indeed history. They belong to the Dame Edna school of picking on hapless, and then helpless, victims of the course. Sometimes put up to it by senior management but often at random, these missiles in a course can do great psychological damage.

The bullshitter/facilitator: For those who have precious little knowledge or skill, or simply those who have done no preparation, there is always the fallback position of the facilitator. In essence this means others (the course participants) do the work. The bullshitter simply encourages them, by a variety of methods, not only to diagnose their own problems but to solve them on the course, and then takes the credit for the solution.

The manual-dependent schoolmarm: Some trainers are rendered guideless, speechless and powerless if their slides and manuals are removed from them. Theirs is the "open your textbooks to page I" approach. Participants are simply required to complete a series of preordained exercises that are supervised and inspected by the strict nanny-teacher. This is the serious and rather boring world of skill acquisition.

Mind-expander and creative: Occasionally one finds the trainer who has taken his or her de Bono rather too seriously. They believe it is their job to think "laterally" on all occasions; to come up with radical, albeit impractical, alternatives. They may do this through brainstorming exercises or public free associations, but the outcome is the same.

Naughty typologies – trainees

Equally there are those on adult training course whose reason for being there extends beyond the straightforward motive to acquire knowledge or skills. The following seven categories represent some of these odd types, all of which are recognizable to adult trainers.

The prisoner: The scowl on the face, the arms tightly folded across the chest, and the folded letter from the boss or personnel manager demanding (requiring) that they have to attend the course, characterize this type. They have probably succeeded at avoiding this course, or ones like it, many times before, but eventually are caught. They are prisoners: they don't want to be there and wish they were somewhere else. They are sour, negative, unhelpful and certainly uncooperative.

The escapee: This type is the course junkie who jumps at the opportunity to get out of the office. They may hate their work or simply enjoy education and training at the company's expense. The escapee is usually rather too experienced at course activities, games and questionnaires and may well have done them before. They are easy to deal with from the trainer's point of view but not good value for money from the perspective of their company.

The old dog: There are various reasons why some people believe they cannot be taught new tricks. Some delegates are on-the-job retirees, in the departure lounge of the organization. They may in fact be quite a long way from retirement, but they are not interested in learning anything. Others believe courses are too abstract, too theoretical, too vague and have nothing to add to their day-to-day working lives.

The eager beaver: This type comes in two forms. The first is the enthusiastic learner, genuinely interested in gaining skills, insights and knowledge. The second is the slightly naive delegate who is happy to take anything on board but has few critical facilities. This makes them too gullible and too unfocused, although certainly easy for the trainer.

The intellectual: Whereas the old dog may reject what he/she is told because it is too vague and theoretical, the intellectual wants to know the empirical and epistemological bases of the data being presented. Many are snobs who think they know more than the trainer (and sometimes do). These high flyers may believe either the content or the style is not appropriate for their level. They may enjoy humiliating the trainer if they can.

The bastard: They are arrogant know-it-alls. They usually believe that personnel departments should be closed, all consultants fired, and the money put into the company's pension fund. In a curious way, they enjoy courses in the way they enjoy meetings, because they have learnt to be maximally disruptive. They may be simple attention seekers and in some organizations are intellectually seriously underpowered. They are a nightmare for trainers because they are solely interested in scuppering or damaging the proceedings.

The ingratiator: Many people are anxious when attending courses because they fear being shown up in front of others. Those who fear being exposed as the product of the Peter Principle tend to be what Americans charmingly call "apple polishers". The ingratiator tries to do a deal with the trainer: "I will be a good boy/good girl if you don't expose or humiliate me". And for trainers it is a good deal.

4.4 Theory and the Classroom

One of the biggest problems with traditional training is that it tends to base its practice on old-fashioned, school-like teaching experiences. Students were placed behind desks, in rows and lectured to. When there were exercises, the teachers would often turn it into some kind of competition with the students – hardly fair, as the trainers held all the cards and knew what the solution was.

Theory and modern practice take a rather different view, but there are still pockets of traditional thinking. Groups take on a character of their own and sometimes do not behave as the trainer might expect them to.

4.4.1 Group development

The size of a class, the length of course and its frequency of coming together can all have an impact on the effectiveness of learning. A trainer needs to be able to recognize what is normal (if not very desirable) and what is unusual and ought to be encouraged or checked. Some training is aimed especially at groups or helping groups to form. But the process of group development may be part of the objective of the course or a consequence of it. This is only important when the group stays together for some time, will work together at a later point and sees themselves as a group.

Tuckman (1965) believed that groups go through a series of stages before becoming mature and effective. This concept suffers from such problems as not clarifying how long each stage lasts, what determines the change from one to another, whether the sequence is always linear, whether one can skip a stage, and so on. Nevertheless the idea has become popular, partly because it allows group participants to understand the process through which their group is going. It is important to note that the trainer for these purposes is usually part of the group. The stages are described below.

Forming

In the forming stage, members focus their efforts on defining goals and developing procedures for performing their task. Group development at this stage involves getting acquainted and understanding other member's roles. In this stage members might:

▷ Keep feelings to themselves until they know the situation
▷ Act more securely than they actually feel about how the team functions
▷ Experience confusion and uncertainty about what is expected of them
▷ Be reserved and polite, at least superficially
▷ Try to size up the personal benefits relative to the personal costs of being involved in the group.

At this stage they are concerned with "sniffing" out and around other group members.

Storming

Conflicts often emerge over who should do what, relative priorities of goals, who might be the "dominant" force. Some members may withdraw or try to isolate themselves from any emotional tension generated at this stage. The trainer needs to be wary of suppressing conflict, as this may create bitterness and resentment. Some groups genuinely have little to "storm" about, but if they do and the feelings are suppressed, there can be problems later.

Norming

Behaviors in the norming stage usually evolve into the sharing of information, acceptance of different opinions and positive attempts to reach mutually agreeable (or compromise) decisions on the group's rules for how they will work together. Emotions often focus on empathy, concern and the positive expressions of feelings, leading to a group cohesion. Cooperation within the group is a dominant theme, while a sense of shared responsibility for the group develops. However, it is both noticeable and surprising that different groups under similar circumstances find different solutions to their psychological processes and, hence, develop spectacularly different behavioral norms.

Performing

This is when the group starts to demonstrate together and individually how they have learnt and show in exercises and in discussion what they have learnt. By this stage, members usually understand when they should work together and when they should help each other. Groups differ at this stage in their performance. Some continue to learn and develop. Other groups may perform only at the level needed for survival. A minimally adequate performance at this stage might be the result of excessive self-oriented behaviors by some members of the group, poor leadership or professional qualities of the trainer or there may be other factors.

Adjourning/mourning

On training courses there is usually a well-defined point of adjournment. This stage has also been called the mourning stage, as it is not unusual for courses to depart leaving members sad and nostalgic (Furnham 1999, pp. 432–4).

Trainers contribute a great deal to how the group develops. They set the standards and potentially can influence values and behaviors much more than a team leader in a management context. Trainers have an unusual degree of power over their students. The wise trainer recognizes this and uses it to create the kind of atmosphere which is conducive to learning, Knowles (1998) principles of adult learning being a good starting point.

4.4.2 Course size

The numbers of participants on a course usually range from 4 to 20 or even more, while 6–12 is perhaps the most common size. There is considerable literature on the consequences of group size. For instance, as size increases, the verbal participation of each member decreases. Size is also related to satisfaction. This is partly because of less communication (not so much time with the trainer) but also because more differing views have to be taken into account.

Table 4.2 is inevitably a simplification and may seem arbitrary to some, but it does highlight some of the more typical effects the sheer size of a course has on its dynamics.

Table 4.2 Possible effects of size on courses

Category/dimension	2–7 members	8–12 members	13+ members
Demands on trainer	Low	Moderate	High
Differences between trainer and learners	Low	Moderate	Moderate to high
Direction required by trainer	Low	Low to moderate	Moderate to high
Tolerance of direction from leader	Low to high	Low to moderate	High
Domination of group by a few members	Low	Moderate to high	High
Inhibition of participants	Low	Moderate	High
Formalization of rules and procedures	Low	Low to moderate	Moderate to high
Time required to reach agreed conclusions	Low to moderate	Moderate	Moderate to high
Tendency for subgroups to form within the course	Low	Moderate to high	High

Source: Adapted from Furnham 1999.

4.5 Program Design

Once the objectives have been established, the trainer has to design a course which helps learners to achieve the objectives within the budget and time constraints set by the practicalities of the business environment. Hardingham (1996),writing in the CIPD's Training Essential series, established 10 fundamental design principles:

1 *Maximize action and interaction.* Allow and program participation throughout the event.
2 *Signpost, signpost and signpost again.* Explain the purpose of each element in the program and how it fits in with the previous and following events.
3 *Vary pace and rhythm.* A slow pace allows for reflection; a faster pace inserts energy and action into the program.
4 *Chunk content.* Break the content down into smaller packages to make it more digestible.
5 *Map the participants' world.* Relate the training to the world of the participants – make it relevant to them. Too often trainers simply take down the last version of a course and apply it, regardless of who they are training.
6 *Give participants choices.* Allow them to decide such things as whether to work in pairs or groups; give them some flexibility over timings of, say, lunch or start and finish times of the working day.
7 *Surface objections.* By encouraging comment on the program at an early stage, the deliverer can take steps to address them, reassure participants or change the program to take the objections into account.
8 *Balance theory and practice.* Too much theory switches many off; only skills and practice and the trainer risks losing credibility.
9 *Design in feedback.* Giving feedback to participants is a crucial part of learning. It is the single most important feature when changing people's behaviors.
10 *Design for closure.* Participants need a beginning, middle and an end.

Table 4.3 compares these principles with the theory discussed earlier.

All have their place somewhere in the theory, although as will be discussed later in this chapter, there are some features which theory suggests should also be included in the course design. Most of the above is self-explanatory, but some are worth more comment.

4.5.1 Chunking

Complex material needs to be broken down into digestible chunks. For example, when faced with teaching someone how to drive a car, the instructor should not reveal all the complications of the process at the same time. Clutch and gearbox should be described separately from the skills of reversing; the importance of the mirror before moving, separately from the use of the headlights. As each part is mastered, then they can be brought together.

Table 4.3 Hardingham's 10 design principles and theory

Hardingham's 10 design principles	How Hardingham's factors relate to theory		
	Knowles' adult learning theory	Kolb and experiential theory	Memory (based on Baddeley's work)
Action & interaction		Encouraging "doing"	
Signpost	Informing learner of relevance of what is happening and therefore potentially some influence		
Vary pace		Allow all four learning styles time	
Chunk content			Break down into manageable portions
Relate to participant	Make training relevant		Provide links
Allow participant choice	Allow some influence		
Surface objections	Allow some influence		
Balance theory and practice		Allow all forms of learning activity	
Give feedback		Encourage thinking and reflection	
Bring to an end	Ensure relevance to workplace		

This leads to modular teaching, which has clear advantages as it gives the learner time to concentrate on each element. The danger is that after a module has been taught, it is not referred to again until the end of the course when the trainer might have a final exercise.

Each module needs to be connected to earlier modules so they can see the whole as well as the parts. In the process the earlier module is reinforced.

The designer needs to be sure that each element has sufficient time and it is properly related to the other parts.

There are a number of methods which course designers can use to

Laurie was given a two-hour session in a helicopter for Christmas by his sister, already an accomplished pilot. Flying helicopters is a serious business and the pilots are enormously professional. Laurie was also impressed with the teaching skills of his instructor, Jeremy.

The first 25 minutes were spent in the center when Jeremy covered various safety factors, explained how a helicopter flies, some radio procedures and then the basic controls. There are three essential devices for maneuvering a helicopter, the cyclic, the collective lever and the tail rotor control/yaw.

help in the process of chunking. A simple pencil and paper or better whiteboard session is often sufficient. Some need do no more than conceptualize the whole and break it down in their minds. Others will use trial and error as they create a program on their computer.

Mind maps or spidergrams provide another method of helping the designer. Tony Buzan (1995, 2004) has written many books popularizing the subject. The claims made for its potential are extravagant: "it harnesses the full range of cortical skills – word, image, number, logic, rhythm, colour and spatial awareness – in a single, uniquely powerful manner. In so doing, it gives you the freedom to roam the infinite expanses of your brain" (www.buzancentres.com).

As far as the course designer is concerned, it helps to identify the main subjects and how each will be developed. It can be used not just

> *They then went out to the helicopter, affectionately known by those in the business as a Robbo 47. After the meticulous checks, they took off and soon enough (in Laurie's case he felt too soon) Jeremy invited Laurie to take over the cyclic. Once that was mastered, Laurie took control of the collective lever.*
>
> *Laurie was then invited to try them in pairs – in the two hours he did not manage to master all three, much to the amusement of his sister, but the principle of chunking was well demonstrated and had it not been for the cost involved Laurie could well have been hooked.*
>
> *Of course there is much more to flying a helicopter than just getting it into the air and flying in more or less a straight line. But the skills of Jeremy as an instructor were such that he did not bother Laurie with the detail at this stage.*

for course design but also in the planning stages of a presentation. Figure 4.4 shows how a mind map of a course for people about to go overseas might look.

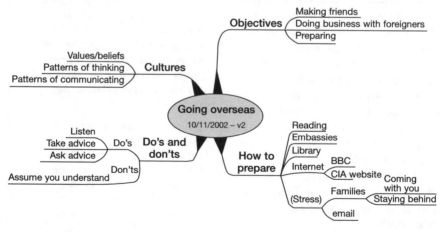

Figure 4.4 **Example of a mind map**

This mind map demonstrates the designer's thinking as he tackled this subject after about 10 minutes. It is easy to put in new thoughts and take out those that are not relevant or at a later stage prioritize the ideas.

4.5.2 Feedback

Feedback is at the center of the learning experience. A learner will listen, hopefully, politely to a trainer explaining where he or she might have gone wrong or how they could perform better, but there is often a resistance to such messages. The trainer may think the learner has taken in the advice, but the learner needs to say more than just "OK fine" for the message to have really sunk in.

If learners are to change, they need to know what they have got right and what was not so good. Sometimes it is blindingly obvious; sometimes people are completely unaware of how they are performing. Joseph Luft (1969) demonstrated this with what he called the Johari window ("Johari" derives from his first name and the first name of a friend Harrington Ingham).

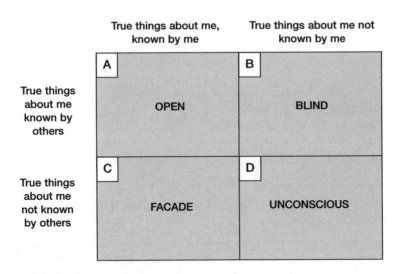

Figure 4.5 **The Johari window**

The whole "window" represents all the information about an individual and each pane represents the knowledge of self and others combined. Thus pane A, the "open" window, is all those things which an individual knows about themselves and which other people also know. In Pane B, others can see something which the individual is unaware of; pane C represents that knowledge which only the individual knows and pane D is about those things that neither the individual nor any observers are aware of.

The purpose of training and feedback can be seen as increasing the size of box A, certainly to the right and into box B, but there may also be advantage of extending it into box C. If, in the process, learners broaden their experience and knowledge and discover something new about themselves which others were also unaware of, that could be a bonus.

Feedback is not always easy to give. Many trainers suggest that the rest of the group should provide the feedback to an individual's performance. This has some dangers:

▷ The feedback may be wrong, inaccurate, too general
▷ More likely the group will be too gentle and refuse to make the necessary points
▷ The individual may be hurt by insensitive comments
▷ The feedback may not be constructive
▷ Some individuals are more fragile than others.

If the trainer is going to use the group as the main giver of feedback, then he or she should moderate and facilitate the comments, keeping a close eye on the recipient to ensure they are accepting it well. The trainer needs also to have his or her own comments on the performance.

▷ Feedback is more likely to be received properly in private, one to one with the trainer or a colleague. Hackett (2003) suggests four ground rules:
  ▶ Ensure feedback is related to the course objectives
  ▶ Be objective in giving feedback
  ▶ Base comments on evidence
  ▶ Identify alternative positive behaviors.

Many trainers use the mnemonic BOOSTS to guide them:

▶ *Balanced:* feedback should give good and bad comment. Use the good to help develop other areas.

▶ *Owned:* there are two parts to be owned. The giver of feedback should give their own views and comments. They should avoid saying things like "others felt that..." or even worse "of course I don't agree but some thought that...". The second part is that they should also own the feedback. It is important for them not just to nod their head, ask them how they thought the session went or how they think they are getting on.

▶ *Objective:* Avoid relying on feelings or instincts.

▶ *Specific:* This one is closely related to the previous one – feedback should be specific and objective. The key is to provide evidence. For example: what specifically did the learner do or say and at what time which produced the conclusions described.

► *Timely:* As with all feedback, it should be given soon after the event.

► *Solutions:* Provide a comment on how any shortcomings might be corrected or what the individual might have done to improve their performance.

A frequent mistake in giving feedback is for the giver to talk too much. Encourage the learner to analyse their own performance and pick up on their comments as well as giving your own. It is also possible to overload a learner by going through every point, good and bad. The memory can rarely cope with more than just a few critical points, probably three at the most.

Finally, a word of warning on giving feedback. The above guidelines are not appropriate for giving really bad news, such as asking someone to leave a course or telling them that they have failed in the course assessment. Feedback is designed to advance the development and learning of an individual. In the end they should feel "boosted", which is not the objective of giving bad news.

4.5.3 The four stages of learning

There are two aspects of theory not covered in Hardingham's analysis (Table 4.2) which should be considered in course design. The first is to ensure that learners have the opportunity to learn using all four styles of learning described by Kolb (1984) and reinforced by Honey and Mumford's work.

It is presented here in a fixed pattern but designers can be flexible and as Kolb identified, there may be times when it is best to change the order so that the learner experiences earlier in the process. Here it is presented in the traditional training order:

▷ Describe the subject to be learnt. This helps the learner to understand the point of the process and helps put the whole thing into context (in Kolb – "thinking")
▷ Demonstrate what is to be learnt. This can be done with a video/DVD or by the trainer/coach doing it in the classroom. Coaches should also find a way of demonstrating what they are helping the coachee to learn (Kolb – "watching")
▷ Invite the learner to do it but with some help and advice from the trainer/coach (Kolb – "feeling")
▷ Invite the learner to do it on their own (Kolb – "doing").

It is easy to miss out a stage. The one which is often skimmed over or missed completely is the demonstration. Section 4.6 demonstrates how helpful this stage can be in the process of learning.

4.5.4 Reinforcement, reviews

Designers should also be sure to introduce regular reviews into their programs. In most courses there is a flood of information; hence it is important to ensure that the material is memorable. Chunking is encouraged, but the disadvantage is that by the time the learner has finished the third or fourth module, memories of the first will have receded and unless learners have a chance to review the earlier lessons, it will easily have been forgotten.

Exercises can help to reinforce, as can discussions in the classroom. Formal reviews can be introduced into the program at the beginning of the day or week. Participants can be asked to jot down on Post-it notes what they remembered from the previous day and what they still need more of. In this way they reflect on what happened but also have the opportunity of telling the trainer what they are still unclear about.

As well as the formal program slots, trainers and presenters should regularly remind participants what has gone on before. In other words, trainers need to build on, reiterate and repeat from previous sessions in order to ensure that the central message and skills are fully remembered.

4.5.5 Summary of the main features of program design

Taking the principal elements of learning theory and how practitioners such as Hardingham go about designing courses, the following are the most significant:

▷ Give learners/candidates/delegates a copy of the program and ensure they know what is happening at each stage of the program and why
▷ Break the material down into modules or chunks
▷ Allow learners to learn through description (theory), demonstration, experience, both with help and on their own
▷ Allow participants the opportunity to influence how they are to learn and to surface any problems, either in the material being learnt or in the course administration
▷ Encourage participation and wherever possible relate the learning directly to the experience or background of the participants
▷ Ensure there is time for proper, honest and helpful feedback
▷ Ensure there is a formal time for review and reinforcement of central messages and skills
▷ Introduce as much variation into the course as possible.

4.6 The Tool Box

One of the principles of good design is to ensure variety; another is to allow

people to learn in each of the four learning
styles. Eleven fairly common techniques are
discussed in this section.

> *College professor – one who*
> *talks in other people's sleep.*
>
> Bergen Evans

4.6.1 The presentation or lecture

This is the traditional and probably the most common form of training. It
serves an important purpose. Visiting speakers can often provide a good
introduction to the subject or interesting slant, but care needs to be taken if
the quality of their presentations is not appropriate.

There is much written about how to deliver a good presentation and this
is not the place to go into that vast subject in detail. The chapter ends with
an essay describing an inspirational lecturer. It is something all trainers
should aspire to.

A particularly useful form of presentation is the case history. Given by
someone in the company or organization who is both experienced and
respected, it can have a powerful influence on learners' beliefs and values as
well as proving a useful demonstration and reinforcement of lessons learnt.

4.6.2 One-to-one discussion with trainer (tuition)

Wherever possible, trainers should spend some time with participants individually and with some privacy. The advantages are clear:

▷ it makes the participant feel special
▷ nervous more introvert learners can express their views and ask questions
  in the more comfortable zone of a one-to-one conversation
▷ it allows the trainer to explain subjects not quite fully grasped in more
  detail, without boring those who have already grasped it
▷ those who are not so quick can be given a little more training
▷ it is the best way of giving feedback, particularly negative feedback.

Conversations can be formally programed and may occur in the corner of a
classroom, a syndicate room or an office. They can also be less formal over
lunch, in a coffee break or in the bar if it is a residential course. In any event,
these are valuable times for the learner and the caring trainer.

4.6.3 Video/DVD

Video Arts, the BBC and other companies have for many years now
produced videos to help learners. Some suggest that all that is needed is the
video itself, although most often it will be part of course on the same subject.
DVDs offer a great deal more flexibility. They provide an excellent method
of demonstrating a skill or particular practice.

For many, however, the costs are prohibitive. Producers want to produce a smart product with well-known actors to make it more attractive. Sometimes their fame and humor can get in the way of learning (that's not to say there is no place for humor, of course there is, but not when it is the dominant theme and the audience is waiting for the next laugh). Furthermore, they can engender a sort of passive mode that some people experience when watching videos. This can occur particularly noticeably when it is necessary to darken rooms in the afternoon. Energy levels seem to drop as candidates feel they need not be as alert in case they are asked questions.

It can be more effective if the trainer uses only parts of the film and encourages discussion of those parts. Some DVDs and their manuals encourage this.

4.6.4 Observing others

Observing each other is useful to demonstrate and reinforce learning. Often it is done with interpersonal activities such as presentation or interviewing skills. Some participants are nervous about performing in front of others and this needs careful handling. Often people become supportive of each other and very attentive. They can easily be encouraged to "steal" ideas and "tricks" from each other when they see something done particularly well.

Role models can come in many forms. Other students can inspire as well as the trainer or others introduced to the group. When attempting to build people's beliefs and values, learners pick up a lot from observing others – good and bad habits.

It is possible to record participants and play that back as part of the learning. The group needs to be quite robust and agreement should be sought beforehand. With carefully managed feedback, the group as a whole learns from each other; and it is not just the mistakes, the better ones will be good demonstrators of how to do something.

4.6.5 Demonstration by trainer/coach

This is pretty standard practice for something practical such as stripping down a Browning 9mm pistol or making picture frames. However, trainers faced with demonstrating interpersonal skills become a little nervous and often shy away from the experience if at all possible. They should not! Learners like to see how things are done and a trainer's credibility is not going to be shattered if they go wrong. It just produces a more lively discussion. Further, it is important not to give the impression that trainers are always extremely insightful or skillful. Being oneself, clumsy or shy helps to convey humanity.

4.6.6 Computer (interactive training program)

There is a new industry dedicated to bringing IT into the classroom. "Blended learning" is one of the buzz phrases around HR conferences at the beginning of the 21st century. Or perhaps they are bringing traditional training techniques into IT training. Either way, IT can contribute greatly to learning and trainers should be looking for ways to enhance their programs.

The obvious example is in computer software courses, but some CD-based learning programs allow people to experiment their newfound skills. Larger companies could put IT programs on their intranet and the internet has courses and information available to all.

Pilots and the military regularly employ simulators to train staff on the more expensive equipment. Open learning centers will have a number of programs which can be usefully introduced into a course either formally during the day or as something participants can take home to practice on their own.

4.6.7 Exercise preparation and delivery

At some stage learners need to practice what they have learnt in the theory sessions. Some would argue that this is the important part of learning – it is in effect the first stage of Kolb's original theory – experience. Exercises can be short or complex, running over many days. They are the workhorse of most courses.

Many trainers enjoy writing exercises. It brings out the creative side in them and they are in effect writing short stories. Some guiding principles for writing exercises are as follows:

▷ Write objectives in a similar manner to course objectives, using the SMARTS criteria. Give the objectives of the exercise to the participants.
▷ Wherever possible tie the exercise objectives into a specific course objective.
▷ Put the scenario into the work situation of the participants. Taking the action into some neutral territory risks making the participants feel it is not relevant to them.
▷ Keep the situation as simple as possible. The new skills being tested will be hard enough. If the background situation is too complex, participants have to devote a lot of energy into remembering the script and not therefore focussing on practicing the skills needed. The cognititive load theory suggests we should avoid overcomplicating learning unless it is necessary.
▷ Where role players are used, ensure that they are properly briefed and know the objectives of the exercise. Care should be taken to avoid overstretching the role players.
▷ Wherever possible, trainers should moderate role player feedback. Role players will have their own ideas about how a situation can be played and however well briefed, something is bound to arise which the exercise designer has not foreseen.

4.6.8 One-to-one discussion with trainer (feedback after exercise)

Like one-to-one sessions with trainers during the "learning" stage, these sessions represent quality time. How to give feedback was discussed in detail earlier. For learning, the essential point is to ensure that the individual recognizes where they might improve or have weaknesses and they have some solutions, an action plan or ideas on how they might change to improve.

4.6.9 Syndicates and group discussions

Where the objective (session or course) is mainly about knowledge, then these sessions effectively become the "exercise" part of other skills-oriented courses. They can also be used as an experience, for example at the beginning of a session, encouraging them to think about the meaning of the subject.

Having acquired knowledge through lectures or reading, a seminar or group discussion provides students with the opportunity to practice. Participants may be asked to describe a particular aspect of the issue and the remainder comment on the presentation. This is common in universities and is the thinking behind "action learning groups" and the like.

4.6.10 Reading

Material can be sent out to the participant(s) before the learning starts. The advantage is that time is saved and the learners can do it at their own pace. The disadvantages are that learners may not bother to read the material or won't comprehend it.

Reading is a useful supplement to a lecture and many learners ask for handouts or a bibliography to help them absorb the lecture. PowerPoint provides some useful tools to provide good handouts.

Where the deliverer is using a different language from the mother tongue of the learners, care should be taken to include additional notes and not rely on the summaries put up on the screen with PowerPoint. Listening in a foreign language is hard work and all the nuances will be lost unless the audience is particularly strong in the language.

And finally learners need time to think through what they have discovered. All too often trainers forget that people, some more than others, need time to reflect on what has been learnt. They need cognitive space.

4.7 Blended Learning

The successful trainer will use all the techniques available and suitable, given the resources, participants and nature of the course. There is at present considerable emphasis on introducing IT into the classroom and produce blended learning. This is good and is discussed in more detail in Chapter 6. For the purposes of this analysis, learning in groups requires a mix of techniques if deliverers are to satisfy the demands placed on them by learning theory and good course design. IT has a big part to play and it could be used a lot more, but there are more arrows in the trainers quiver than just the lecture and IT. Blended learning should introduce what is relevant to the material and the participants.

4.8 Popularity of Training Methods

Seventeen experienced trainers responded to a questionnaire asking how much time was devoted to each of the items discussed above on courses that they ran. Data was provided on 42 courses ranging from city and guilds machine embroidery to senior management courses (IT software courses were excluded). All the courses had been run at some stage during 2004. All the trainers had been through some kind of modern training in how to train. As part of their objective, the vast majority had to acquire knowledge, skills, beliefs and attitudes. The course lengths varied considerably from one day to three weeks. The results are shown in Table 4.4.

Table 4.4 Popularity of training methods

Method of training	Average usage on all courses % (with lows and highs)	
Lecture or formal presentation	**14**	(0–47)
One-to-one discussion with trainer (tuition)	**4**	(0–15)
Video/DVD	**2**	(0–5)
Observing others	**5**	(0–10)
Demonstration by trainer/coach	**6**	(0–15)
Computer (interactive training program)	**3**	(0–15)
Exercise preparation and delivery	**27**	(15–45)
One-to-one discussion with trainer (feedback)	**13**	(5–20)
Syndicates and group discussions	**14**	(5–20)
Reading	**4**	(0–25)
Time to reflect	**7**	(0–15)
Others	**1**	(0–5)

> *It is often presumed that a skills-based course requires increasing amounts of time spent on perfecting skills whereas in fact, achievement at the highest level is determined by knowledge and a focus on radical and confident attitude.*
>
> Pamela Watts, city and guilds trainer
> questionnaire respondent
> December 2004

An image of training emerges which involves considerable participation, in exercises (27%), discussion with the trainer (17%) and syndicates (14%). Lectures and formal presentations take up only 14% but they do spend a further 13% observing videos, demonstrations by the trainer or each other.

The group concerned may not be truly representative and it is noticeable, for example, that little use is made in this group of IT and therefore "blended learning". The use of IT in the classroom may therefore be underestimated compared to the national averages.

The statistical base is also not strong enough to draw firm conclusions about differences between popularity of methods when a course was primarily concerned with knowledge, skills, beliefs or values. However, it is clear (unsurprisingly) that courses which are heavy on basic skill acquisition spend more time on exercises (up to 45%). But, as the skills become more advanced, less time is spent on exercise and more on one-to-one time with the trainer. In some cases, there are no lectures or formal presentations when taking learners up to the top levels of their skill or profession.

Those involved in knowledge spend more time listening to presentations and reading (62%). Syndicates and discussion groups were also popular with this group.

It was not possible to identify a particular trend for those courses primarily concerned with developing beliefs and values, except that they tended to use the full range of methods available.

Technology does not play a major role in the classroom.

> *I find that real value from development can be attained the more the learning is integrated with real issues in the workplace. This both presents reality to the individual and makes them confront change in a way that they might not otherwise.*
>
> David Vere, Development Partnership
> questionnaire respondent
> December 2004

Some respondents commented that they would like to use more technology, particularly short DVD clips demonstrating a particular skill (interviewing, rapport building, meaning of body language) which trainers could use in their own presentations rather than handing the class over to some smooth but slightly off target video/DVD costing many hundreds of dollars.

The image is not that of a sedentary existence rooted to a classroom desk. Training courses are dynamic and tend to make full use of a range of materials and techniques.

4.9 Conclusion

Training in groups is alive and well. It still forms the mainstay of most organizations' learning effort and it is popular with many students. More work should be done to bring accessible technology into the classroom and there is scope for more detailed research into the methods used in training. The emphasis in recent years has been on the coach and e-learning. They are important and have an important role to play in learning, but more traditional forms will continue to play their part. The challenge will be to modernize and keep trainers up to the mark.

Much of this chapter has been about the methods used by trainers – the processes in the classroom. But the most important element of any training course is not the technology, the visual aids, or program design. The person who stands at the front of the class is key to the whole process and can make or break the success of the learning.

4.10 Characteristics of a Great Lecturer

Teachers can and do, change lives. They can determine the choice of university and degree course. They can have a direct impact on career choice. They can light candles in the darkest mind. They can model attitudes, beliefs and behaviors, setting an example to follow.

Practically everybody can nominate such a person using a secondary school teacher or university lecturer. Many maintain contact, partly out of thanks, but also looking for continuing inspiration.

Often the teachers are not among the most successful. Nor are they necessarily the Mr. Chips of the school. Inspirational teachers in universities probably spend too little time in the library and laboratory scribbling for those all important publications to help them to promotion. Some don't care for high (management) positions, because they know where both their strength and joy lie.

So what are the characteristics of the inspirational? First, there is unbounded *enthusiasm*, even *passion*, for their subject. They show the thrill, the joy and the sheer pleasure of acquiring skills and knowledge in a particular area. And they are able to communicate this. Indeed they cannot hide it. You can't easily fake passion or at least not over a sustained period. All great teachers are passionate. Work becomes play for them.

Second, they are *evangelists* trying to convert minds rather than souls. They want others to share their joy and passion, believing it to be good for them. They really want to communicate the good news. One of the characteristics of the inspirational evangelist is that they never retire. Neither they nor their employees wish it. They are simply too valuable. And good administrators know it. They soon become "Emeritus" but usually eschew the titles, preferring simply to carry on, ignoring the passing of the years.

Third, they *set high standards*. Inspirational teachers are not merely benevolent, kindly parental substitutes. They want to bring the best out in people. They do not compromise but they do encourage. They understand the learning process and the markers along the way. Thus they are able to get the best out of people and it is often for this that they are profoundly admired.

Fourth, they *update their material*, metaphors and methods. Every generation needs a different introduction to the discipline. The pupils come with different experiences and expectations. Their hot (and cold) buttons are different. They need to be approached differently. The inspirational teacher is always in fashion, able to appeal to many throughout their careers. It goes without saying that they have to update their knowledge as well.

Fifth, there is the issue of *adaptation and flexibility*. This means knowing how to "package the brand" differently to appeal to different individuals and groups. The intelligence, social background and values of students dictate that they have to be approached differently. Brilliant teachers can and do do this.

There is a business passion for coaches. A great teacher is, of course, both a coach and a model. All great teachers bring their topic alive by constantly referring to current events and how knowledge of the subject enables better understanding of the world we live in. They show its relevance.

Inspirational teachers inspire by intrinsic motivation. Their students voluntarily stay on after school, write essays that "don't count", and do additional reading. They paint the big picture, and direct students to excellent sources.

Skills-based teaching, as in the performing arts, crafts and technology, is no different. Students apprenticed to a master will often acknowledge his/her insight and dedication in shaping their skills. It is no accident that the "master class" is so popular in business.

And why are inspirational teachers the way they are? Intelligence, knowledge, multiskilled ... all of the above. But most say they became teachers or lecturers because they themselves had an inspirational teacher. So it's not genetic but it certainly is passed on.

5 One-to-One Learning

5.1 Introduction

Coaching is growing more quickly than any other training technique available to companies in the UK (CIPD 2004) as well as the rest of Europe. The picture in the US is the same. But one-to-one learning covers a wide range of styles and methods. Learners have different needs and come from a wide range of backgrounds. The choice of "help" (be it advice, support or "therapy") and methods used by practitioners also varies; matching the two is not easy.

There are many reasons why executives may want a coach. They include:

▷ Loneliness; they need to share confidential ideas
▷ Sounding board; for difficult decisions
▷ Outsider's perspective; unbiased advice
▷ Stress resolution; express weaknesses, learn some coping skills
▷ Education; be taught new skills.

But some managers may also want a coach as:

▷ A trophy
▷ A fashion accessory
▷ A crypto member of the board.

But it is tough at the top and managers need help. Typical, acute and chronic sources of senior management stress are:

▷ Work overload
▷ Time pressure and deadlines
▷ Driving through change
▷ Being in the media spotlight
▷ Understanding the dynamics of the board
▷ Career planning
▷ Work–life balance
▷ Keeping up with legal and technical change
▷ Strategic planning
▷ The vision thing.

A common characteristic amongst the plethora of books and articles on any aspects of one-to-one learning is the certainty and confidence of the authors in the methods they propose. This is natural, but it does not assist the reader or purchaser, trying to work out what will help him or her most or that of their peers or staff. What they need is a way to make better informed choices. Nor does it help the systematic investigation of what each has to offer or how effective each may be.

The problems are exacerbated by the lack of accepted definitions. Figure 5.1 gives some examples of definitions offered by various authors or authorities. Each is meant to be exclusive and reflects the authors' own preferences or style. Often they stray into adjacent fields.

▶ "Effective coaching in the workplace delivers achievement, fulfilment and joy from which both the individual and the organisation benefit" and "Coaching is the art of facilitating the performance, learning and development of another" (Downey 2003, p. 21).

▶ "Someone from outside an organization uses psychological skills to help a person develop into a more effective leader. These skills are applied to specific present-moment work problems in a way that enables this person to incorporate them into his or her permanent management or leadership repertoire" (Peltier 2001, p. xx).

▶ "Coaching is both an assistance and a collaborative construction offered to a person (or a team) through a time limited intervention or, more often, as support spread over a period of time. This assistance and co-construction is in keeping with a professional situation, and/or a managerial and/or organizational situation" (Lenhardt 2004, p. 281).

▶ Learning and coaching is "based on principles that could be summarized in three words: *awareness*, *trust* and *choice*. Elaborated slightly, the principles were (1) non-judgemental awareness is curative; (2) trust self 2 (my own and the student's); and (3) leave primary learning choices with the student (Gallwey 2000, p. 10).

▶ Coaching is unlocking a person's potential to maximize their own performance. It is helping them to learn rather than teaching them (Whitmore 2002, p. 8).

▶ Mentor: an experienced and trusted adviser. An experienced person in an institution who trains and counsels new employees or students *(Concise Oxford Dictionary)*.

▶ "Mentoring is offline help by one person to another in making significant transitions in knowledge, work or thinking" (Clutterbuck 2001, p. 3).

▶ "Mentoring: creating possibilities and providing guidance and support to others in a relationship of trust; it includes facilitating, bringing vision to life and enabling people to achieve" (Cranwell-Ward 2004, p. 26).

▶ "Counselling is a process which helps an individual clarify their motivations, worries and hopes; it helps them to come to terms with their feelings, and enables them to take responsibility for, and begin to resolve their difficulties" (Institute of Management 1999).

▶ "Life coaching is about gap analysis that closes the gap between life and dreams ... [it] is based in the present and the future. It is founded on the premise that the past need not equate to the future" (Martin 2004, p. v).

Figure 5.1 **Definitions in the one-to-one learning business**

To add to the confusion, there are many words in the English language which refer to people in the business of learning, coincidentally all beginning with "C" or "T":

Coach: private tutor (n). One who instructs or trains a performer or sport players. To train intensively by instructions, demonstration and practice (v)

Confessor: a person who gives heroic evidence of religious faith, but does not suffer martyrdom. A priest who bears confession is one's spiritual guide

Confidant: one to whom secrets are entrusted

Consultant: an expert who gives professional advice or services

Counsellor: a person who gives professional advice

Teacher: one who teaches or instructs

Therapist: a person trained in methods of treatment and rehabilitation other than the use of drugs or surgery

Trainer: someone who trains, being prepared for test or contest and bringing a desired degree of proficiency in specified activity

Practitioners do not make it any easier because they imply that their approach is superior to all others. This chapter aims to describe what is available, bring some light to the terminology and describe the principal techniques used by the various practitioners. In this sense, it attempts to educate potential consumers.

5.2 Coaching

The most common form of coaching is that which takes place on the job and is usually concerned with improving the skills and knowledge of staff. The subject matter is directly concerned with the job at hand. It might be to help with someone's drafting, writing a budget, stripping down a gearbox or writing a speech for the CEO or minister. But it is also about how they see their job, how they deal with uncertainty and how they cope with pressure.

It can also be about values and beliefs. Helping new salespeople do their job involves not just the mechanics of selling and knowledge of the product but is also about developing persistence and resilience to potential clients saying "no". A young curate will

Coaches come in many shapes and forms. Writers have had fun at their expense. McAdam (2005) lists seven:

▶ *The trophy coach: Having your own coach is the modern-day equivalent of having the keys to the executive cloakroom in some corporate cultures.*

often discuss with and listen to the priest or bishop about the meaning of God's word. An employee will look to his or her boss for advice on working (or not) long hours, the ethics of business in that company or what attitude to adopt to competitors.

5.2.1 Origins

Coaching has some of its origins in the apprentice schemes in Europe and America. No doubt our earliest ancestors trained their children in the skills of hunting and self-protection in a similar way. In medieval Europe apprenticeships were established by the guilds for young craftsmen. The Industrial Revolution provided a stimulus to apprentice schemes as the only realistic way of meeting the heavy demand for skilled labor.

> ▶ *The terminator coach: Beware the terminator coach where an individual is offered a coach as part of outplacement by stealth*
>
> ▶ *The coach as surrogate manager: This is a variant on the terminator, where the boss tells you: "as you know I'll be away on secondment for the next six months. Don't worry, a chap from a coaching outfit has been hired to give you some help if you need it."*
>
> ▶ *The adhesive coach: This coach tends to emphasize how expert they are. They alone are able to help you: "never mind the chemistry, just trust me".*
>
> ▶ *The coach on the couch: Offers a huge amount of empathy but little positive help. Probably confusing intuition with judgement, they will relive their experience through yours: "That's just what happened to me – here's what I did."*
>
> ▶ *The absentee coach: Prefers to coach via the telephone rather than face to face. They see themselves so phenomenally successful, you should consider yourself lucky to get even this.*
>
> ▶ *The borderless coach: With little sense of boundaries or ethics, this type of coach blithely goes where others will not. Lacking technical training and experience, they are best avoided.*

Commenting on the period 1870–1914, Charles More (1980, p. 41) wrote: "while apprenticeship was not the only means of acquiring skill ... it was the single most important". Sheldrake and Vickerstaff (1987, p. 4) add: "Apprenticeship placed an obligation on the employer to teach the apprentice the trade, and it was assumed that during the early years of their apprenticeship (running from five to seven years) the apprentice would receive more by way of training than they gave in terms of production".

The state did not play a major role in these early years. The Statute of Artificers of 1563 is the first example of state intervention. By making a seven-year apprenticeship compulsory and restricting entry to certain craft trades, it provided the legal basis for vocational training until 1814 when the "laissez-faire" attitudes of the time opposing any state regulation brought about its abolition.

The craft trade unions that emerged from the mid-19th century insisted on apprenticeship qualifications for membership, and used craft status as a means of gaining and maintaining influence and power. World War I disrupted apprenticeship training.

From 1925, the government, concerned about a possible shortage of skilled workers and mass unemployment, introduced a series of measures including the interrupted apprenticeship scheme which enabled those whose apprenticeships had been interrupted by the war to resume them. Apprentice schemes still exist and the word has some modern popularity, but it is a different model from the early days of guilds (CIPD fact sheet: "Training: A Short History", January 2004, http://www.cipd.co.uk).

History does not relate in any detail how the apprentice was taught or what methods of teaching the master craftsman employed. It was the famous master–pupil relationship that we still see with musicians (and indeed academics). It is reasonable to assume from stories of the time that the apprentice learnt by observation and his gradual deployment on increasingly difficult tasks. That it took seven years suggests that either the tasks were very complex, the teaching might not have been the efficient or the employers wanted to delay paying the full rate for as long as possible.

Even where formal apprenticeship relationships did not exist, the manager probably took some responsibility for helping staff to acquire the necessary knowledge, skills, beliefs and attitudes. In the modern era, the task of coaching junior staff is increasingly seen as an important skill for managers. They are inscribed into competency frameworks and there are many courses available for the manager to learn the skills of the coach.

5.2.2 Choosing a coach

Chapter 8 discusses how to assess providers of learning in general. As far as coaching is concerned, various observers have tried to help the potential purchaser of coaching to make a judicious decision and choice. The Federal Consulting Group has a helpful *Coaching Guide* (2002) which includes some considerations to think about when deciding whether or not to coach and how to judge a potential coach:

▷ The coach's typical clients and developmental issues – Has the coach worked with situations similar to mine?

▷ General technique or approach to coaching – Am I willing to work within these techniques or approaches? Do I prefer to work face to face, by phone, or email? How flexible am I on the "meeting" format?

▷ Experience coaching Federal managers – Has the coach worked with Federal managers so that he/she is familiar with the dynamics unique to Federal organizations or my organization in particular?

▷ Business/organizational knowledge – Does the coach understand the business/organizational issues related to my situation?

▷ Values – sensitivity to confidentiality, ethics, and freedom from gender and culture bias – Am I comfortable that the coach can work for my best interest?

▷ Interpersonal skills – listening, straightforwardness, rapport, trust, warmth, compassion, humor – Is the coach someone I can trust? Does the coach listen to understand?

▷ Assessment skills and awareness of instruments applicable to your situation – What other information will the coach use to assist me?

▷ Flexibility and ability to work effectively with a broad range of executives – My issues involve relationships with other executives; can the coach work with me effectively, and help me understand how to work effectively with them?

▷ Ability to plan, conceptualize, implement and manage a coaching relationship over time – How will the coach keep me accountable for results and assure that I keep making progress?

▷ Demonstrated knowledge of learning theories and the dynamics of change – Does the coach understand the personality and temperament issues related to my situation or organization?

▷ Credibility and authenticity – Can I trust this coach to be honest with me?

▷ Political savvy – Is the coach savvy enough to understand the politics of my situation?

In the UK, Gillian Cribbs, writing in the *Financial Times* in 2003, produced the following shorter guide:

▷ Training: Have they had formal independent or accredited training?

▷ Experience: What experience do they have of coaching and the business?

▷ Style and chemistry: Do they inspire trust, seem similar in energy, politics and humor?

▷ Intellectual framework: What do they know about the theoretical/epistemological approach and process?

▷ Measuring success: How will outcomes be measured, when, why and how?

▷ Supervision: Is the coach supervised and supported by others?

▷ Self-awareness: How aware is the coach? What is their motivation?

One of the most important decisions is whether a coach is the most appropriate way of learning and if so which type of coaching. To make a judgement on these questions, some understanding of the processes involved and the options available is useful.

5.2.3 Coaching processes

There are a number of processes which coaching specialists promote. Some of the ones described in this section are also used by executive coaches, life coaches and others, although it is sometimes uncertain how they differ.

The degree of direction that a coach should give is a controversial area. Many modern and respected writers favor the non-directional approach. In the days before they entered the field, coaches tended to tell their charges what to do and how to do it. What is meant by non-directional coaching?

For Gallwey, coaching is "unlocking a person's potential to maximize their own performance. It is helping them to learn rather than teaching them" (quoted in Whitmore 2002, p. 8). These authors are in effect moving coaches from the instruction end of the learning spectrum to facilitation. It encourages coaches to see people's potential rather than their past performance and weaknesses and therefore encourages self-belief and confidence.

This has a number of advantages. Chapter 2 demonstrated how adult learners like to have some influence over their learning and using these techniques the learners are much more likely to relate it to their own experiences. Furthermore, we know that experience is an important way of learning. Letting the learner take the initiative and try out some of their ideas first will stimulate learning effectively.

However, senior managers on coaching courses worry that the non-directive approach takes a long time. Surely, they argue, it is much quicker to explain precisely what should be done and how to do it. Asking questions and waiting for the other to come up with the answer is not a good use of time.

Parsloe argues that there are times when a hands-on, directive approach is more appropriate. "The more inexperienced the learner is, the more 'hands-on' the coaching style will have to be. With complete beginners, the coach may well have to adopt the style almost of an instructor" (Parsloe 1999, p. 9).

> *True learning begins with unlearning.*
>
> Fred Kofman,
> *On Becoming a Leader*

One of the dangers with the directive approach is that the subject will do as they are told, but without understanding why. They will have to rely on their memory to keep doing it that way and they will eventually remember it through many repetitions, by which time it has become deeply engraved in their memory. If they want to learn how to do it differently, they will need to "unlearn" their previous methods.

Faced with an expert who follows the "instructional" style, learners will do as they are told – in effect they comply. Compliance can be induced through respect or liking the person. Belief in the person's abilities means logically that he or she knows how to achieve and therefore their example is worth following.

Compliance can also be induced by fear. A coach who uses pressure or who is feared will achieve some learning. A staff member could feel threatened by a manager who is responsible for their annual appraisal. This pressure may be explicit or implicit. The effect is the same. Fear of the coach or trainer or ridicule in front of others is all too often seen in the workplace and is seriously deleterious to learning.

The fact is that fear does work and instruction with or without pressure is an effective means of learning. Before the modern trend towards non-directive learning, such techniques were common and people at schools, universities and in the workplace learnt skills, knowledge, values and beliefs, some of them effectively and efficiently. It may not be ethical to use pressure, challenge or peer evaluation but coaches should not deny its effectiveness.

Nor should they believe that they never use such techniques themselves. Having striven to create a good positive relationship with a client, the coach is effectively putting the learner under some pressure to achieve, because the client will not want to let down their teacher. The desire to please is a powerful incentive – coaches should recognize its presence and the pressure it produces.

Where, however, does instruction have a place in the coach's armory? Knowledge is at the core of most things learners do. On the sports field a novice tennis player needs to know some of the rules of the game before they start. As they become more skilled and engage in matches, they need to know the finer points of the game. They could learn about the advantages of the drop shot or the lob by waiting until it happens to them on the court or they happen to do it by chance, but a description by someone else will speed up the process of learning.

What about the values or in the language of sport, the etiquette? Is the game purely about winning points at any cost? To what extent can a player engage in disrupting tactics to put the other off? Golfers have many rules about etiquette, but not all are written down. Behavior around the green as the other takes a putt is very considerate about the putter. But they are not all obvious to the newcomer. Should he or she wait until they are ostracized by the other members of the club before realizing that this behavior is not accepted? The learner can refer to books but an easier way is often to ask, or be told, that is, instructed.

> *Often the most effective facilitators in learning processes are not professional trainers but line managers themselves.*
>
> Peter Senge *The Leader's New Work*

Beliefs are a little different. The importance of believing in one's self was discussed in Chapter 3. Self-confidence is an important element of learning and it does not matter how often a learner is told they can do something, they will not necessarily be able to do it. If the confidence and belief in the coach or teacher is absolute, the learner may acquire courage from that person and go ahead on the basis of what they are told. But often that confidence is not there. Other more subtle approaches have to be deployed to persuade the player they have the potential. The job of the sports coach is thus to train skills but also attitude; hence all the modern literature on such subjects as the "Inner Game".

Beliefs and values have to be nurtured in business and management as well. Take, for example, writing skills. Not many graduates, even from the best universities, leave with a good, let alone perfect knowledge of grammar (many cannot even spell well). In some organizations, the written word is important and a high value is put on good grammar and spelling. The British civil service is a good example of this kind of culture. Grammar does not lend itself to a non-directional approach. Learners need to know how to conjugate verbs and even that a sentence should have a verb in it. The huge success of Lynne Truss's (2003) *Eats, Shoots & Leaves* is a tribute to this.

But the skills of good writing go further than good grammar. The style is important. Short sentences are often more effective than long complex structures. Too many adjectives and adverbs tend to detract from the message and a split infinitive, while acceptable to the strict grammarian, is (or at least was) an anathema in the civil service. These touch on skills as well as the values and beliefs of an organization. Learning through experience takes time and can be emotionally painful. A new entrant willing to learn is happy to be told what to do.

There are also skills which are inherently dangerous which favor an instruction method. A personal protection course for journalists going to danger areas may include some firearms training. The instructor is unlikely to let the learner use the weapon alone without some clear instructions on basic safety issues and how to hold it without causing harm to others or themselves. Indeed most learners would not want to pick up the weapon without some careful guidance beforehand.

Scuba diving is dangerous and the instructors take great care to demonstrate how the equipment is to be used safely as well as effectively. Furthermore, they want people to follow some procedures in exactly the same way in case of an emergency so others will know what is happening and what to do to help.

The question becomes what is being taught, to whom and at what stage. This should help determine how they might best learn. It is a matter of matching the person to the job.

5.2.4 Instructional techniques

The skill of the coach faced with having to "instruct" is to present the skill or knowledge in such a way that the learner is eager and able to learn (and puts in all the necessary effort). The principles of adult learning discussed in Chapter 2 together with some of the theory of learning will help. Chapter 4 describes how trainers use a four-stage approach to introducing new skills (p. 79). Parsloe (1999, p. 20–1) provides a similar "practice cycle" technique for coaches.

Stage 1: explain and demonstrate: At this stage the coach is usually advised to:

▷ Summarize what is about to be explained and demonstrated
▷ Emphasize why it is important

▷ Outline how it is going to be done
▷ Explain and demonstrate, following a logical sequence
▷ Summarize, re-emphasizing why it is important
▷ Allow time for questions, clarifications and feedback to check under-
   standing"

Stage 2: reflect on the learning

Stage 3: review progress

Stage 4: plan to practice again.

5.2.5 Non-directive learning

While directive methods or instruction have a place, the arguments in favor
of the non-directive methods are powerful in practice and in theory. The
coach is not looking here for compliance but for learning, which is self-
generated. Something which is learnt through an individual's own experience is much more likely to be remembered and used. The fact that it does
not necessarily comply with the coach's methods or own way of doing
things is not important. If it works, then the learner should be able to use
those techniques.

   Kolb's theory of learning showed us this. A child touching a hot radiator
is going to remember not to touch it again much more effectively than if
told not to do so by caring parents. Computer skills can be learnt in the
classroom with an instructor or at the workplace with a coach. Much can also
be learnt by experiment and the use of logic. Occasional reference to an
instructor or manual might be helpful but learning through trial and error
will have a lasting effect.

   Learning how to manage others or yourself can be done effectively
through non-directive methods, that is, by asking the coach a series of
questions which lead the learner to a conclusion that works best for him
or her.

   This technique was brought to prominence in the US and the UK by
the American Tim Gallwey (2000). Others such as Downey and Whitmore
have proved to be enthusiastic disciples in the UK. Gallwey pioneered his
views in the world of sport with *The Inner Game of Tennis* and *The Inner
Game of Golf*. In both he encouraged learners of the games to discover for
themselves how best to hit the ball and move. He rejected the traditional
instructors' methods of telling people how to hold the club or racquet and
how to swing it. He let people discover for themselves. *The Inner Game of
Work* followed.

In *The Inner Game of Work* Gallwey (2000, p. 177) describes the role of the coach as:

"Coaching is an art that must be learned mostly from experience. In the Inner Game approach, coaching can be defined as the facilitation of mobility. It is the art of creating an environment, through conversation and a way of being, that facilitates the process by which a person can move toward desired goals in a fulfilling manner. It requires one essential ingredient that cannot be taught: caring not only for external results but for the person being coached.

"The Inner Game was born in the context of coaching, yet it is all about learning. The two go hand in hand. The coach facilitates learning. The role and practices of the coach were first established in the world of sports and have been proven indispensable in getting the best performance out of individuals and teams. Naturally, managers who appreciate the high levels of individual and team performance among athletes want to emulate what coaching provides.

"The coach is not the problem solver. In sports, I had to learn how to teach less, so that more could be learned. The same holds true for a coach in business."

As a tennis coach, Gallwey realized that his clients were distracted by an internal dialogue, between, on the one hand, the person wanting to hit the ball in a certain direction and with a force or spin and another who constantly questioned whether the client could actually do it.

> It occurred to me that there was a dialogue going on in the player's head, an internal conversation not unlike his external conversation with me. In a commanding tone , the voice in the head would issue teacher like commands to his body: "get your racquet back early. Step into the ball. Follow through at the shoulders." After the shot the same voice would deliver its evaluation of the performance and the performer: "that was a terrible shot! You have the worst backhand I've ever seen". (Gallwey 2000, p. 6)

Gallwey's conclusion was that this dialogue was unhelpful. It did not occur in great athletes and furthermore he, as a coach, was contributing to the distractions. He was in effect providing much of the source material for the internal voice casting judgements on a performance. Gallwey called this voice "self 1". The one it was talking to he called "self 2".

Gallwey then applied these lessons to the workplace:

> I realized companies had much to gain by learning to access the great reservoir of Self 2 talent in their workforces. Success in this effort would depend on their ability to recognise and reduce the many ways in which their culturally accepted practices contributed to Self 1's interference with that talent. (Gallwey 2000, p. 17)

He then produced the formula:

$$\text{Performance} = \text{potential} - \text{interference}.$$

Performance in any activity, from hitting a ball to solving a complex business problem, was equal to one's potential *after* the interference factor had been subtracted from the equation. Performance rarely equals potential. A little self-doubt, an erroneous assumption, the fear of failure was all it took to greatly diminish one's actual performance (Gallwey 2000, p. 17).

Given that the coach's instructions effectively made up much of that interference, Gallwey's solution was to remove it and trust the learner's instincts in work as in sport.

Taking this as the inspiration, other coaches developed what is known as the GROW technique, perhaps best described in *Coaching for Performance* by John Whitmore (2002). Before describing the GROW model, Whitmore urges coaches to build awareness and responsibility in their coachees:

> While awareness includes seeing and hearing in the workplace, it encompasses much more than that. It is the gathering and the clear perception of the relevant facts and information, and the ability to determine what is relevant ... When we truly accept, choose or take responsibility for our thoughts and our actions, our commitment to them rises and so does our performance. (Whitmore 2002, pp. 33 and 37)

Having established the context of awareness and responsibility, Whitmore then describes the GROW process. Using open questioning techniques, Whitmore (2002, p. 53) suggests following the GROW sequence of headings:

▷ GOAL setting for the session as well as short term and long term
▷ REALITY checking to explore the current situation
▷ OPTIONS and alternative strategies or courses of action
▷ WHAT is to be done, WHEN and by WHOM and the WILL to do it.

The unusual point about this model is that goals are set before investigating the reality, that is, the background or issues involved. Whitmore argues that goals based on reality alone are liable to be negative, a response to a problem and limited by past performance. Setting goals first encourages coachees to look forward and therefore be more inspiring, motivating and creative.

Myles Downey (2003, p. 25) takes up the issue of setting the goal first and while he does not change the order, he does put in an extra element at the beginning which is to establish the topic for consideration first: "What you want is to understand what territory you are in, the scale of the topic, the importance and sometimes the emotional significance for the player. It is sometimes useful to establish what the player's longer-term vision or goal for the topic is."

Downey also urges coaches to be demanding in the goal-setting stage.

The commonly accepted formula for setting goals or objectives is that they should be SMARTS (Armstrong 2001, pp. 478–9):

Specific   – clear, unambiguous, straightforward, understandable and challenging

Measurable   – quantity, quality, time, money

Achievable   – challenging but within the reach of a competent and committed person

Relevant   – relevant to the objectives of the organization so that the goal of the individual is aligned to corporate goals

Time-framed   – to be completed within an agreed timescale.

5.3 Executive Coaching

The popularity of executive coaching has taken many by surprise. Clearly it fulfilled some important need. Just as the rich and powerful (at least in America) once needed a personal therapist both as a trophy and an adviser, so managers now appear to have the need for an executive coach and their very expensive conversation.

Writers on executive coaching tend to produce their own definition. For example, the Australians Zeus and Skiffington (2002, p. 9) define it as:

> a collaborative relationship between an executive and a coach, the aims of which are to bring about sustained behavioural change and to transform the quality of the executive's working and personal life.

The Frenchman Vincent Lenhardt (2004, p. 17) describes coaching as:

> help, guidance and co-construction that is offered to a person (or a team) through timely intervention, or more often long term support.

Presenting a largely US perspective on coaching, described by them as development coaching, Lucy West and Mike Milan (2001, p. xvii) in their book tellingly titled *The Reflecting Glass*, define it as:

> one-to-one consultancy with senior executives, which has as its objective the development of optimal effectiveness in a leadership and managerial role. It is an activity by the creation of a structure in which the individual can stand back from his or her context, learn through a process of reviewing that context and his or her performance within it, and then act on that learning.

It is in fact hard to come up with a single definition that would generate any kind of agreement amongst those who describe themselves as executive coaches. Some things appear to be common. In general they talk about helping senior managers or executives rather than more junior people; they generally put themselves at the non-directive end of the spectrum; they tend to be external rather than senior members of staff. But even in presenting those statements, they have to be qualified by words such as generally or mostly.

Part of the problem may be that if defined too narrowly, some coaching opportunities would be excluded. Thus a junior but potential high flyer might not fit in with the definition if it was limited to senior people. Some would expect that in their role they might need to be directive (because that is what the client wants or because the situation demands it). Some writers certainly accept that senior board members can be an effective executive coach.

> *You can always tell a Harvard man, but you can't tell him much.*
>
> Attributed to James Barnes, 1866–1936, America author

There is a chameleon-like quality to some coaches. Often they define themselves in the context of other similar professions. Thus Chapman et al. (2003, p. 15) put coaching between counseling and mentoring. West and Milan (2001, p. 29), however, describe it as a marriage between the two disciplines of consultancy and counseling.

Table 5.1 Comparison of coaching processes

The process	West and Milan	Hudson	Starr
The beginning	Contracting and relationship management	Establish the coach–client relationship – form trust	Establish the context for coaching
		Formulate a coaching agreement – establish what is inside and outside the agreement	
The middle	The work	Move from problem orientation to a vision orientation –the future the client would prefer	Create understanding and direction
		Construct a change scenario – develop a future-oriented personal or organizational strategic plan	
		Resist resistance – the focus is on resistance	
		Challenge, probe, confront – connecting a sense of purpose with a vision of a coaching "result"	
	Ongoing review and evaluation	Coach the new scenario while deepening the relationship – details, timing, priorities, training, integration, revision	Review/confirm learning
The end	Ending and managing feedback to the organization	Conclude the formal relationship, begin follow-up coaching	Completion

Source: Starr 2003, p. 58; West and Milan 2001, p. 58; Hudson 1999, pp. 26–31.

Each of these disciplines is discussed later. What, however, are the processes that executive coaches (broadly defined) follow in their trade. Do they differ from those of the performance, largely skills-driven coach?

Three processes are compared in Table 5.1. Two (Starr, and West and Milan) have a simple four-stage process covering similar although not identical ground. Hudson breaks his process up into eight stages. All emphasize the importance of creating a good relationship at the beginning and bringing the business to a close.

On the face of it these are similar to the GROW model. The issue of when exactly goals should be set is not addressed specifically and the models considered here do not discuss the advantages and disadvantages of asking clients to talk about their aims before they discuss the problems.

Chapman et al. (2003) approach the question of methodology in a different manner. They consider the reaction of the client first and provide a series of case histories to demonstrate how each situation needs slightly different handling. They base their argument on Adams' transition curve.

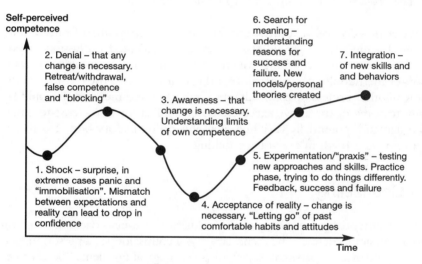

Figure 5.2 **The transition curve**
Source: Chapman et al. 2003, p. 27, adapted from Adams et al. 1976.

The case histories given by Chapman et al. are instructive and have some common features with the procedures described by West and Milan, Hudson and Starr. There is an introductory session where the coach and client get to know each other, the client explains the issues of interest or concern and goals are set. Although not specified in Starr, West and Milan and Hudson, in nearly all of Chapman et al.'s case studies there are a series of diagnostic tests, such as 360° assessment, Myers-Briggs, FIRO B and 16PF.

The use of diagnostics is not an essential part of executive coaching but it is a regular feature of sessions. There are some real advantages and dangers in their use and Chapter 7 discusses the use and variety of diagnostic tests in some detail.

What then differentiates executive coaching from other caring and facilitating professions? The answer is bound to be set with conditions and qualifications. Each executive coach sees their role differently from others and some quite radically so, but the following features are generally true:

▷ Clients tend to be senior executives who have a budget for this activity
▷ The sessions are focussed on one individual's aspirations or performance, but others (stakeholders, line managers, peer group or subordinates) may also take part
▷ Goal setting is an important part of the process and usually takes place at the first session
▷ The contract is usually limited in time or number of sessions
▷ The coach is usually external to the organization
▷ The process of coaching tends to be non-directive.

These factors do make executive coaching different from other forms of one-to-one learning. Having said that, there is no accepted professional body regulating executive coaching which means there are no established standards or methodology. Furthermore, others muscle in on the territory in the name of other professions: consultants, counselors and mentors all would lay claim to some of the above executive coaching features. Low cost-to-entry, high demand, potentially very high pay plus no regulatory body has meant an explosive growth in executive coaching.

5.4 Counseling

There is potentially something of the counselor in every coaching situation and it is easier to define. The dictionary says a counselor is: "a person trained to give guidance on personal, social, or psychological problems". Many one-to-one sessions will surface problems which are not relevant to the workplace and do not form part of the job description of the coach, line manager, colleague, trainer or personnel officer.

Quite reasonably, many fear that they are not qualified to deal with such situations, although if the problem is sorted at the beginning and quickly, its harsher manifestations can be avoided. Nevertheless everyone at some stage gets involved in helping people with problems, be they family, friends or in the workplace. But the questions for the professionals are important here. The first is to differentiate between counseling and therapy. Table 5.2 provides a helpful set of comparisons.

Table 5.2 Differences between counseling and therapy

Counseling	Therapy
Caring, enabling, facilitating, supporting	Con/de/re-constructing, interpreting, intervening, treating
Explore, discover, clarify issues	Develop new ways of solving problems
Alleviate suffering	Improve functioning
Focus on here and now	Focus on past and present
Evolutionary change	Revolutionary change
Short term, clients seen frequently	Long term, clients seen frequently
Therapy low on theory	Therapy high on theory
No need for personal therapy	Usually need for personal therapy
Everyday, average, "mundane" problems	Abnormal, serious chronic, acute problems
Person-centered	Problem-centered

The second question is what style/type/or school of thought to choose. The most obvious question naturally concerns efficacy. Interestingly, researchers have shown that all techniques work roughly equally. They do so because there are common factors to all counseling processes which explains why they have beneficial effects:

1 *The therapeutic alliance:* through therapy, patients and clients gain acceptance, attention, care, respect and support. It is this sense of being understood and assisted that is essential to the cure.
2 *Self-examination:* the whole therapeutic process encourages greater self-monitoring and self-analysis which often in and of itself suggests solutions.
3 *Morale:* clients often report feeling happier and more optimistic because they believe that their coping mechanisms and strategies have improved and the overcoming of their personal difficulties is possible.
4 *Commitment to change.* Agreement to and indeed attending therapy voluntarily and paying for that therapy is a reaffirmation of commitment to change which is the best predictor of change.

What is its role in the workplace and more specifically in helping people learn? West and Milan (2001, p. 33) believe that counseling is a crucial skill for a coach, and the following is necessary:

▷ Acceptance of the client
▷ Empathetic understanding of his or her experiences
▷ Congruence in providing honest feedback regarding his or her way of being.

According to West and Milan, these are necessary if a coach is to create a climate of trust and safety. Furthermore, personal, social or psychological problems can interfere with work and therefore impact on performance and so it is necessary for the coach to surface such problems. The coach has then to be able to judge at what stage if any the problems are beyond their ability to handle. Should the client be seeing a fully trained counselor or therapist? An important skill of anyone engaged in one-to-one learning is to be able to judge when they are out of their depth. Their reaction must be to advise the person to seek professional help: they should not open questions they cannot answer nor should they sweep the issue under the carpet as being too difficult.

The process of helping is worth some study, as it has similarities to that of the coach. Gerard Egan, a leading authority on counseling, provides a three-stage model, each stage being divided into a further three:

Stage I: Identifying and clarifying problem situations and unused opportunities

Step I-A: Helping clients tell their stories – relationship building is crucial.

Step I-B: Focussing – to include screening (is the problem worth the time and effort of an expensive helper?), focussing (in a complex situation, which are the highest priority problems – which patterns need to change in their life).

Step I-C: Blind spots and new perspectives – one of the most important roles of a helper is to help clients to identify blind spots and new unused opportunities.

Stage II: Goal setting – Developing a more desirable scenario

Step II-A: Constructing a new scenario – need not be a wild-eyed idealistic state of affairs but rather a conceptualization of what the situation would be like if improvements were made.

Step II-B: Critiquing the new scenario – ensuring the goals are clear, realistic, adequately related to the problem situation, in keeping with the client's values and capable of being accomplished within a reasonable time frame.

Step II-C: Choice and commitment – while the choice should remain with the client, the helper can help by guiding them in the search for incentives.

Stage III: Action – Moving toward the preferred scenario

Step III-A: Discovering strategies for action – a strategy is a means to an end. Clients need to explore the different ways in which a goal can be achieved.

Step III-B: Choosing strategies and devising a plan of action – the chosen strategy or strategies need to be broken down into a step-by-step plan; what to do first, second and so on.

Step III-C: Action – implementing plans and achieving goals – the counselor helps clients to foresee difficulties, provides support and challenges.

(Egan 1986, pp. 36–54)

In presenting this model, Egan insists that it should not be followed slavishly, for example in a chronological order. The skilled helper will use it flexibly.

There are many similarities to the various coaching models explored so far. In parts it is more rigorous and it might well serve some coaches well in their approach to a client who needs help, albeit of a work-oriented nature.

5.5 Consultant

Management consulting has been a feature of business for a long time. Management theory was still in its infancy when James McKinsey founded the firm that bears his name in 1926. He had left his academic career as a professor of accounting at the University of Chicago to build a firm that provided finance and budgeting services, but quickly gained a reputation

> *I don't like to hire consultants. They're like castrated bulls: all they can do is advise.*
>
> Victor Kiam (1926–2001)

for providing advice on organization and management issues. In 1933, the arrival of Marvin Bower provided James McKinsey with a strong advocate and a fellow visionary. Bower held both a J.D. and an M.B.A. from Harvard University. He adamantly believed that management consulting should be held to the same high standards for professional conduct and performance as law and medicine (http://www.mckinsey.com).

From the beginning, consultants have provided advice to clients, not just on what they should do but how. They tend to be employed by the company and have a contractual relationship with the company as opposed to individuals. Their main concerns are business processes and the strategy. West and Milan (2001, pp. 30–2) put coaching between the two disciplines of consulting and counseling. The development or executive coach needs to understand something of the business before they can be of much help. The message is simple enough, but no less powerful for that.

Human resource consultants – typical activities:

▶ *Diagnosis* – searching for the real cause usually of a behavior problem, for example absenteeism, turnover, theft.

▶ *Measurement* – psychometric assessment of things such as candidate personality, staff attitudinal survey, training course success, client responses. This is done at its best in an assessment center.

▶ *Instruction* – training education, updating, informing on state-of-the-art issues in things like motivation, teleworking, and so on.

▶ *Process* – quasi-group psychotherapeutic-type activity where consultants seek to understand psychological processes responsible for particular outcomes like conflict. It can also have a quite different application, meaning the understanding of business processes like how consumers are dealt with.

▶ *Systems* – the setting up and maintenance of things such as performance management systems which often involve considerable computer expertise.

5.6 Mentoring

On the one hand, Chapman et al. (2003) put coaching between the professions of counseling and mentoring. Mentoring is in the same zone as coaching – development – but is further away from relationships of greater intensity, as demonstrated in an interpersonal or therapeutic counseling context. The "mentor may often seek different objectives [from the coach] and be in less frequent contact with the participant" (Chapman et al. 2003, p. 15). Experts in mentoring see it a little differently.

Mentoring used to be quite easy to define. It represents help given to an individual by someone usually more senior and the conversations were more about beliefs and values than actual skills. The essential quality, however, was that the mentor was not in the line of command for the individual concerned. Some of that may still hold true but mentoring, in the hands of those who write about it, has taken on rather more ground.

The word does have distinct meanings in the US and Europe. In American companies a mentee is more the protégé of the mentor. The latter guides his charge through the institutional promotion ladder, by providing advice on not just how to develop but who he or she should know and how to develop them.

David Clutterbuck (2001, p. 3) defines mentoring as "offline help by one person to another in making significant transitions in knowledge, work or thinking" and then goes on to offer the following definitions (pp. 4–5):

Mentoring is a partnership between two people built on trust ... Addressing issues and blockages identified by the mentee, the mentor offers advice, guidance and counselling and support in the form of pragmatic and objective assistance.

Mentoring helps mentees and mentors progress their personal and professional growth.

The mentoring relationship is confidential ... For this reason the mentors are rarely in a line relationship.

Mentors can help individuals reach significant decisions about complex issues ... Mentors are not there to solve problems but rather to illuminate the issues and to help find a way through them.

Mentoring is a positive development activity ... mentoring has proved to be very effective in transferring tacit knowledge within an organization, highlighting how effective people think, take decisions and approach complex issues.

Sharing views and ideas builds understanding and trust.

The similarities with coaching are easy to see. Furthermore, writing on mentoring sees the same four-stage process in the relationship, but slightly different language is used: both parties spend time getting to know each other and setting a direction; progress is made; wind down and celebrate success and finally the relationship continues informally if infrequently as a sounding board (Clutterbuck 2001, p. 101). One of the major difference with a program like this compared to coaching is that it can last many years.

So what are the distinguishing features of a mentoring relationship? There are no real absolutes but there is a tendency for the following:

▷ The mentor is outside the line
▷ The mentor usually comes from inside the organization
▷ The mentor is more experienced and tends to be more senior
▷ The period often lasts a number of years
▷ The relationship often develops into a genuine friendship and can therefore move into more personal matters.

> *Learn from the best while they're good and move on.*
>
> Robert Waterman *The Frontiers of Excellence*

5.7 Life Coaching

Life coaching is not necessarily concerned with the workplace and may not have anything specifically to do with learning at work. It is briefly included here because many people may have issues at work which impact on learning and they turn, independently of their employers, to a life coach. It is important to recognize what a life coach can do to help and where he or she might fit in.

Martin (2004, pp. 57–9) identifies nine essential aspects of life that she asks clients to assess before embarking on a life coaching session. These are health, wealth, family, relationships, contribution to the world, spiritual, career/job, playtime and finally what is lacking. It is clear from this that work is only one of nine and not a high priority.

There are some interesting features that unite life coaches. Perhaps in an effort to dispel any allegations that they are all rather too "touchy feely", most of the books on the subject stress the importance of commitment. Most ask clients to sign a contract, which defines when and how many times the two will meet as well as specifying the objectives. If the client falls down on his or her side, the relationship is by implication brought to an end. Harrold (2001, p. 11) describes the process as follows: "Coaching moves people forward, fast and easily. Some people call it "bootleg Coaching", and I admit that I am demanding and I can be tough. I'm not going to be soft on you. I want action, not excuses."

Life coaches are not interested in the past, but the future. According to Martin (2004, p. 3): "Life coaching is about gap analysis that closes the gap between life and dreams ... [it] is based in the present and the future. It is founded on the premise that the past need not equate to the future." Like many other forms of one-to-one help, it is based in the non-directive camp.

Martin (2004) introduces a development of the GROW process described by Whitmore and discussed earlier. She uses a model based on I CAN DO:

Investigate: what is important for the client and what does the coach need to know about the client?

Current: what is the current situation, briefly described?

Aim: what are the client's aims in life?

Number: how many alternative ways of achieving the aims are there?

Date: by what date should the aims be complete?

Outcome: what are the outcome indicators?

An interesting feature of Martin's approach is that the first three stages are completed by the client on paper, with the help of a questionnaire/chart before the first meeting.

5.8 Lessons from Sport

Sport produces heroes and heroines who have some very clear qualities, most of which equate to the kinds of skills and qualities which business executives and managers seek in their own staff. Sport is also big business and athletes can command large fees for books and personal appearances. Away days, leadership seminars and management courses seek out a sporting hero, not just to hear good stories from a great sportsperson, but also to learn from their techniques, to try and apply what sportspeople have done in the workplace. What can their experience do to help the learner?

Many sports coaches are responsible for teams and in that sense fall outside the strict subject matter of this chapter. But the skills of the sports coach are relevant and many individuals in teams receive one-to-one coaching from the coach.

There is considerable literature on sports coaching. Figures who dominate the early 21st century – Tiger Woods (US golf), Jonny Wilkinson (England rugby) and Andy Roddick (US tennis) and many other sports stars – have all produced bestselling books. Of specific interest to those who are interested in helping others achieve, and who might also aspire to greatness, is how the top sports stars motivate themselves and, in the context of this book, learn how to motivate themselves and develop beliefs and values which help them to focus on that achievement.

The processes are similar to those already outlined in this book. The top stars have a great knowledge of their own game and many of sport in general. They know the rules and the tactics. They will spend much time and effort examining the strengths and weaknesses of their opponents.

All sportspeople want to build up their skills. The word is well used and understood. It is just the same in the workplace. People need skills but they do not always recognize what they have and need.

Finally, they need the right beliefs and values. In sport this is variously described as "mental attitude", "motivation" "self-esteem" or "confidence". It is in this area that the sports coach has most to offer one-to-one providers, be they coaches, managers or executives.

For sports coaches, building confidence is an essential part of ensuring victory. The sportsperson can acquire all the knowledge of the game, its rules, the tactics, the strengths and weaknesses of the opposition; they can also build their skills to the highest degree, but on the day they have to have developed the right beliefs and attitude to achieve the ultimate. Davies (1989, p. 153) describes confidence as "a belief, a self-assurance in one's own abilities. It is essentially a feeling of having an expectation of success."

There are those who believe that such confidence is not learnt or acquired, it is something which people have or do not have. To quote Davies (1989, p. 153) again:

> there is a feeling that confidence is a quality beyond voluntary control. This is not so. The ability to do justice to one's ability, to be confident, to be physically relaxed yet mentally alert in highly stressful conditions is a skill which can be acquired through appropriate practice and experience, though clearly it takes some people longer than it does others.

The importance of developing the right attitude in sport is underlined by Clive Woodward in his book *Winning* which followed the England rugby team victory in the World Cup. In 1999 Woodward took his squad to the Royal Marines base where they were put through some gruelling exercises for four days. On the last day of the visit, Woodward asked several of the senior offices for an honest assessment of the players. Their response after some hesitation was: "There are men in your squad whom we would not go into battle with.... It's not about their skills. It's about their attitudes and the effect on the team. One team player can sap all the energy from the group" (Woodard 2004, pp. 261–2). Like Davies, Woodward believed that the problem of attitude could be addressed: "the energy sappers were all sorted out. Some I managed to turn around. In every case none of them had actually realized that what they were doing behind the scenes had caused so many problems" (Woodward 2004, p. 264).

Clive Woodward is exceptional in a number of ways. Not many would have put much money on England winning when he took over as coach. He brought to a very traditional, not to say old-fashioned club an approach that had more to do with business than any British sporting traditions. He was also a fine sportsman in his own right, having played rugby for England some 21 times. Few coaches of international standing can claim such sporting prowess.

Gallwey recognizes the importance of self-esteem or at least the effect lack of esteem has on the mind at work:

> If a worker is viewed by one or more fellow workers as being less than competent, it tends to reinforce self-doubt, increase self-interference with the worker's potential, and thus creating a self-fulfilling prophesy for all who are looking for and expecting to find the perceived deficiency. (Gallwey 2000, p. 30)

For Gallwey, the issue becomes one of focus, allowing the real self the space to perform, without the distractions of the inner mind or others who might doubt.

Much of the work on self-confidence is based on Bandura's theory of self-efficacy (the surety of producing the desired effect). According to Bandura (1977) there are four sources of this self-efficacy:

1 Performance or mastery experiences. To achieve, people have to have the skills, the better the skill level the greater the potential to achieve
2 Vicarious experiences. People need to have role models; in an athlete's world someone to watch
3 Verbal persuasion. The role of the coach is to provide reassurance and interpretations of what is happening
4 Physiological information states. For an athlete this is information about the body and what it is doing.

For the one-to-one provider in the workplace this is reasonably familiar: develop skills, watch those who are successful around you, provide reassurance, explanations and guidance and finally be physically and in the case of the workplace emotionally intelligent.

Self-confidence is not the only thing that sports psychologists are concerned with. Williams and Krane (1993) concluded that certain mental skills and psychological attributes have been repeatedly found to be associated with superior performance in athletes. They included:

▷ Goal setting
▷ Higher self-confidence
▷ Heightened concentration
▷ The use of visualization and imagery
▷ Self-regulation of arousal
▷ Well-developed coping skills for dealing with unforeseen events and distractions
▷ Mental preparation plans
▷ Well-developed competitive routines and plans
▷ High levels of motivation and commitment.

(quoted in Elliott 1999, p. 73)

5.8.1 What makes a good sports coach?

Davies (1989) lists a number of qualities of the successful coach. These are:

▷ A sincere interest and genuine like of the people he or she is involved
  with, which enables the coach to follow development closely
▷ Extensive knowledge
▷ Commitment, ability and desire to create strong relationships
▷ Enthusiasm and a concern with all aspects of performance and training
▷ Being well organized
▷ Conscientious
▷ Ability to create a stable and relaxed environment, especially for teams in
  order to create strong team cohesion
▷ Creating a happy environment for all
▷ Provide a direct relation to the goals of the individual/team/organization
▷ A confident stable person, who is able to generate optimism, self-belief
  and commitment within his/her teams or individuals
▷ Flexibility, and the ability to observe and function in various environments.

This list, although discussed in reference to sporting coaches, carries
many personal and target-based statements that are important in the
workplace.

Davies stated that the function of a sporting coach is to "mould theoretical and practical understanding into a coherent pattern to develop an
athlete." This is used to emphasize what is highlighted as the single biggest
factor in sporting coaching, that of extensive knowledge. The relationship
between coach and athlete, or coach and worker, is one which in nearly all
cases is based on mutual respect. For the learner in each of these dyads, the
respect is generated through an appreciation of the knowledge that the
coach is trying to pass on.

Davies explains how the sports coach uses this knowledge in a number of
ways. An in-depth knowledge of training methods allows the generation of
training, technique drills and so on, which hold the learner's attention. The
coach becomes the translator of complex knowledge into units which the
learner understands, and knowledge of the situational aspects of sport allows
the coach to handle outside influences on the athlete's life, such as family,
friends, home life and the media. All the good coaches, mentioned above,
are renowned within their specific sporting fields for having an encyclopedic
knowledge of their own sports.

A coach's knowledge carries with it much of his ability to gain respect,
and thus it is important that this knowledge is based in a number of sound
principles. These principles transcend the sport and business environments
to be universal features of a good coach.

Coaches should seek to avoid habituation and should at all times display
the ability to perform in any environment and under any circumstance. This
is particularly important to the consultant coach, who will in the course of

his day-to-day work be in a number of places in a short space of time, and so must be highly flexible. This flexibility is aided in its development by high-level knowledge.

A second ability of the coach is the accurate diagnosis of success and failure. A coach must be able to see what factors have influenced both success and failure, and this common ability is again highly applicable to both sport and business. Davies provides some evidence to show how a sporting coach has a specific advantage in this field. The sporting coach spends a majority of his days in the company of his athletes. In doing so he learns the specific weaknesses and strengths of each individual, what motivates and demotivates, when a player is up or down, happy or sad. This type of specific knowledge of individuals is something which sporting coaches gain through time spent with individuals – luxury few business coaches have.

Davies also highlights the importance of communication and interpersonal skills for the good coach. This is evidently important in sports and business. A quick glance through newspaper job advertisements shows an abundance of employers asking for various levels of written and verbal communication skills and interpersonal skills. Davies discusses this in particular reference to the problems of communication breakdown. He describes three ways in which communication can break down (Table 5.3).

The final aspect of good coaching Davies discusses is motivation and coaching. As mentioned above, good coaches should be able to generate optimism and self-confidence in the learners, whether they are sportsmen or businessmen. Davies proposes that good coaches employ a level of self-

Table 5.3 Communication breakdowns

Breakdown	Sporting example	Business example
Basic breakdown – speak or listening	A player receiving a transfer to a new area of the country will instantly have to learn colloquialisms for various footballing terms. This could easily result in misunderstanding	Excessive use of "buzz words" or business "lingo", may make presentations and conversations difficult to understand to those who are not used to the phrases
Breakdowns as a function of the environment	An athlete may have problems hearing a coach from across a track due to the physical distance, or particularly windy conditions creating a break-down in effective communication	A conference room booked for a presentation may not contain sufficient microphones for individuals in the back of the room to be able to hear what is being said clearly. Again leading to a communication breakdown
Breakdown between source and recipient	This could include a falling out between manager and player, leading to a complete break-down in communication	A direct report could have switched roles without a replacement being appointed, leading to a breakdown between source and recipient

Source: Adapted from Davies 1989.

analysis to ensure that their own personal ethos does not cloud the individualistic needs of the learners, organizations and situations. To do this a
number of steps are suggested:

▷ Awareness of the different motivations of the individuals, groups, teams
  and squads.
▷ Use goal-setting behavior to maintain focus in these various groups.
▷ Appropriate feedback should be used in adjusting, controlling and regulating performance for all these groups.
▷ Practice should simulate reality as closely as possible.
▷ Through an awareness of individuality, the coach should be able to
  develop the self-confidence of each individual, and therefore training
  should become meaningful to each individual.

A good coach will have the knowledge and communication skills to
develop these practices in order to generate a motivational environment
for work/training. Davies (1989) states that the characteristics that both
top players and coaches share are their analytical ability and a motivation
to succeed.

Some evidence for the importance of these interpersonal traits in business
comes from Chatman et al. (1999), who highlighted social skills, likelihood
to arouse liking, social perception, honesty and the ability to see to the heart
of problems as key to employment. They also noted that individuals who
were rated as more poised, were socially perceptive and had the ability to
arouse liking received larger increases in pay (p. 533).

Here though again, the examples of the good coaches may prove coun-
terintuitive to this argument. Brian Clough, a prominent British football
coach, although a man highly respected by his players, was not renowned for
his social skills. Alex Ferguson, one of the most successful managers in
British football, is another example of a man who at times shows little in the
way of social skills.

5.8.2 Coaches and learning

As mentioned above, there are a number of factors, such as the time a coach
has with learners, which differ between sport and business. Another example
is the learning situation or type of learning. The question we must ask, is do
coaching skills transfer across learning situations?

Many authors have noted the difference between formal learning and
coaching. Formal learning involves training courses and qualifications,
most often held away from usual working environments and in hotels or
institutes. These courses use seminars, lectures, tests and projects as part
of the learning experience. Many consultants believe formal learning is
highly beneficial:

What many of these institutes have in common is the country house atmosphere, the idea of a withdrawal from the active participation in the affairs of industry and commerce, to discuss management matters with other managers, to exchange experience and compare notes. (Ferguson 2002)

Ferguson (2002) notes how coaching in business is less formal, with an ad hoc quality, but at the same time it has equal importance as more formal training. It must have a supportive element, be strongly based in experience and hence knowledge, it is seen as vital to overall success but it can be fallible, in the sense that each independent coach will give his or her own degree of depth, breadth and quality of coaching.

This dual process is emphasized still further by the proposed three models of management education and training put forward by Handy et al. (1988). These were:

1 *The corporate approach* – used primarily in larger organizations. It focuses on meeting the business needs and immediate functional requirements of the organization, by developing its own training departments. These now constitute in-house training schemes.
2 *Academic approach* – replication of the American system in which a multitude of courses are available from different institutions. These are often organized on a micro-level, with various ways to progress through a certain set of courses, but little criteria to compare them to one another on a macro-level. This represents formal learning.
3 *Professional approach* – "earn while you learn", a mix of education and training aimed at becoming a member of an institute.

So do great coaches have an ability to work in both formal and ad hoc environments? Some of those mentioned above would not fall into this category. Brian Clough would have used very few formal learning methods. However, the new breed of coach, for example Clive Woodward and Jürgen Grobler, use formal learning far more than their predecessors in the training of their athletes. In rowing in particular, the sport of Jürgen Grobler – the GB national coach – video analysis of technique and races, and detailed monitoring of individual athletes' power, is very much a part of day-to-day coaching.

Although it is important to highlight these different forms of learning, it seems that the use of both of these techniques is neither necessary nor sufficient to be a great coach in sport or business. However, we may currently be in the middle of a change in trend that is strongly encouraging the use of both techniques.

5.9 Conclusion

The types of one-to-one learning have many similarities, but each does have distinguishing features. The common features are in many ways more power-ful than those which separate them out. Common features include:

▷ It is a one-to-one relationship
▷ They are designed to help people learn, adjust, grow and cope
▷ And become more effective, usually in the work context.

Writers tend to use a linear scale to show where their discipline sits. Two dimensions do it better (and if technology allowed three might be even more helpful!), because there is so much to connect them all (Figure 5.3).

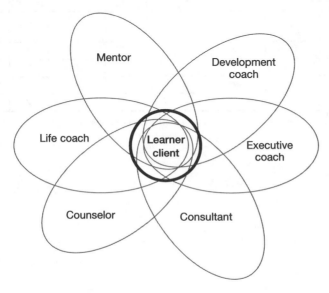

Figure 5.3 **Commonality of the six disciplines**

The differences are perhaps more controversial and difficult to define. Indeed they all probably have more in common with each other than they are likely to want to admit. There are, however, three broad categories where there are some differences: the degree of direction which is acceptable, whether the help is provided internally or externally (with the added differ-ence of whether it is provided by a line manager or not) and whether the help is exclusive to work or not. Table 5.4 summarises the six manifestations.

Much has been written about one-to-one learning in all its manifestations and many claims are made about how it can help and advance the recipients. In the learning business, coaching is the fastest growing industry and the demand for the other forms of help is in much demand. While not doubting its value, very little rigorous research has been done on the value of the various processes and the evidence is anecdotal. A possible exception is the work that has been done on counseling and therapy. Much of the work is based in psychoanalysis and therefore tends to have a strong base at universities. Few serious universities have involved themselves in the world of one-to-one learning and the research carried out tends to be about the volume and nature of learning. The subject is important: a great deal of money is spent on this kind of learning and its impact on staff could be enormous.

Table 5.4 Summary of the three main differences

Category of one-to-one help	Directive	Non-directive	Internal		External	Work focus	Life/ personal
			In-line	Out of line			
Performance coaching	✓	✓	✓	✓	≈	✓	X
Executive coaching	≈	✓	X	✓	✓	✓	≈
Mentoring	≈	✓	X	✓	≈	✓	✓
Life coaching	≈	✓	X	X	✓	X	✓
Counseling	X	✓	≈	≈	✓	≈	✓
Consultancy	✓	✓	X	X	✓	✓	X

Key: ✓ Generally accepted practice; X Not generally accepted; ≈ Possible, especially if qualified staff are available or required

6 Learning with Technology

6.1 Introduction

Some coaches, mentors and trainers might be tempted to skip this chapter. They would be wrong to do so. Technology has a lot to offer all educationalists. It has had enormous impact in the past helping people to learn. It will do so in the future: and more and more cheaply and effectively.

When Caxton established the first printing press in England in 1476, learning was made easier and available to many more people. Books and pamphlets became available to many more people and in the process, the business of learning was transformed. Radio and television did something very similar in the 20th century. In the 21st century, computers and the internet are making their contribution to the learning of billions of people all world. No one medium replaces another. They simply add to the options.

The internet is making a huge impact on research and the spread of information; business exploitation of the new technologies is vast and the providers of learning are showing their creativity and determination in delivering solutions for learners. But how far can the latest technology go in providing solutions for learners?

The American Society for Training and Development (ASTD) has reported significant increases in the use of technology for delivering learning, more than half of it from online sources (Sugrue and Kyung-Hyun 2004). The Chartered Institute of Personnel Development (CIPD) survey on training and development reported that e-learning had increased in the UK by 47 percent second only to coaching (CIPD 2004).

There is some evidence that this increase is beginning to level off. Learning Circuits, part of the ASTD and specializing in e-learning, conducted a survey in the autumn of 2004 and found that "the number of companies that have been using e-learning for quite some time fell from 41.7 percent in 2003 to 35.3 percent in 2004" (Ellis 2004). The author puts this down to respondents being more incisive about how they define e-learning. It is also worth noting that the survey, like so many others, on these subjects has sought its evidence exclusively on-line. This will automatically exclude those who are instinctively uncomfortable with at least this part of technology.

The CIPD in its report *E-learning: The Learning Curve* (2003) recognized this as well:

Early on, we witnessed a series of claims that e-learning was the ultimate panacea, but at the time of writing (October 2002) many commentators are suggesting that this early optimism was grossly misplaced. There is now sufficient evidence to show that the growth of e-learning in corporate organizations has plateaued following a variety of implementation problems. (CIPD 2003, p. 1)

Clearly training chiefs think it is a good thing – but what is e-learning? Is it different from earlier technology-based systems? Are they that much more powerful or useful than more traditional methods of helping people to learn? Do they base their products on learning theory and do they follow best practice in helping people learn? Are they good value for money?

This chapter will explore these questions, look at the most common technologies used, and analyse their effectiveness and the professionalism of the makers of such learning aids.

> As so often in the world of training and development, researchers are bedeviled by the variations in definitions. The CIPD (2003 p. 1) defines e-learning as: "learning that is delivered, enabled or mediated by electronic technology".
>
> The ASTD published a report (Dublin 2004, p. 1) which neatly summarizes the definition dilemma:
>
>> The truth is that the term *e-learning* means different things to different people. When the term was first popularized in 2001, it most often referred to computer-based training (CBT) delivered over intranets and the Internet. *E-learning* replaced *Web-based training* (WBT), which, during the highflying dot.com days, was just not sexy enough. It was a time when we were putting an e in front of everything: e-letters, e-toys, e-commerce, e-banking, e-pets and the e-list goes on and on. But the constant was a reference to delivering courses online, intranets, or over the Web.
>>
>> By 2002, many of the industry's experts were offering a more robust definition of e-learning. E-learning is "the use of technologies to create, distribute and deliver valuable data, information, learning and knowledge to improve on-the-job and organizational performance, and individual development."
>>
>> By 2003, we had begun to play with the e and extend the definition even further. One of the definitions I came to like was "enabling, enhancing, and extending learning through the use of technologies." So, it is no wonder then that learners, managers, and executives are confused about what we mean when we talk so confidently of *e-learning*.

Martyn Sloman (2001, p. 7) makes a distinction between technology-based training and e-learning:

E-learning/e-training – the delivery of learning or training using electronically-based approaches – mainly through the Internet, intranet, extranet or Web (the "e" is a shortening of electronic", originally popularized for e-mail, the transmission of messages digitally through a communication network). The terms m-learning/m-training are emerging, with the "m" denoting "mobile" for wireless technology using mobile telephones.

He uses the term "technology-based learning" as the generic.

The concern is whether people replying to surveys such as the CIPD or ASTD understand the difference. Some may only be referring to "connected" learning, that is, through the internet or their own intranets rather than the library of DVDs and CD-ROMs that they have built up over the years.

For the purposes of this book, we refer to the clearer (although admittedly less stimulating) term "technology-based learning"(TBL). Technology is of course used in many training and learning situations, but the distinguishing feature of TBL for this chapter is that a learner can be alone with the piece of technology for a significant period of time and learn without the presence of another person, coach, trainer or mentor.

This includes CD-ROMs and DVDs specially produced to help people to learn (such as language tuition or Mavis Beacon's *Teach Yourself Typing*), videos and DVDs such as those from Video Arts and IT programs put on the intranet to help staff to come to terms with new systems or upgrades.

6.2 History of TBL

While the printing press was probably the most important technological advance in history for learners, the modern era began with the development of electronic techniques, starting in earnest with the radio. Film, television and the Open University soon added their weight. People would listen (and still do) to a variety of informative programs. During World War II film was used again to inform people, as well as teaching skills such as how to fit a gas mask.

In the 1950s television started to reach the masses and opened up significant new possibilities for learning. From its early days, Lord Reith, the first director general of the BBC, established its public service aims to educate, inform and entertain. At the lighter end of the scale, cooking programs such as Fanny Craddock in the UK, with the long suffering Johnnie, taught many thousands of people new techniques in cooking.

This early period is significant because it used technology to bring enormous amounts of information to a wide range of people at little cost. In terms of helping people to acquire new knowledge, it was truly revolutionary. Radio and television played a significant role during World War II in keeping people informed.

The computer, the internet and intranet systems have brought another revolution in how people learn. Sloman (2001, p. 36) describes the emergence of technology-based training (TBT):

> TBT can be said to have emerged in the 1970s when the emphasis was placed on computer-assisted learning using mainframe computers. A National Development Programme in Computer Assisted Learning (NDPCAL) was in existence between 1970 and 1974. Also in the mid-1970s, Barclaycard introduced an extensive computer-assisted training programme for its data entry staff.

In the 1980s developments in computers gave an enhanced structure to TBT. The micro-computer emerged; graphics and color could be introduced to programmes. A national computer-based training forum was established in 1982 with the support of the National Computer Centre. The Government (in the form of the Manpower Services Commission) established a project (Project "Author") in 1983–4 to encourage the spread of the approach. New products in the form of laser disks and interactive video appeared.

6.2.1 The Open University

The Open University in Great Britain has been a pioneer of e-learning for some time. Their learning and teaching strategy is:

> open university courses are delivered as an integrated combination of media and methods, each chosen for its unique contribution to the learning experience. It is essential to provide the appropriate balance of media – text, audio, video, interactive simulations, data base resources, IT tools and communication environments. (www.corous.com, 2004)

In 1926 the educationalist and historian J.C. Stobart wrote a memo, while working for the infant BBC, advocating a "wireless university". By the early 1960's many different proposals were being mooted. R.C.G. Williams of the Institution of Electrical Engineers argued for a "teleuniversity", which would combine broadcast lectures with correspondence texts and visits to conventional universities – a genuinely "multimedia" concept. September 1967 saw the crucial Cabinet decision to set up a planning committee "to work out a comprehensive plan for an open university". The package consisted of radio and television and correspondence material, summer courses and the provision of computer facilities. The emphasis was on independent learning (www.open.ac.uk, 2005).

The methods used by the university produce good results. In their annual national test of teaching quality the *Sunday Times* rated them 5th in the whole of the UK in September 2004. The ranking is based on official judgements of teaching quality made by the Quality Assurance Agency for Higher Education. Its inspectors rated the teaching quality in 86% of Open University departments as "excellent".

6.3 Recent Developments in TBL

In the 1990s the widespread use of PCs (and later laptop computers) meant that the

> CD-ROM (compact disk read only memory: a form of high-capacity storage using laser optics rather than magnetic means to read data) emerged as a powerful form for distributing training material. The storage capacity available permitted data to be presented in a multimedia context. (Sloman 2001, p. 36)

Soon organizations were spawning "open learning centers", some were renamed rather awkwardly "knowledge center training facility". More recently, they have become "learning resource centers". Usually these are places where TBL material can be found as well as books and advice from trainers themselves.

6.3.1 E-learning

Learning which uses the web or intranet is generally described as e-learning. As we saw at the beginning of this chapter, definitions might go further, but that is essentially how e-learning is differentiated from other TBL. Professor Allison Rossett paints two pictures in the opening chapter of *The ASTD E-Learning Handbook*, which she edited: "I've been having these two parallel dreams about E-Learning. One is rosy and rich with possibilities. The other isn't quite a nightmare, but it has people running down corridors and bumping into walls" (Rossett 2002). She admits that had she edited the book 18 months earlier, the first glorious vision would dominate.

The problems seem to be that the workers are not voting with their feet. Those involved with the technology are excited and enthusiastic. They like it. But then they would, it is learning brought to their world. The challenge is bringing e-learning to the world of the non-computer expert.

Rossett quotes Pat Weger, vice-president of learning and organizational development for AT&T Broadband: "She lamented the quality of the on line training she was reviewing. 'Much of it is bad, worse than the late 1970s page turning CBT'" (Rossett 2002, p. 6). At the same time, Weger was optimistic about the potential of e-learning and recorded many positive developments.

> *The "e" in e-learning stands for education – we too often forget that – it is not about bandwidth, servers, and cables. It is about education – first and foremost.*
>
> Ken Gates, East-West University, quoted on www.masie.com 701 e-learning tips

E-learning is being taken seriously by organizations and governments. The UK government is seeking a unified e-learning strategy and in its consultation paper (DfES 2003, p. 7) wrote:

E-Learning exploits interactive technologies and communication systems to improve the learning experience. It has the potential to transform the way we teach and learn across the board. It can raise standards, and widen participation in lifelong learning. It cannot replace teachers and lecturers, but alongside existing methods, it can enhance the quality and reach of their teaching, and reduce the time spent on administration. It can enable every learner to achieve his or her potential, and help to build an educational workforce empowered to change. It makes possible a truly ambitious education system for a future learning society.

Essentially, E-Learning is about improving the quality of learning through using interactive computers, online communications, and information systems in ways that other teaching methods cannot match. It is relevant to all subjects and to learners at every stage of learning or training. E-Learning can even reach out and re-engage people who are currently not involved in education because it is interactive, and can adapt to their needs.

E-learning is here to stay but it presents real problems for the deliverer. The theory of learning cannot be ignored and there are a whole new range of problems, some technical, some creative, which have to be addressed.

Dublin (2004, p. 4) concludes his article with the following trenchant words for the designers:

> The initial stage in demonstrating this return on expectations is to focus on installation. You must make sure that, technically and organizationally, your e-learning works. Adults have a very low tolerance for technologies and new processes that just don't work. The second stage is to focus on implementation, on getting learners to use it and the organization to support it. The third and final stage is to focus on integration. Through integrating with the business of the business, your e-learning efforts become interwoven into the fabric of your organization's culture and activities; in effect, your e-learning becomes invisible.

In order to ensure your e-learning is used by your learners and embraced by your organization, remember the following:

► It's about business and providing a business solution.
► It's about providing a return-on-expectation, not just a return-on-investment.
► It's about enabling learning and driving performance, not training.
► It's about people – learners, managers, and executives – not technology.
► It's about motivating learners and energizing organizations.
► It's about becoming invisible, interwoven into the very fabric of your organization and its culture.

6.3.2 Blended learning

The only surprising thing about the concept of *blended learning* is that anyone might have imagined that a significant learning strategy could be anything other than "blended". There may be some subjects that can be learnt on one course, using one particular method, but they are the exception. TBL in any format has much to offer but it cannot provide all the answers.

Despite the earlier hopes and expectations, with some manufacturers possibly beginning to believe their own sales literature, computers and the internet could not teach everything. Other methods, some technical but most involving trainers or as they are often called, "facilitators", could do some learning functions better. The concept of blended learning took hold.

It is worth recalling the strategic teaching aims, mentioned above, of the

Open University courses which are "delivered as an integrated combination of media and methods, each chosen for its unique contribution to the learning experience... text, audio, video, interactive simulations, data base resources, IT tools and communication environments" (www.corous.com).

The ASTD define blended learning as "Learning events that combine aspects of online and face-to-face instruction"; the CIPD "These programmes combine a variety of different methods within one programme to maximize the individual development and the available learning opportunities in a cost effective manner" (Stoddart 2004).

In a strident article posted on the ASTD website, Don Morrison, an e-learning consultant, suggests that the majority of blended learning is a reaction to disappointing e-learning initiatives. He goes on to suggest that the reason for these failures is because implementers did not think hard enough about why they were implementing it. He challenges readers to name one enterprise with an exemplary record in traditional training that fouled up its e-learning implementation.

Morrison (2003) believes that

> it takes uncommon imagination and creativity to create distance learning engaging and powerful enough to change behaviors... Unimaginative distance learning cannot change behaviors but neither can unimaginative classroom learning. What determines the effectiveness of learning is the quality of the instructional design and content not the choice of channel.

Will blended learning become "blurred learning", a phrase that already appears in serious literature? The issue is not just about learning. The proposition is that everything in the electronic age is moving so fast and responding to so many different demands that everything is becoming a blur, in Martyn Sloman's (2001) words, "the connected economy gives rise to a blurring of activities and boundaries". The challenge must surely be to help learners to acquire clarity and focus.

6.4 Effective TBL: the Five Dimensions

Helping people to learn needs passion, involvement and commitment. The best coaches and traditional trainers have personalities which attract and influence the learners around them. They know about the subject, they know about learning and they know how to help people.

Compared to learning where people are directly involved, TBL has two disadvantages which need to be overcome. The first is that the computer, the DVD player and the television are not blessed with personality, style, charm or flexibility. Some people might welcome this. Emotion can get in the way of learning and they prefer an inanimate teacher who is consistent, efficient and works to their hours, not something imposed by concepts such as normal office working hours. However, most people like human interaction:

note the dislike of automated phone systems. People like to interact with human beings. That is not to say there is no place for technical help, but not all the time.

The second disadvantage is that a third element is introduced to the business of getting the messages over – knowledge of the mechanics of producing good video, software authoring programs or how to make a simulator. For successful learning, the providers have to ensure:

▷ They know about the subject (some coaches would argue that this is not always essential, but for the purposes of this chapter that discussion is put to one side)
▷ They know about how people learn, the theory and how it works in practice
▷ For TBL, how to translate that knowledge to the media being used.

This triangle of knowledge is essential to produce effective TBL (Figure 6.1).

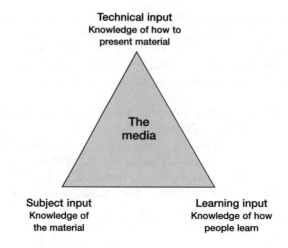

Figure 6.1 **The triangle of knowledge**

All too often designers have two of the three and only a smattering of the third. A knowledge of all three is rare. If they start as trainers, the technical quality may be poor to average. If they start as technicians, the content may be weak. But whichever it is that is weak or missing affects the effectiveness of the project.

6.4.1 Technical knowledge and skill

Trainers can often talk their way through a problem; the nature of their business means that they have to be quick on their feet and hold the interest of a group of people, however tough the question or difficult a particular participant is. Few have the knowledge of the software authoring program expert, the film editor or video producer.

The media produced has to be technically proficient; the best has to be creative. Technical designers not only have to know their stuff, they need to be good listeners so they can find out what the other two parties are saying and turn their ideas into reality, even adding to them by producing ideas which the technical expert will know is possible but which the others have not even thought of yet.

6.4.2 Subject knowledge and skill

Someone has to know the subject matter. Rarely is a TBL product lacking in expertise about the subject matter. Other subject experts may disagree about the approach or interpretation taken by the designers but expertise of one kind is nearly always available. The trick is to turn that expertise and knowledge into a video or interactive learning program and use the best learning theory.

6.4.3 Learning knowledge and skill

To suggest that the learning skills expert is the Cinderella of the three would imply that the technical and subject experts are the two ugly sisters, which would be wrong; but too often the expertise and enthusiasm of the other two dominates and compromises the learning input.

The three are equally essential to a successful project. There are many writers who recognize the importance of applying learning expertise. Clive Shepherd's *Learning Object Design Assistant* is a good example of this (Shepherd 2003b). The demonstrations he provides at the end of this book and the text show a clear understanding of many of the learning essentials. The introductory screens of each demo provide good objectives: "when you have completed this tutorial, given the characteristics of an animal you'll be able to correctly identify whether it is a mammal" (Shepherd 2003b, p. 119). This follows the SMARTS guidelines laid down on pp. 27 and 101. Each page explains where the learner is and what is going to happen next and so follows the principle of adult learning described by Knowles that adults like to know what is happening (see pp. 34–5). There are many other examples of good practice from Shepherd's work.

There is much to be learnt from trainers and coaches as well as from learning theory. The following are some of the more significant.

6.4.3.1 The introduction

First impressions are important and what happens in the early screens of an interactive program or the first few minutes of a DVD is just the same. They should cover the following:

▷ Create some impact or interest early on
▷ A description of the program, how is it structured, how the learner will be involved, what they will be expected to do, what he or she can expect
▷ Provide objectives in the SMARTS way. Care needs to be taken. DVD and video are good at passing on knowledge and can affect people's beliefs and values. It is harder for TBL to develop some skills, the learner needs to practice them, experience the skill before he or she has really got to grips with it
▷ How long it will take the average person to complete it
▷ Why the learning points are important or significant
▷ How the learner might follow up if he or she has questions or wants to know more. This might be best left to the summary or included in both parts
▷ Give the big picture – introduce the subject to be learnt.

The general principle is to try and reassure learners and answer any questions they may have at the beginning. Remember they can't put their hand up and ask, the designer has to try and anticipate what learners will want to know. It is also important for the designer to remember that people forget easily. Gentle, subtle reminders are in order.

6.4.3.2 Developing the learning points

This is the meat of the business. The design is similar to that of any training course (see p. 74). In Chapter 4 the following design points were recommended:

▷ Break the material down into modules or chunks. In TBL the principle is no different.
▷ Allow learners to learn through description (theory), demonstration, and experience, both with help and on their own. These are the four elements of Kolb's (and many others) basic learning points. In a video or DVD, it is possible to do the first two very effectively. Experiencing a skill is often difficult with TBL. If it is an IT skill, for example typing or software, then the computer can do the job very well. If it is project management or quality control, technology finds it more difficult.
▷ Allow participants the opportunity to influence how they are to learn and surface any problems, either in the material being learnt or in the course administration. This is one of the great strengths of TBL. The learner can move around the program, fast forward the video or go straight to the DVD scene he or she wants.
▷ Encourage participation and wherever possible relate the learning directly to the experience or background of the participants. In some cases, it may be possible to write programs specifically for the organ-

ization; mostly they come off the shelf and are generic. This loses some impact. It is important then to have a tutor nearby to help.

▷ Ensure that there is time for proper feedback. Feedback is not possible on a closed circuit program, but technology has advanced and broadband connections can now make online discussion possible. On the internet, many providers offer telephone contact – video conferencing, possible for some of the big companies, will not be far away for individuals working at home. But feedback online is never really going to be able to satisfy the learner whose case is complex.

▷ Introduce as much variation into the course as possible. Let the IT designer run riot with his or her technical knowledge! Use good sounds, lively pictures and clever animations. Humor is more difficult, but vary from light to heavy.

▷ Introduce plenty of reviews and reinforcement as the program develops.

6.4.3.3 The summary

Round off the subject by summarizing the main points. Remind the learner how more can be found out or answer questions. Give a bibliography, including websites.

6.4.4 The fourth dimension: words and looks

The three elements of subject, technology and learning expertise are the core of the design business and will lead to effective learning of knowledge and those skills which lend themselves to technology. Can TBL do more and if so, how?

The instinctive answer from many will be a negative. But the importance of technology has been recognized by many great and infamous leaders in the past. Hitler and the Nazi regime used radio and film to great effect in the 1930s in their propaganda war and some of Churchill's most important speeches were listened to on the radio by a rapt British audience. Roosevelt's fireside chats were deeply significant in influencing the American people. These are not examples of training skills but they do show how even this basic technology can influence people's beliefs and values; an aspect of TBL which is rarely considered.

Following the destruction of the twin towers in New York in September 2001, Osama bin Laden used the media to great effect, partly to worry the US and the West but also to rally his followers, given his enforced state of hiding. His words not only carried knowledge and meaning, they influenced his followers through rhetoric. The lesson is clear; properly used, technology can help to influence people even when they are distant from the creator or speaker.

The written word is an essential medium for passing on knowledge, but it also inspires and there are many examples of how the written word has changed people. TBL can combine the power of the voice and the written word (although not at the same time – see below) and add some. It has real potential for changing beliefs and values.

Having put together the core elements, someone needs to look at the whole and ensure excellence in language, quality of voice and other sounds as well as visual impact (Figure 6.2).

Harvey Thomas and Roy Lilley are both experts in the spoken word and have advised prime ministers and CEOs on communication skills. Their golden rule is: "If they haven't heard it – you haven't said it!" (Thomas and Lilley 1995). People do not take on board everything that is said or written and they have an alarming tendency to hear things that have not been said or interpret it in other ways.

There are four basic rules to any communication, written or spoken:

▷ *Simplicity.* Unusual words may show the writer or speaker to be clever and well educated, or more often a show-off, but simpler words have more impact and are therefore easily understood.

▷ *Brevity.* Any person can only absorb a finite amount of information. Only a small part of a long text or statement will therefore be remembered. Murphy's law will ensure that the important parts are the ones not committed to memory.

> *If language is not correct, then what is said is not what is meant; if what is said is not what is meant, then what ought to be done remains undone.*
>
> Confucius

▷ *Human.* Style is a contentious issue and people will hold on to their views. In office communications, a degree of humanity helps the reader or listener to relate to the messenger and the message. It should be friendly, sympathetic and natural.

▷ *Accurate.* An obvious statement perhaps but all too easily shaded or, in the modern idiom, spun out of recognition (Furnham and Taylor 2004, adapted from Gower 1987, pp. 12, 24).

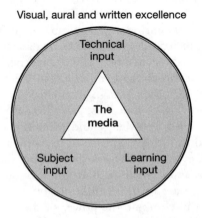

Visual, aural and written excellence

Figure 6.2 **Putting in the fourth element**

Designers are creatures of habit. Once they discover something works they tend to stick to it. This is particularly so with those without formal training. They get a good idea but soon everyone is using it and then it becomes ordinary. Employ the best. There are companies which take a pride in listening to their clients and "combining marketing expertise, creative flair and technical excellence to bring you the full spectrum of e-commerce solutions" (www.abstracts.co.uk, 2005).

In attempting to use the full range of multimedia, designers often put text on the screen and then have someone read the text out. Trainers for trainer courses and presentation skills courses almost invariably point out that this habit is bad practice. Morrison (2003) notes:

> Neither should we glibly provide a spoken narration with all text displays in order to cater to both auditory and visual learning preferences. To do so flies in the face of research into Cognitive Load Theory which shows that delivering the same content simultaneously in two channels impedes assimilation.

6.4.5 The fifth dimension: business

Technology rarely comes cheaply. There may be some TV recording which serves a good purpose or research and the acquisition of knowledge can be done on the internet. That aside, the development of bespoke DVD or an intranet to carry training packages is expensive. The training manager is looking at hundreds of thousands of dollars and that is often on the low end of the scale.

The cost of the project is one aspect. Wherever the product is being developed, there will be a budget. If the product is to be sold on the market, the marketing team will have to see the product and they may have comments on the packaging. An area of potential conflict is what the packet says the product can do. The instructional objectives will be couched in specific and quite limited terms. The marketing team will want to put the objectives in much more extravagant terms. Too often the compromise is to couch the objectives in maximum terms but use words that cannot be measured. Words such as "understand" and "fully appreciate" will creep in. The marketing team and the legal experts are happy; the former because they can use more flowery language and the legal experts because they will fear actions against the company under the Trade Descriptions Act if more specific language is used.

In any event, the business case has to be made and the product sold without legal action against the producers. Figure 6.3 shows all five parties in the design.

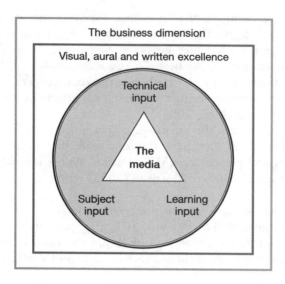

Figure 6.3 **The five dimensions of creating TBL**

6.4.6 Can they communicate?

Although there are five distinct parts to the team (and in some organizations they may be broken down even further and add some such as a specific project manager), there will be some overlap. The person with learning knowledge may also know the subject matter. The subject matter expert may also have some business and marketing skills.

> *There are people who, instead of listening to what is being said to them, are already listening to what they are going to say themselves.*
>
> Albert Guinon (1863–1923)

The issue becomes one of communication between the five disciplines. Will the subject expert be able to explain exactly what he or she is trying to achieve? Will the technical expert be able to explain what is possible? While it might go against the grain, it should fall to the training expert to facilitate the discussion. They would identify early on what the learning objectives are, encourage the subject expert to provide a general overview and then identify how to break the subject matter down into chunks. All this can be done before involving the technical expert. Listening skills are at a premium.

6.5 Technology Options for the Learner

The options available are surprisingly limited, but they all carry a punch when properly developed. The six options are now briefly discussed.

6.5.1 Radio/audio/electronic book

All three are good at passing on knowledge and while they can also influence skills and attitude, their strength is in the information arena. The radio has a slight disadvantage over the others because it relies on scheduled programs. Of course they can still be captured by recording and increasingly broadcasters are making previous programs available over their internet sites. But listeners still have to take extra action to obtain the program they want.

Audio has the advantage of being portable so learners can listen in the car or on the train. There is a variety of forms. The old-fashioned mechanical cassette tapes are rapidly being overtaken by electronic systems which have no moving parts and a huge memory. Programs can be recorded on them easily and quickly and they can travel anywhere. The tape and CD may be around for a while however, as this is still the easiest form for program makers to distribute their material.

Mention should also be made of using this type of media to learn languages. In these circumstances, they go a stage further and demonstrate to the listener how a language is spoken and the learner can then practice on their own. For a few this may be enough but for the vast majority help from other sources is necessary.

The electronic book can be read on PDAs (personal digital assistants – small TV-like handheld devices with a screen which can be read) but for the most part these are not convenient for using over long periods. Reference manuals such as dictionaries, encyclopedias and technical books do have a place on the PDA. More common is reading a book or manuscript on a screen, PC, laptop or TV. The disadvantage is that the screen is tiring to watch and may harm the eyes. A book is less tiring to the eyes because we use reflected light to see the pages. Screens emit light and reading from them is like looking at thousands of small torches. If people do a lot of reading from the screen, it is advisable to have a dark background and put the text in a light color, which reduces the damaging effect.

6.5.2 Television

Like radio, users of TV have to work around a schedule and either watch them or record. Recording is now so common that this is not much of a disadvantage, as long as the learner remembers and can follow the recorder instructions!

TV, videos and DVDs (simple recording versions) are all excellent at passing on knowledge and demonstrating skills. Like radio, they can be used to influence attitudes but this is not their strength. TV (unless recorded) has the disadvantage of being continuous and you cannot turn it off for a break or to absorb the message. But all have been used to great effect in teaching skills from cooking and golf to presentation and interviewing skills.

6.5.3 CD-ROMs/DVD

Along with intranet systems, CD-ROMs and interactive DVDs are potentially powerful systems for some learners. They are portable and provide
freedom to use when and where individuals want (assuming a PC or laptop
is available). They can also choose how long they want to learn and they
move at their own pace. In a traditional training class, learners have to go
along at the speed determined by the trainer and that depends on the abilities of the group. The quicker and slower learners have to tolerate this – with
the CD-ROM and DVD this problem is eliminated.

Programs are also capable of testing the learner so they can only progress
when they have successfully completed a module. Readouts can be produced
to assess the student.

6.5.4 Intranet

Internal linked systems can deliver the same potential as a CD-ROM or
DVD. But there are two important provisos: staff are limited to the office
and the systems can be heavy on memory and central processing unit usage.
A company's system needs to be robust enough to manage.

6.5.5 Internet

Theoretically, the internet should be able to everything that an intranet does,
but download and upload times can limit the internet's value. There are
however many sites now offering good educational and learning opportunities. They tend to be more about acquiring knowledge but more sophisticated
and ambitious sites are available. Many are free. Good sites include
www.learndirect.co.uk, www.vision2learn.co.uk and www.derby.ac.uk/learn-
ing. The BBC is also worth a visit at www.bbc.co.uk/learning.

The added advantage of the internet and to some extent the intranet is
that they are often combined with tutors or email facilities so that learners can
consult people directly with problems. Contact groups may be established
and live conference calls established. Few companies will have the resources
for this, but, like broadband, it will not be long before that technology is
readily available. It does and will add another dimension to e-learning.

6.5.6 Simulators

Aircraft pilots spend a lot of time training using simulators. They provide an
almost real opportunity to fly, without risking a crash, possible loss of life and
heavy costs. They are effective, but costly. The technology is becoming gradually more accessible. Game arcades and software already exist to amuse the

would-be flyer or driver of cars. Some sports are also replicated using computers to produce skiing or horse riding effects; a technology to watch for in the classroom.

The market for simulators will become increasingly accessible to the learning profession. The US army has recently produced an online game for those considering a career with the army – it is in effect a pre-induction course. The site is worth a visit: http://www.americasarmy.com/.

It is worth making a special mention here of learning about a computer's software through any of the above IT-based systems. Packages which teach Word, Java, typing skills or any of the other programs lend themselves uniquely well to TBL. For this kind of learning, ticks would appear in all the boxes in Table 6.1 including beliefs and values. Not only can programs take the learner through the whole cycle of learning, passing on knowledge and skills, they can also directly influence the user in matters such as password security, health and safety issues concerning posture and taking regular rest and the desirability of producing quality work.

6.6 How Good Is It?

Some material available to the learner is very good, but sadly there is an awful lot which fails to deliver. A glossy cover, the reputation of the publishers or high cost of the product are no indicator of quality.

The ASTD 2000 report is interesting in recording that, while investment in TBL systems is still large, there may be a leveling off. The report's authors go on to comment:

> This leveling off in the growth of learning technologies suggests that perhaps organizations are finding technology-based training difficult to do well. Challenges that companies may be facing include technological barriers, cultural resistance to a new way of learning, and the challenge of ensuring that technology-based training is cost-effective and produces results that truly enhance individual and firm performance. (McMurrer et al. 2000, p. 15)

One of the problems is that some program designers do not have a sufficient understanding of training theory. Too many are seduced by what the technology can do rather than focussing on what is most likely to help the learner.

Table 6.1 considers the potential of the six principle and broadly defined vehicles of TBL. It makes a judgement against two sets of criteria. The first is how well each can help people to learn new knowledge, skills, beliefs or values. The second is how far down the learning track they go. In Chapter 2, we established the four necessary stages of learning: describing the subject, demonstrating what is to be learnt, helping learners to practice the newly learnt item and then letting them do it on their own.

Table 6.1 Potential value of TBL systems (assuming high-powered PC/laptop/recorder)

TBL system	Know-ledge	Skills	Beliefs and values	Describe	Demon-strate	Do with help	Do alone
Radio/tape/electronic books	✔	≈	≈	✔	≈	✗	✗
TV (scheduled programs such as Open University), Video/DVD	✔	✔	≈	✔	✔	✗	✗
CD-ROMs/DVD/specific programs written onto the hard disc	✔	✔	≈	✔	✔	≈	✗
Intranet	✔	✔	≈	✔	✔	≈	✗
Internet	✔	✔	≈	✔	✔	≈	✗
Simulators	≈	✔	✔	✔	✔	✔	✔

Key: ✔ useful; ≈ of some but limited value; ✗ of little or no value

6.7 Future Trends

Technology is alive and well, and will always serve the learner well. Predictions that it will take over or dominate the learning business are probably exaggerated. Even the most ardent technophile accepts that it cannot do everything nor will it suit everyone.

There are many buzz words in the technology business, mostly associated with e-learning. Some claim that they have new technologies and concepts to offer. We are conscious that this chapter has not included many that may eventually become accepted in the workplace. The intention was not to produce a comprehensive analysis of every aspect of TBL, but to describe some of those already established, and, on the basis of this, to draw some general conclusions about how TBL might be developed and used in the workplace.

The industry has some consolidation and restructuring to do if it is to bring some order to the profession. There are a number of areas where there is a potential deficit:

▷ Combining the theories of learning in the technical design, together with the creativity of media designers and the business skills of the marketing departments.
▷ The ability of e-learning to take learners through the full learning cycle, that is, to include the chance to practice and experience their learning.
▷ It needs to be able to give more effective feedback.

The answer to the first will be simulation. This already exists in the military and for training aircraft pilots. But simulators are still enormously expensive.

The market already has part of the solution in the games market. Sports such as football, golf and tennis have games which are amazingly lifelike and are beginning to teach kids how to play the game as well as something of tactics and skills. The application of these kinds of technologies in an affordable package for the learning business cannot be far away.

As far as feedback is concerned, the technology already exists to link learners to an online tutor. This reintroduces the human face to the equation.

It is hard to judge the comparative impact on the learning world of the printing press and the spread of bookshops or the computer and its bookshop equivalent of the internet. Both are big and to be welcomed. The particular challenge of the computer and the internet is the speed of its development. It is hard to keep up and envisage its future in the next 10 years, let alone the 550 years that the printing press has been influencing us. Both media will continue for some time. The learning profession should work together to incorporate the new technologies.

6.8 Conclusion

There is more technology can do and there is more that those involved in more traditional forms of learning, trainers and coaches can do to exploit the potential of technology in all its forms. At present, technology is best at passing on knowledge of any kind and teaching IT skills. Arguably it can do so better than books or lecturers. This is no mean achievement. It has the potential to change beliefs and values, but has some way to go to achieve this consistently. This is not a question of technology, purely design.

The real challenge comes in training skills, particularly interpersonal skills. The solution may be elusive. It is hard to believe that technology can teach someone the skills of baseball or cricket to the point where they can walk onto a pitch and deliver a ball or take the strike without practicing with other humans; similarly with interpersonal skills such as speech giving or counsel-type interviews.

The future does lie in a combination of learning materials and TBL designers could usefully listen to and observe their colleagues in the other learning professions. All learning facilitators learn from the theory. The psychology of learning has not changed – the means of delivering it now has become much bigger.

7 Assessing Learners

7.1 Introduction

The personality of individuals is a fascinating subject – people talk about it all the time, although without some of the scientific precision, which psychologists seek to impose on their work. People talk about each other and use terms such as reliable, delightful, outgoing, anxious, curious, all terms which psychologists recognize but they tend to use more particular phraseology: conscientious, agreeable, extravert, neurotic, openness.

Trainers, consultants and coaches frequently use tests to discover more about the people they are working with and then help them change for the better. They are popular with learners for a simple reason: everyone is fascinated about themselves and many of these tests produce insights into their own character. Indeed, it is often the task of much management training simply to increase self-insight and self-awareness.

But are they any better than the star signs to be found in magazines and newspapers? Are they more about commercial gain and profit than scientific study? To what extent are the results written in an ambiguous way so that the reader can take from it what he or she wants (the Barnum effect, see pp. 171–2)? In short, are learners being conned or is there some substance to the stories?

As well as answering these questions, this chapter looks at the whole picture of testing learners, not on their performance on the training course (this was done when describing feedback, pp. 77–9) but as a way of providing insights into their personality, their abilities and their preferred role in the workplace in all its various manifestations.

7.2 The History of Psychological Testing

Trainers, recruiters and selectors all use psychological tests. To the newcomer the topic of psychometric testing can be a confusing area. What do these tests measure? Do they work, that is, are they valid? Are they good value for money? What do the numbers mean? This chapter will look at various psychological tests to give the would-be trainer a helpful "which guide" to choosing and using tests.

Cook (2004) maintains that you can trace psychological testing to the Old Testament. In Old Testament times, Gideon was the commander of the Israelite army, and he had an unusual problem – too many volunteers. He needed to reduce their numbers, but not at random; he wanted only experienced and courageous men. He used two rough-and-ready tests for distinguishing good soldiers from bad. He first told the volunteers how dangerous war could be and how great the risk of death and injury: "Whosoever is fearful and afraid, let him return and depart early". About two-thirds of the volunteers changed their minds and went home. But there were still too many volunteers. Gideon now told the remaining volunteers to take a drink from the nearest stream. Those who lapped the water "putting their hand to their mouth" passed the test, but "all the rest of the people bowed down upon their knees to drink water" (Judges 7: 3–6) and failed because experienced soldiers keep watch for enemies at all times, even when slaking their thirst. This was a selection test. Perhaps not too impressive by today's standards but he had the right idea.

Later the Chinese (as early as 2200 BC) instituted a selection program for public officials. They attempted to measure proficiency in music, archery, horsemanship, writing and arithmetic. For instance, candidates composed a poem and wrote on an assigned theme while being confined for a day and a night in a test booth. About 5% passed this test and they were required to retake it every three years, a sort of psychological MOT. Over the years all sorts of training institutions, from schools to hospitals, monasteries to the military, attempted to devise their own rough-and-ready methods to select and train the best candidates.

By the late 19th century, the discipline of psychology, as it exists today, could be recognized. Francis Galton measured over 9000 people on things like memory, color discrimination and so on and showed how they were closely related to each other.

In the early 20th century Binet, a Frenchman, began work on intelligence testing, to be used in "institutions for the feeble-minded" to establish which inmates (children and adults) would benefit from how much and what sort of formal education. This has been recognized to be the "official" state of psychometric research into cognitive ability.

It was both world wars, however, that provided the biggest impetus to psychological testing. What any army needs is a reliable, valid and efficient screening method. World War I brought with it not only the need to screen the intellectual functioning of recruits, but also the need to screen for personality problems.

Today there is a branch of psychology called psychometrics that is concerned specifically with test measurement and theory. Over 100,000 tests of various types and quality exist and the testing industry is a worldwide, multimillion pound undertaking.

Until the early 1980's, the use of psychological tests of ability and personality in British industry was comparatively unknown. The British have been sceptical about psychology and believed one could "sum up" a person pretty well at the traditional interview, with a glance at a CV, the grip of the handshake, the steadiness of the eye and a few perspicacious questions about sport, hobbies and parents.

But four things happened in the early 1980's to make testing not only popular, but almost a requirement for HR professionals to talk about best practice and level playing fields:

1 The sudden rise in unemployment produced such unprecedented job applicant numbers that the old system could not cope.
2 There were stories, perhaps apocryphal, that executives supposedly used tests (more to fire than hire people) to turn around the company.
3 Equal opportunities legislation became more prominent and its effects placed selection center stage and, as a result, transparency and fairness became dominant requirements.
4 These three influences created the ideal growth medium for the establishment, and aggressive marketing, of test publishers, one of whom, Saville and Holdsworth, still dominates the market in the UK.

Consultants soon jumped on the bandwagon and, by the late 1980's, testing was all the rage. Graduates on the milk round sometimes reported that they had taken the same test six times, while middle-aged executives could be seen on trains reading paperbacks like "know your own personality" and "know your IQ" in anticipation of a terrifying testing session to determine whether they were to be "let go" in the new round of restructuring.

Demand was met by supply. There was sudden growth in test publishers and Americans found for the first time that the British were interested in using tests. Ironically, massive popular interest in tests and testing was occurring just as both personality theory and classic psychometrics were in decline in academia. But authorization to use psychological tests was one of the grounds fought over in the establishment of chartered psychologist status at the time by British Psychological Society, and this exclusivity added to the tests' mystique and appeal.

And the "rage of testing" soon moved to trainers. Trainers found that people enjoyed taking tests; after all they provided feedback on the most interesting of all topics – oneself. Indeed many managers' introduction to tests was via training rather than selection. They got to talk and think about their preferences and preferred team roles; they examined their thinking and learning style, some even glanced furtively over the wall into their emotional stability.

Testing was not a flash in the pan. Certainly, some people remained skeptical; a number even became cynical but too many people had too much at stake. Consultants made a lot of money either testing people and writing reports or else training HR people to "certify" them to use the tests themselves. Test creators and publishers had a field day. And HR professionals enjoyed the credibility that testing gave them. Trainers were, however, among the first to see the usefulness of tests.

Trainers found tests helped in decision making and gave users a new vocabulary to describe and analyse people. Subsequent enthusiasm for the concept of competency in fact revived interest in testing rather than quenched it.

There have been blips in the field. Some damming evaluations have been published in top research journals. Employers have been sued; others have been publicly ridiculed by their choice of test, but more frequently by the use of items in the test.

So what is state of the art twenty years on and a decade into the new millennium? Did raised expectations lead to a major decline in interest? The answer appears to be no. And every so often a new idea comes along that helps the testing business. The latest of these is emotional intelligence. Despite or perhaps, because the concept was all-things-to-all-men, it soon appeared how, when, why and which tests are used depends extensively on the type of business that people are in and now they can be downloaded from the web, almost free of charge.

7.3 The Uses of Psychological Test Data

Psychological test data from all sorts of tests – ability, intelligence, personality – can be put to all sorts of uses (legitimate-illegitimate; sensible-senseless). These can be classified by settings such as:

▷ *Educational settings* for the early detection of certain problems; selecting people for various classes; streaming or classifying candidates; vocational guidance.
▷ *Counseling settings* tests can help to counsel all sorts of people; identify areas of problem or concerns; match abilities to jobs; establish preferences and competences in a wide range of everyday tasks.
▷ *Clinical settings* including private psychotherapy to give a comprehensive overall picture of personality functioning. They can be used in diagnosing a particular problem to determine if it is neurological, psychological, lack of ability or some combination. A consultant hired by an insurance company may want to detect if a person is malingering or really has a problem. A psychologist appointed by a court might use tests to see if a client is indeed fit to stand trial. A psychologist in a prison might be asked if a prisoner really is rehabilitated and can safely be set free.
▷ *Business settings* are widely used in business and industry to assess the knowledge and skill of potential employees; assess the wisdom of promoting people to senior positions; determine the extent to which people can cope with the prospect of regular transfer; establish the necessity or eligibility for further training in specialized or new skills.
▷ *Training settings* can be used to evaluate skills, knowledge and attitudes before and after courses; give insight into oneself and others; help educate people in the language of psychological process within and between people. Mostly they are used to help the individual and the coach or trainer to identify areas which the learner wants to change to become more effective in their job. In the training context, they are about increasing self-awareness.

7.4 Different Kinds of Tests

Psychological tests can be classified or grouped in a number of ways: historically, theoretically, in terms of what they are measuring. But what are psychometric tests and how do they work?

A few simple clarifications. First, "psychometrized" or "evaluated" tests are analysed for features such as reliability and validity, which are crucial. However, many tests have not been through such a process. The "Are you a demon or dodo under the duvet?" tests found in popular magazines have no known psychometric properties. They are devised by journalists, not statisticians. Their aim is to amuse, not measure.

Next, tests are crudely divided into tests of power and tests of preference. The former are essentially ability tests with right or wrong answers. They may measure general intelligence or specific abilities and are often timed. The score is such that more is good, less is bad.

But preference tests, at least in theory, have no evaluation dimension, for they measure personality or values. In fact we all know that it is better to be stable than neurotic, conscientious rather that indolent. It is debatable whether it is better to be extravert than introvert: but most of the literature on happiness and confidence supports that position.

7.4.1 Personality questionnaires

There are a large number to choose from. However, there are a number of features that can be differentiated. Some tests, especially those most used in clinical psychology, have been devised specifically for the testing of abnormal populations (for example MMPI), while others have been devised to reveal the basic dimensions of normal functioning adults (OPQ, 16PF).

Some personality questionnaires set out to measure one single specific trait like altruism or the need for achievement while the majority measure a whole system of traits. However, multi-trait tests claim to measure quite different personality dimensions, although each claims that their list is the most fundamental, comprehensive and exhaustive.

Some personality questionnaires measure personality dimensions or traits like extroversion or neuroticism which are supposed to be consistent over situations and stable over time (unvarying). On the other hand, some measure thinking styles such as the extent to which people characteristically blame themselves or others when things go right or wrong.

There are those visually based on Freudian or neo-Freudian ideas and which measure dynamic aspects of personality such as deep-seated needs or fears, while others measure styles of behavior.

Personality questionnaires are of many different types. They differ in length from a dozen or so items to over 600; some demand binary answers while others give a wider choice; some require ranking, others rating of items.

Methods used to test vary as well. The most common methods used are:

▷ *Projective techniques.* These tests give testees rather ambiguous stimuli (usually pictures, but also sounds and verbal scripts) that they respond to. The idea is that because people either will not, or cannot tell the truth about themselves, they should be encouraged to *project* something of themselves into pictures or stories, so revealing their true personality. A well-known example is the inkblot or Rorschach test but there are many others. Sometimes pictures are presented tachistoscopically (very fast) so that they are on the threshold of awareness or recognition. A more popular version is the sentence completion task. People are asked to complete the simple statement "I am....." twenty times. On the other hand, the question might be "my greatest fear is..." or "what I learnt from my parents is...". These are then content analysed for specific themes. Those tests are not widely used because it is argued that there is no proof that tests actually measure deep-seated aspects of personality; reliability on the part of the testee and scorer is low; and, curiously, a number of extraneous variables like mood affect results.

▷ *"Objective" personality tests.* These are performance tests measuring actual behavior. For instance, because it was observed that tense people press hard when writing, compared to easy-going, more carefree people, a handwriting pressure test was developed. Tests have measured saliva flow, skin conductance, pupil dilation, along with a high number of human abilities. Some people prefer objective tests because of the resistance to faking, response sets and self-delusion. However, they do have serious validity problems because although it is possible to get a nice, clean objective measure, there is not always good evidence that this relates in any meaningful way to personality functioning. A lie detector, or the polygraph, is a sort of objective personality test.

▷ *Measures of moods and states.* Whereas traits are supposed to be relatively stable, mood states fluctuate over time. But these states may have fairly regular patterns and are powerful determinants of behavior. Thus one can have state anxiety brought on by testing or public performance as well as trait anxiety that is a general level of anxiety. In a sense, one needs to "multiply" the two together. There are a number of mood checklists and a measure of drive that measures states. Sometimes, need states such as the need for achievement is put under this category.

7.4.2 Intelligence tests

There are many intelligence tests, some of which concentrate on verbal intelligence, others numeric intelligence and still others spatial intelligence. The use of cognitive ability tests is filled with controversy despite the fact that it appears to be the case that intelligence is perhaps the best predictor of success at work. Two things are worth considering, however; one is the distinction between *general* and *multiple intelligence,* and the other, the distinction between *fluid* and *crystallized intelligence.*

According to Sternberg (1990), researchers in the controversial field of intelligence tend either to be *lumpers* or *splitters.* The former emphasize that people who tend to do well on one sort of IQ test do well on practically all others. They talk of general intelligence (g) and see the IQ score (derived, of course, from a good test) as highly predictive of educational, business and life success.

Splitters, on the other hand, tend to be more impressed by different types of intelligences. They notice that while being equally bright, some (arts) students are good at words while others (science students) are good at numbers. Splitters have, of course, made very different distinctions; perhaps the most well known is that of Gardner (1983), who talks of seven multiple intelligences. He distinguishes between language abilities, musical abilities, logical and mathematical reasoning, spatial reasoning, body movement skills and social sensitivity. The lay person also likes to believe intelligence is multi-faceted – despite evidence to the contrary.

However, since the turn of the century, another distinction had been made between fluid and crystallized intelligence. The analogy is to water – fluid water can take any shape, whereas ice crystals are rigid. Fluid intelligence is effectively the power of reasoning and processing information. It includes the ability to perceive relationships, deal with unfamiliar problems and gain new types of knowledge. Crystallized intelligence consists of acquired skills and specific knowledge in a person's experience. Crystallized intelligence thus includes the skills of an accountant, lawyer, as well as mechanic and salesperson. Fluid intelligence peaks before 20 years and remains constant, with some decline in later years. Crystallized intelligence, on the other hand, continues to increase as long as the person remains active.

These two types of intelligence are highly correlated, although they are conceptually different. Usually what you have learnt (crystallized intelligence) is determined by how well you have learnt (fluid intelligence). Inevitably, other factors like personality do play a part – introverts like to read, study and learn, while extraverts like to socialize and have fun, but bright extraverts who like learning often do better at tests of crystallized intelligence. And, self-evidently, motivation is important – a highly motivated adult will learn more efficiently and effectively than an adult less interested in learning.

7.4.3 Attitude and value tests

There are a whole range of tests that are aimed at measuring attitudes to various topics like health, nuclear power, sex roles, and so on. There are also scales that attempt to measure a testee's values and value system. These are often popular with trainers.

They are essentially attitude measures and may be relevant to work. Thus, they may include things like belief in the work ethic, which is the idea that work is inherently good and brings many psychological beliefs. It may involve belief about personal control of one's destiny at work. These measures might include even such things as addiction to work. Many are interested in work values particularly such things as beliefs about equity and equality. These include terminal values (desirable end states) and instrumented values (desirable modes of conduct).

Tests and assessments can be aimed at people's performance at work or used to identify what roles they prefer in the workplace – 360° assessments and others such as Belbin's team role inventory are common instruments in the trainers' armory. The learning style inventory discussed in earlier chapters is also frequently used on training courses.

7.5 Personality Trait Measures

There are a vast number of tests available – too many to cover in a book like this. The following summaries are selected because of their popularity or because the authors believe they have some significant qualities. Each summary provides a brief description of the objectives of the instrument, in effect what it is trying to assess, examples of how it might be used and a comment. The mechanics of the tests such as time taken, number of questions and so on are not discussed here (for more on tests, see Furnham 1999). Table 7.4 provides a summary of the eight tests discussed at the end.

7.5.1 Myers-Brigg types inventory (MBTI)

The MBTI provides a method for understanding people by looking at eight personality preferences that everyone uses at different times. The eight are organized into four opposite pairs. The four preferences describe four activities:

▷ *Energizing* – how a person is energized, either extraversion (E) or introversion (I)
▷ *Perceiving* – what a person pays attention to, either sensing (S) or intuition (N)
▷ *Deciding* – how a person decides, either thinking (T) or feeling (F)
▷ *Living* – the lifestyle a person adopts, either judging (J) or perceiving (P)

MBTI is best used in management development where it can provide a useful stimulus to increasing people's self-awareness and an appreciation of of others so as to make constructive use of individual differences. It can be used for team building to identify the strengths and weaknesses of a team. Some companies and organizations use MBTI as a selection tool. This is more controversial as the tendency may be to recruit clones rather than a healthier, balanced workforce.

The theoretical background to the measure of personality is derived from the theoretical work of Jung (1923). The test was devised by a mother and daughter team and has been aggressively marketed ever since the 1950's. The test is undoubtedly popular, but psychologists' views vary on its validity. Most of the discussion centers on the eight variables identified in the MBTI. Is there really a clear distinction between the sensing/intuition and judging/perceiving types?

One significant and well-established personality trait is also not measured in the MBTI: that of neuroticism or stability/instability. While it may be uncomfortable to be told that you are unstable, it is an important piece of information for managers, teams and perhaps most of all for recruiters. Those who have a neurotic tendency do have qualities to bring to the workplace (sensitivity, creativity). This omission has led some commentators to wonder whether MBTI success is partly due to the fact that it delivers only good news.

7.5.2 16 Personality factors (16PF)

Another popular and fairly easy to use instrument is the 16PF. Devised by Cattell in the late 1940's, the 16PF is based around the proposal that an individual's personality consists of 16 personality factors, outlined in Table 7.1. 16PF is most frequently used as a selection tool, although it is found in some management development sources, hence its inclusion here. It provides useful material for discussion of an individual's personality, but because it covers some of the darker sides as is clear from Table 7.1, care needs to be taken in giving feedback.

Table 7.1 The 16 personality factors with score meanings

Personality factor	Low score	High score
1. Sociable	Reserved	Warm, cooperative
2. Intelligent	Dull	Bright
3. Mature	Affected by feelings, undemonstrative	Emotionally stable, calm
4. Dominant	Obedient, submissive	Assertive
5. Cheerful	Sober, serious	Enthusiastic
6. Persistent	Disregards rules, undependable	Conscientious
7. Adventurous	Shy	Venturesome
8. Effeminate	Tough-minded, realistic, vigorous	Tender-minded, sensitive
9. Suspicious	Trusting	Suspicious
10. Imaginative	Practical, conventional	Imaginative
11. Shrewd	Forthright, naive	Sophisticated, shrewd
12. Insecure	Self-assured	Guilt-prone, timid
13. Radical	Conservative, traditional	Experimenting
14. Self-sufficient	Group-dependent	Self-sufficient, resourceful
15. Controlled	Uncontrolled	Controlled
16. Tense	Relaxed	Tense

A review of the literature shows that there is some controversy over 16PF, perhaps the most strident being between Cattell and Eysenck, another prominent psychologist. Furnham (1992) identified it as follows:

> These two figures have occasionally taken swipes at each other. For instance, Eysenck (1985) has claimed that Cattell's 16 factors are unstable: when results are thus completely unreplicable, it would seem that the theory based on the original analysis is unacceptable, and that such scales should not be used in theoretical or practical scientific work. (p. 9)

In reply, Cattell (1986) quotes 41 published studies that replicated his system. He notes:

> Eysenck's resort to three factors is shown to be theoretically faulty and unable to equal the criterion predictions obtainable from the 16PF primaries. (p. 153)

In fact both men, graduates of London University, have developed questionnaires useful in the world of occupational testing.

7.5.3 The Eysenck personality questionnaire (revised) – (EPQ(R))

Despite Cattell's comments quoted above, most commentators agree that Eysenck has produced the most sophisticated trait personality theory. It has survived some rigorous investigation and is considered to be robust. The EPQ(R) measures three variables, those claimed by Eysenck to be the most important personality dimensions: extraversion (E), Neuroticism (N), Psychoticism (P).

Kline (2000) describes these three as follows:

▷ *Extraversion.* The extravert is sociable, lively and in terms of Eysenck's theory stimulus hungry.
▷ *Neuroticism.* Eysenck calls his second factor neuroticism since he regards this as basic to neurosis although empirically it is certainly identical to the factor labelled anxiety... This factor is trait anxiety.
▷ *Psychoticism.* This is the somewhat exotic label given to a factor in which high scorers are cruel, hard, ruthless and entirely lacking in empathy. They like risk taking and danger and this factor is related to criminality and is generally lower in females.

The EPQ(R) is used in management development and has some value in selection processes. Its only flaw, according to Kline (1993, p. 505), and this only affects personnel selection, is that "the factors are broad, and that more detail is required for the discriminations that have to be made in job selection".

Eysenck provided the basis for many of the psychometric tests that exist today "in brief it is a benchmark personality test" (Kline 1993, p. 505).

While it may be well known amongst psychologists and other experts in the field, it is not so well known amongst trainers and coaches. It perhaps lacks the commercial promotion which the MBTI and 16PF enjoy.

7.5.4 NEO-PI

The direct inheritor of the Eysenckian and Cattellian traditions are the Americans Costa and McCrae, whose work in the 1980's and 1990's has revived the world of personality theory and testing. Working in the psycho-metric trait tradition, they settled on three and then five dimensions of personality. Based on this theory, NEO-PI measures the "Big 5" factors of personality in the five factor model. According to this model, there are five orthogonal dimensions of personality, neuroticism, extraversion, openness to experience, agreeableness and conscientiousness:

▷ *Neuroticism* reflects a tendency to experience negative emotions, like anxiety, anger, hostility and depression. Individuals who score high on neuroticism tend to be anxious, self-pitying, tense, touchy and unstable.
▷ *Extraversion* reflects a tendency to experience positive emotions and behave sociably. Individuals who are high on extraversion tend to be active, assertive, energetic, enthusiastic, outgoing and talkative.
▷ *Openness to experience* reflects a tendency to engage in intellectual activi-ties, and experience varied sensations and new ideas. Individuals who score high on openness tend to be artistic, curious, imaginative, insight-ful, original, and tend to have wide interests.
▷ *Agreeableness* reflects a tendency for altruism, trust and friendly compli-ance. Individuals who score high on agreeableness tend to be apprecia-tive, forgiving, generous, kind, sympathetic and trusting.
▷ *Conscientiousness* reflects a will to achieve, persistence, dependability and self-discipline. Individuals who score high on conscientiousness tend to be efficient, organized, reliable, responsible, thorough, and have a good planning ability.

NEO-PI is used in management development courses and can be usefully applied in coaching situations where coachees need some data on their personalities and on which they can focus their minds. It is also used in selec-tion processes.

There is now broad agreement from many sources that the five factor model has credibility, although as might be expected in the world of psychology, there are some detractors (for example Kline 1993). It is in the world of organizational behavior that the five factor model has become most popular amongst researchers. NEO-PI suffers like some of the other tests from a lack of marketing skills, but it remains one of the simplest and most effective tests available today. Its selling points are reliability, validity and comprehensiveness.

7.5.5 Hogan's personality inventory (HPI)

The Hogan personality inventory (HPI) is a seven-factor personality inventory developed specifically for the business community. HPI contains seven primary scales and six occupational scales:

Primary scales
▷ *Adjustment* – self-confidence, self-esteem, and composure under pressure
▷ *Ambition* – initiative, competitiveness, and the desire for leadership roles
▷ *Sociability* – extraversion, gregariousness, and a need for social interaction
▷ *Interpersonal sensitivity* – warmth, charm, and the ability to maintain relationships
▷ *Prudence* – being planful, self-disciplined, responsible, and conscientious
▷ *Inquisitive* – imagination, curiosity, vision, and creative potential
▷ *Learning approach* – enjoying learning, staying current on business and technical matters

Occupational scales
▷ *Service orientation* – being attentive, pleasant, and courteous to customers
▷ *Stress tolerance* – being able to handle stress, even-tempered, calm under fire
▷ *Reliability* – honesty, integrity, and positive organizational citizenship
▷ *Clerical potential* – following directions, attention to detail, and communicating clearly
▷ *Sales potential* – energy, social skills, and the ability to solve problems for customers
▷ *Managerial potential* – leadership ability, planning, and decision-making skills

The Hogan measures (there are others) are rapidly growing in popularity due to their easy application to the world of work. However, it is probably the Hogan dark side measures of personality disorders that are proving most popular, in part because they have no serious competition.

7.5.6 Fundamental interpersonal relations orientation – behavior (FIRO-B)

FIRO-B originated in the US in the 1950's having been originally written by Dr William Schutz for use in the American armed forces. The aim of the test is to help people become more aware of how they behave towards other people and how others behave towards them.

FIRO-B measures three areas of interpersonal needs: inclusion, control and affection. Each need area takes the form of "wanted" and "expressed". The resulting six cells are summarized in Table 7.2.

Table 7.2 The six scales of FIRO-B

	Inclusion	Control	Affection
Expressed	I make efforts to include others in my activities. I try to join social groups and be with people as much as possible	I like to organize and control other people's activities. I try to take charge of others and be the leader of any group I am in	I make efforts to get close to people. I am comfortable expressing personal feeling and I try to be supportive of other people
Wanted	I want other people to include me in their activities and invite me to belong. I enjoy it when others notice me	I feel most comfortable working in well-defined situations. I like to have clear expectations and instructions	I want other people to show warmth towards me. I enjoy it when people share their feelings with me, and when they encourage my efforts

It is used for personal development, career counseling, management development and team building.

The emphasis in this test is on interpersonal relationships. People's feelings and sensitivities are highlighted. Courses which need to investigate these issues will find the test useful. There is not much literature on its validity and it appears to be rather weak. But it does offer a unique point, namely the difference between expressed and wanted.

7.5.7 Occupational personality questionnaire (OPQ)

Many would argue that Saville and Holdsworth (market leaders in the UK for occupational psychometric tests) have succeeded in producing a series of instruments on various behavioral aspects of work, which are both commercially successful and have some validity.

The most comprehensive versions of the OPQ measure 30 scales, derived from existing personality inventories, repertory grid studies and criteria for occupational success. The scales are grouped into three categories associated with relationships with people, thinking styles and feelings and emotions.

The OPQ is popular amongst consultants as it is directly relevant and designed for assessing personalities in a work situation. The OPQ looks at team types (based on Belbin's work, see below), leadership styles (directive, delegative, participative, consultative or negotiative leader) and subordinate styles (receptive, self-reliant, collaborative, informative or reciprocating subordinate) (Jones 1993, p. 68).

As we have seen, academics often openly criticize each others' work and it is not surprising that there has been some careful scrutiny of the OPQ. These have focussed on two aspects. The first is whether the underlying dimensions (relating, thinking and feeling) are independent of each other. The second is to question whether the OPQ does really predict occupational behavior. Jones (1993, p. 73) also notes that it "can be seen to be superficial by a small minority of purist psychologists".

7.5.8 PA preference inventory (PAPI)

Like the OPQ, PAPI is a largely commercial instrument and forms a key element of the range of assessment services offered by the PA consulting group. The results are presented in a wheel design, providing a useful focus for discussion. There are 20 different factors broken down into seven key areas. There are 10 needs and 10 roles.

Table 7.3 The 20 factors of PAPI

Key areas	Needs	Roles
Work direction	To finish a task To achieve	Hard intense worker
Leadership	To control others	Leadership Ease in decision making
Activity		Pace Vigorous type
Social nature	To be noticed To belong to groups For closeness and affection	Social extension
Work style		Theoretical type Interest in working with details Organized type
Temperament	For change To be forceful	Emotional restraint
Followership	To support authority For rules and supervision	

PAPI is increasingly popular and is used to help in many development courses and situations. It is directly relevant to the workplace and therefore attractive to many consultants, coaches and trainers.

PAPI receives even less attention in the academic literature than OPQ or FIRO-B, however, its popularity and marketing makes it a leading instrument for consultants.

Table 7.4 Summary of some personality tests

Test	What is measured	Context in which useful	Comments
MBTI	Extraversion/introversion Sensing/intuition Thinking/feeling Judging/perceiving	Self-awareness, team building, management development, more controversially it can be used in selection	A popular test, and testees can easily identify with the results. Neuroticism is not assessed
16PF	16 personality factors: social, intelligent, mature dominant, cheerful, persistent, adventurous, effeminate, suspicious, imaginative, shrewd, insecure, radical, self-sufficient, controlled, tense	Mostly used in selection but has a place in management development	Well researched and validated
EPQ(R)	Extraversion, neuroticism, and psychoticsm	Management and leadership	The factors are broad and the test would usefully be included with others. It is one of the benchmark tests both for its theoretical foundation and its validity
NEO-PI	Neuroticism, extraversion, openness, agreeableness and conscientiousness	Management and leadership. It is also used in selection processes	It is based on the work of the EPQ(R) and assesses the generally accepted five factors
HPI	Adjustment, ambition, sociability, interpersonal sensitivity, prudence, inquisitive, learning approach: Occupational preferences: service, orientation, stress, tolerance, reliability, clerical, potential, sales potential, managerial potential	Individual development also used in selection and assessment	A useful, practical test that is being used more and more in applied settings
FIRO-B	Six personality variables based on inclusion, control and affection, combined with "wanted" and "expressed"	Personal development, career counseling, management development and team building	Concentrates on interpersonal skills and therefore limited in its uses
OPQ	Team, leadership and subordinates styles	Directly applicable to behavior in the workplace	Commercial but with considerable data now to support its validity
PAPI	Work direction, leadership, activity, social nature, work style, temperament, followership	Directly applicable to behavior in the workplace	Commercial and popular

7.5.9 Raven's progressive matrices

Although designed before the differences between fluid and crystallized intelligence were fully recognized, Raven's matrices are an effective test of an individual's fluid intelligence. It has also been used to judge someone's approach to problem solving.

Raven's is generally accepted as one of the best tests of fluid intelligence currently available. The only slight flaw identified by Kline (2000, p. 462) is that only one type of diagram or matrix is used in the test. Other items should be used to minimize the effects of specific factors.

7.5.10 Watson-Glaser critical thinking analysis (WGCTA)

The WGCTA is a well-known and well-established verbal reasoning series of tests. It looks at patterns of intellectual thought according to five main areas:

▷ Inference
▷ Recognition of assumptions
▷ Deduction
▷ Interpretation
▷ Evaluation of arguments.

The tests are used extensively in selection but also as a useful tool for individual development. They help to increase awareness by identifying strengths and weaknesses. They assess crystallized thinking and, as with Raven's, most commentators rate its reliability and validity to be high.

7.6 Other Forms of Assessment

There are a number of other tests and assessments frequently used and which should be mentioned. They are not strictly speaking personality tests but some use the science of personality assessment.

7.6.1 Belbin team roles

In the course of many years research, Dr. Meredith Belbin discovered nine specific team roles. All teams are made up of these and no others (Jones 1993, p. 187). The roles, together with a brief description, their strengths and allowable weaknesses, are shown in Table 7.5.

Table 7.5 Belbin's team roles

Team role	Contribution	Allowable weakness
Plant	Creative, imaginative, unorthodox. Solves difficult problems	Ignores incidentals. Too pre-occupied to communicate effectively
Resource investigator	Extravert, enthusiastic, communicative. Explores opportunities. Develops contacts	Overoptimistic. Loses interest once initial enthusiasm has passed
Coordinator	Mature, confident, a good chairperson. Clarifies goals, promotes decision making, delegates well	Can be seen as manipulative. Offloads personal work
Shaper	Challenging, dynamic, thrives on pressure. The drive and courage to overcome obstacles	Prone to provocation. Offends people's feelings
Monitor/ evaluator	Sober, strategic and discerning. Sees all options. Judges accurately	Lacks drive and ability to inspire others
Team worker	Cooperative, mild, perceptive and diplomatic	Indecisive in crunch situations
Implementer	Disciplined, reliable, conservative and efficient. Turns ideas into practical actions	Somewhat inflexible. Slow to respond to new possibilities
Completer/ finisher	Painstaking, conscientious, anxious. Searches out errors and omissions. Delivers on time	Inclined to worry unduly. Reluctant to delegate
Specialist	Single-minded, self-starting, dedicated. Provides knowledge and skills in rare supply	Contributes on only a narrow front. Dwells on technicalities

The test itself consists of two parts, the first invites the individual concerned to complete the form. This produces a self-perception report. The second invites observers of the individual in the workplace to comment as well. Comparison of the two provides the basis of a useful discussion on self-awareness. Belbin has extended the use of the software produced in association with the questionnaires to analysing job specifications and then to selection and recruitment.

Belbin's team role inventory does provide teams with some useful data on which to consider their own strengths and weaknesses. Discussion in a team invariably leads to new insights into what is happening and what might make an excellent team.

There are some technical criticisms of Belbin's approach which do undermine its scientific validity. This should warn managers away from making important recruitment or appointment decisions based only on a Belbin analysis. However, as an instrument to stimulate discussion and demonstrate how teams might effectively be structured, it is of real value.

7.6.2 Honey and Mumford learning style questionnaire (LSQ)

This was discussed in the context of David Kolb's work on learning styles in Chapter 2. The LSQ is frequently used in training courses, particularly those involved in training such subjects as training itself. Honey and Mumford have produced an easily accessible and easily interpreted questionnaire which shows people's learning preference. These are:

▷ *Activists* like to be involved in new experiences. They are open-minded and enthusiastic about new ideas but get bored with implementation. They enjoy doing things and tend to act first and consider the implications afterwards. They like working with others but tend to hog the limelight.
▷ *Reflectors* like to stand back and look at a situation from different perspectives. They like to collect data and think about it carefully before coming to any conclusions. They enjoy observing others and will listen to their views before offering their own.
▷ *Theorists* adapt and integrate observations into complex and logically sound theories. They think problems through in a step-by-step way. They tend to be perfectionists who like to fit things into a rational scheme. They tend to be detached and analytical rather than subjective or emotive in their thinking.
▷ *Pragmatists* are keen to try things out. They want concepts that can be applied to their job. They tend to be impatient with lengthy discussions and are practical and down to earth.

The significance for trainers, coaches and consultants is that by knowing their own style they can counterbalance any instincts they may have when trying to teach someone who has a different style to their own. An activist coaching a reflector is likely to become frustrated by the latter's desire to have everything explained before trying out whatever it is they want him or her to do. This "halo" or "horns" effect is well known. The LSQ helps the provider to anticipate potential problems with clients.

7.6.3 Emotional intelligence

Few concepts have grabbed the attention of researchers, theorists and in particular practitioners in the field with the intensity and suddenness of emotional intelligence (EI). As it has caught the imagination of the public and is often used in learning environments, it is worth providing some detail.

The roots of EI can in fact be traced back to E.L. Thorndike's (1920) social intelligence and Gardner's (1983) intrapersonal and interpersonal intelligences. The term EI itself was discussed in the literature several times before Salovey and Mayer proposed the first formal definition and model of the construct in 1990. This early model was soon followed by several other concepts, the most influential and the one largely responsible for launching the field was Daniel Goleman (1998).

Salovey and Mayer (1990) defined emotional quotient (EQ) within a developmental model of intelligence. Their model of EQ comprises four hierarchical tiers that define a person's ability to recognize and group emotions:

1 Individuals learn how to *identify emotions in themselves* and others as well as how to discriminate between expressions of emotions.
2 Individuals use emotions to aid the *decision-making process*.
3 The ability to *employ emotional knowledge*, that is, the capacity to recognize the relationships among emotions and transitions from one emotion to another
4 The ability to *manage emotions by behavior* associated with the information those emotions convey.

In contrast to Salovey and Mayer (1990), Goleman (1998) proposes a theory of EQ that is performance-based. Specifically, he relates EQ to 20 competencies in four clusters of general abilities, consisting of self-awareness, social awareness, self-management, and relationship management. Each of the four clusters is seen as distinct from cognitive abilities and each other.

1 Self-awareness is defined as knowing what one feels.
2 Social awareness encompasses the competency of empathy and the ability to read non-verbal cues.
3 Self-management relates to the ability to regulate distressing emotional responses and inhibit emotional impulsivity.
4 Relationship management is defined by one's ability to understand or influence the emotions of others.

Having caught the imagination of the public and those in the business of learning, it was not long before the concept was spawning a large number of tests and models. There was no coherent operational framwework and the development of the constructs was haphazard, with numerous apparently conflicting findings.

There was another problem in the early days because there was no distinction made between self-report measures and those using performance measurements. More specifically, the fundamental distinction between self-report and performance measurement went unheeded, thus leading to conceptual confusion and contradictory results. The choice of measurement method has a direct and significant influence on how to devise a questionnaire and thus the empirical findings.

Petrides and Furnham (2001) proposed a conceptual distinction between two types of EI based on the measurement method used to operationalize them:

1   *Ability EI* (or "cognitive-emotional ability") concerns the actual ability to perceive, process, and utilize affect-laden information. This construct pertains primarily to the realm of cognitive ability and should be measured via maximum performance tests.
2   *Trait EI* (or "emotional self-efficacy") concerns a constellation of emotion-related self-perceptions and dispositions. This construct pertains primarily to the realm of personality and should be measured via self-report questionnaires.

It is important to understand that ability EI and trait EI are two distinct constructs differentiated by the respective measurement methods used to operationalize them rather than by the content of their sampling domains.

There exist only a few measures of ability EI, most of which are iterations of pilot tests developed in the 1990s. The problems of developing a wide range of EI items that can be scored according to objective criteria are considerable and as yet no reliable construct is available.

Progress has, however, been made on trait EI. Petrides et al. have designed and published a "trait emotional intelligence questionnaire" (TEIQue) on the internet. Respondents are asked to answer 153 questions around 15 facets as shown below.

Facets	High scorers perceive themselves as...
Adaptability	flexible and willing to adapt to new conditions.
Assertiveness	forthright, frank, and willing to stand up for their rights.
Emotion perception (self and others)	clear about their own and other people's feelings.
Emotion expression	capable of communicating their feelings to others.
Emotion management (others)	capable of influencing other people's feelings.
Emotion regulation	capable of controlling their emotions.
Impulsiveness (low)	reflective and less likely to give in to their urges.
Relationship skills	capable of having fulfilling personal relationships.
Self-esteem	successful and self-confident.
Self-motivation	driven and unlikely to give up in the face of adversity.
Social competence	accomplished networkers with excellent social skills.
Stress management	capable of withstanding pressure and regulating stress.
Trait empathy	capable of taking someone else's perspective.
Trait happiness	cheerful and satisfied with their lives.
Trait optimism	confident and likely to "look on the bright side" of life.

Source: http://www.ioe.ac.uk/schools/phd/kpetrides/trait_ei1.htm#TEIQue

Much progress has been achieved in the few years since the early models were introduced, at least as far as trait EI is concerned. But practitioners should be wary and scrutinize any programs or instruments they plan to use; many are not based on good scientific research.

7.7 Legal and Ethical Considerations

What kinds of ethical guidelines govern those people involved in testing? In fact most testers have to abide by a strict code of ethics, are well trained and are themselves tested on their testing knowledge.

At times there are heightened periods of public concern about testing, the nature of tests, and so on. Concerns include the following:

▷ The only thing tests measure is the ability to take tests.
▷ Tests discount important features like knowledge or experience in dealing with difficult situations.
▷ Tests are unfair.
▷ Tests are biased against certain groups.
▷ Test scores are overinterpreted, kept on record, and used for purposes for which they were clearly never designed.

Equal employment opportunity acts in many countries stipulate no discrimination by reason of race, color, religion, sex and national origin. Some legal provisions disallow any discrimination in terms of mental and physical hardship. Some legislation demands that testers have some "minimum competency" certificate to be able to administer and interpret tests.

Psychologists are concerned about who has access to tests and who is competent to administer them. Professions are particularly concerned as to how testees are informed about their scores and the need for preventing obfuscating jargon.

To prevent, as much as possible, the misuse of psychological tests, the ethical codes officially adopted by the American Psychological Association and the British Psychological Society devote considerable space to test distribution and use.

7.8 Reliability

For all sorts of reasons, test results do not always accurately reflect a person's actual personality, intelligence, ability, motives or interests. Test scores from testees vary according to:

▷ the amount of test anxiety they are experiencing and the degree to which that test anxiety might significantly affect the test results.

▷ the capacity and willingness to cooperate with the examiner or comprehend written test instructions.

▷ the amount of physical pain or emotional distress being experienced at the time of testing.

▷ the amount of physical discomfort brought on by not having enough to eat, having had too much to eat, or other physical conditions.

▷ the extent to which they are alert and wide awake as opposed to "nodding off".

▷ the extent to which they are predisposed to agreeing or disagreeing when presented with stimulus statements.

▷ the extent to which they have received prior coaching.

▷ the importance they attribute to portraying themselves in a good or bad light.

▷ the extent to which they are, for lack of a better term, "lucky", and can "beat the odds", on a multiple-choice achievement test (despite the fact that they may not have learnt the subject matter).

By and large most, but by no means all, psychological tests are pretty reliable, that is, the correlation (the reliability coefficient) between the scores of people who take the same test twice over a reasonable period of time is quite high. This should be .90 or above.

There are various sources of error that may significantly reduce the reliability of a test and lead to poor consistency. These include:

▷ *Test construction:* The actual range of questions asked as well as things such as the wording of tests actually affects the consistency of people's answers.

▷ *Test administration:* Such things as room temperature, ventilation, noise, writing surface can all affect results. So can the amount of sleep the testee had the night before, the amount of test anxiety present, the drug they may be taking, illness, temporary worries and, for women, the stage of their menstruation cycle can all cause careless mistakes, misreading questions and the giving of uncharacteristic answers. Finally, certain characteristics associated with the tester (age, sex, physical appearance, professionalism) can subtly alter the nature of the test situation as perceived by testees and hence their actual results.

▷ *Test scoring and interpretation:* The advent of computer scoring has largely prevented error creeping in here but some tests still require testers to make an "expert judgement" as to the correctness of an answer. Without rigorous and standardized training, it is possible that different (albeit small) interpretations (and hence scores) will be given by different testers.

Test designers are concerned to ensure reliability; in many ways it is not a serious problem, as the statistics on this indicate that most tests are suprisingly robust and reliable.

7.9 Validity

The most important aspect of most tests is the extent to which they actually measure what they claim to measure, that is, the meaningfulness of the test score. Essentially the validity of any psychological test may be evaluated by scrutinizing the content; relating the score obtained on the test to other test scores and measures; and how the test relates to or predicts other measures, behaviors or beliefs within the theoretical framework originally devised for the test.

There are many types of validity and not all are equally important. It is probably predictive validity that is most important – the ability of test scores to predict later behavior.

At the end of the day, test validity is the single most important issue in testing. Does the test really measure what it claims to be measuring? Clearly, this is relevant in the real world of selection and recruitment. It is also important in training where, although usually the "numbers" do not count as much as the concepts, they remain most important to ensure that people do not get false or misleading feedback about themselves and others.

The problem with good proof of test validity is that it takes time, money and effort. Frequently, the results are disappointing, in the sense that the levels of validity hoped for by test constructors and publishers never quite reach their targets.

7.10 Fakability

People lie on personality tests; most lie to present themselves in a good light, hoping to appear healthily adjusted, intelligent, motivated normal people. Occasionally they present themselves in a negative light to avoid such things as imprisonment or corruption. They also may be trying to malinger and avoid various types of work.

What can one do about faking, good or bad or mad. Essentially five things:

1 *Use a lie scale:* Many, but not all questionnaires, have a lie scale in them. Lie scales usually contain items of high social desirability: Have you ever broken or lost something belonging to someone else? Do you always wash your hands before a meal? Have you ever cheated at a game? The total lie scale can be calculated and if the person has a score well above a certain level, it must be assumed that they are lying on all items.
2 *Correlating items with measures of social desirability:* Another way of detecting lying is to look at the social desirability of every item. This can be done by asking people to rate each item, or they might complete the full test and the results correlated with the test of the general tendency to show social desirability. This at least pinpoints the areas of social desirability where people are most likely to lie.

3   *Having a fakers' profile or template:* Another very useful way to catch
    fakers is to obtain the typical profile of someone faking, good or bad. You
    do this by actually inviting different groups of people to fake what they
    think is the most desirable answer (specifically not give an honest
    answer). From these people you can derive a fake-good template or
    profile which you can use to detect fakers.
4   *Use warnings:* It has been found that people will be more honest if simply
    told to do so. Stress the importance of honesty, the first answer to come
    into the head, and the necessity of not lying. When people are loath to
    admit negative behavior (stealing office stationery, shopping online in
    office time), one way to avoid this is to force them to choose which of a
    pair of equally unacceptable behavior they do most often (ipsative tests –
    forced choice).

Three additional points need to be made. Firstly many people think
psychologists test honesty by checking reliability, that is, whether they tend
to give the same answer to the same sort of question. The answer is they do
not but the more people believe this the better. Secondly, people may lie less
when computer scoring is involved because they feel their actual responses
are not handled by people or seen by others. Thirdly, when people lie, they
tend to move one or two points up from their original scale (like a 45-year-
old claiming to be 42), which has the effect of compressing the range of the
scale rather than actually getting completely different answers. People do
disagree about what is the best answer and thus they do not all fake in the
same way.

7.11 Norms

This refers to the average or mean responses for age and different groups of
the population. It is customary to standardize tests on large representative
population groups, broken down (or split up) by sex, age and class factors.
The test may also be given to specific groups depending on what the test is
measuring, that is, mental patients for tests of neuroticism; managerial
groups for tests of occupational interests and ability. These groups should
be sufficiently large and representative of the category of people they
should represent.

Good norms are crucial because they tend to be the yardstick against
which results are interpreted. For instance, you need to know what a score
of 13 on a dimension means. The norms will tell you whether it is high or
low, for men or women, older or younger people, and so on. Clearly if a test
only has female norms, American norms or is based on students, it may be
much less useful for use on British workmen. Test developers should invest
in good comprehensive normative studies as their failure to do so may
severely limit the usefulness of a test.

7.12 Using Tests Wisely

Frequently, personality tests are used for appraisal training and selection. Many organizations would choose a personality questionnaire to help them in the process. There are a number of questions to ask before proceeding:

▷ What is the object of the test? How is this objective the same or different from existing tests designed to measure the same thing? How will the objective(s) be met?

▷ Is there really a need for this test? Are there other tests that purport to measure the same thing? In what ways will the proposed test be better than existing tests? Will it be more reliable? More valid? More comprehensive? How might this not be better than the other tests? Who would use this test and why?

▷ Who would need to take this test? Who would need the data derived from it? Why?

▷ What content area should the test cover? How and why is this different from the content of existing similar tests?

▷ How will the test be administered? Will the test be individually administered, or should it be amenable for both individual and group administration? What differences will exist between the individually administered version and the group administered version? How might differences between the two versions be reflected in test scores?

▷ What is the ideal item format for this test? Why? Should the test be amenable to computerized administration, scoring, and/or interpretation?

▷ Should more than one form of test be developed?

▷ What special training will be required of test users in terms of administering or interpreting the test? What background and qualifications will a prospective user of data derived from this test need to have? What restrictions, if any, should be placed on distributors of the test and the test's usage?

▷ What types of responses will be required by test takers? What "real-world" behaviors would be anticipated to correlate with these responses? Why will scores on this test be important?

7.13 360° Assessment

360° assessment or multi-rater feedback (MRF), provides evidence of how subordinates, peers, customers and the boss perceive an individual's performance against previously established criteria, which usually relate directly to the core skills and qualities required of the job in question. The individual concerned usually fills in the form as well so that comparisons can be made between his or her perceptions and those of his or her colleagues.

There are three questions which need to be addressed:

▷ Based on the perceptions of others, how valid is the evidence? When should a recipient feel he or she can ignore what is said in a report?
▷ Should the assessment be used for appraisal, in any form, or should it be limited to development only?
▷ Does it work? Does the recipient change their behavior for the good as a result of a 360° assessment?

360° assessment has not always been welcomed with open arms. One permanent undersecretary informed his board of management in 1995 that he proposed to introduce 360° assessment into the department and that the board would be the first to experience this new management tool. There was some discussion in which the procedures were explained, including that of subordinates assessing board members. The board were not happy and the silence at the end of the discussion was broken by one member asking the PUS if they could delay the process six months, by which time their teams might be better prepared to assess him.

Another government department took advice from their colleagues in France. The French were horrified at the idea. It would amount to "insubordination".

But 360° assessment is now with us and is a regular tool in management development programs and courses. Consultants, coaches and trainers regularly use it and to some extent depend on it to focus attention on the areas of development they should concentrate on.

As a serious development tool, 360° assessment is still in its infancy and work continues to test its design, application and validity. It is, however, in regular use and deserves more detailed discussion here.

According to Edwards and Ewen (1996), the history of 360° assessment (also referred to as multi-source feedback – MSF) can be understood in terms of themes developed in various decades of the 20th century:

▷ 1940's   Assessment centers had multiple assessors of multiple task performance (competences) by the same individual.
▷ 1950's   Military leadership assessment and selection used peer and superior ratings on specific courses.
▷ 1960's   Job evaluation processes at the time used multi-raters.
▷ 1970's   Executive selections, succession planning, project evaluation and placement all began to use multi-rater assessment to improve decision making.
▷ 1980's   Talent assessment and performance appraisal both incorporated elements of multiple rater theory.

It was suggested that the relatively slow adoption of 360° assessment occurred because of the visual factors, organizational culture, inertia, budget, unavailable technology to support it and little or no research evidence.

7.13.1 How valid is the evidence?

The key word in the description of 360° assessment above is *perception*. Those asked to rate someone in the workplace will have some evidence but they will not have the full picture. The only person who may have that is the individual concerned and their view is well known to be prejudiced and they may not have the skills to interpret all the evidence that is available to them. Are they able, for example, to interpret all the signals which subordinates send out when they are unhappy? Can they elicit all the information necessary to make a good judgement?

The rater has less information and is plagued by the same inadequacies of interpretation. Are their perceptions worth anything?

Much depends on the question to which they are responding. Take, for example, a question that frequently appears on questionnaires: "To what extent does the person being assessed get to know individuals and their aspirations?"

A rater will be able to answer the question as far as he or she is concerned, and may have some evidence about others in the workplace. Where a boss is not co-located with the person being assessed, he or she will not have much evidence on which to base their answer. Subordinates will usually have the better evidence.

However, with a question like "To what extent is the person being assessed sensitive to wider political and organizational issues?", a subordinate is less well placed than the boss to make a judgement on this issue.

A question such as "To what extent does the person being assessed tackle poor performance or inappropriate behavior?" will provide some observers with a problem, particularly when commenting on a good manager. Many would argue that a good manager will first anticipate problems arising from poor performance and will therefore tackle any issues arising from it quickly before others notice it. Even when poor performance has become established, the manager is unlikely to tell everyone exactly what he or she has done to rectify the situation. The very nature of tackling poor performance demands a degree of discretion and confidentiality, which makes the actions unobservable. Those who handle poor performance well often receive middling marks on this kind of question, because observers have no real evidence to say one way or the other.

None of these observations need make the perceptions of others invalid, but it does put a responsibility on the facilitator of the feedback to help the individual interpret the responses correctly.

There have been a number of studies on the ratings results. Furnham and Stringfield (1993) in a study of three ratings groups (supervisory, self and subordinate) found that there was greater similarity between subordinate and supervisor than between self-ratings with either. This finding was confirmed in a second study, this time adding the effects of consultant ratings (Furnham and Stringfield 1998). In other words, observers from whichever level agree more with each other than the person rating themselves.

The evidence indicates that peers make discriminating judgements about their colleagues and there is substantial overlap between peer and training. Peers are more likely to observe characteristic behavior than training staff or supervisors because they work closely with the individual and therefore have more opportunities to observe behavior. In addition, it is argued that because individuals are likely to censure their behavior when they know they are being observed by training staff or supervisors, it is more likely that peers observe typical behavior compared to training staff or supervisors. The finding is that peer ratings are the best single predictor of job advancement. In summary, the current study together with previous research suggests that, in a training environment, peers are able to make discerning judgements about their colleagues and therefore make a useful contribution (Furnham and Stringfield 1998, p. 223).

Atkins and Wood (2002) used assessment center rating data as a criterion when comparing the accuracy of self, supervisor, peer and subordinate ratings. They conclude:

> Although self-ratings were biased and were the least valid predictors of the assessment center ratings in this study, the possibility of errors in observer ratings should not be ignored. Reviewers of 360-degree programs have commented on the lack of training given to raters and the fact that the criteria used in many programs are not well defined. Concerns about the motivations and competence of raters apply equally to observers and self-raters. In addition, as is true in other forms of appraisal, the more job related and specific the behavioral statements used to define the competencies surveyed, the less error there will be in all sources of ratings. The fact that the 360-degree feedback programs are used predominantly for developmental purposes may contribute to the lack of concern for the rigor of ratings. However, as we have pointed out, inaccurate ratings can have detrimental effects, irrespective of the reasons for collecting them. (pp. 900–1)

7.13.2 Appraisal or development?

The use of 360° feedback for appraisal or development is controversial. Alimo-Metcalfe (1998) gave advice on implementing and using 360° feedback based on her own experience of using multi-rater feedback in the public sector. She demands seven points in the early phase, the first three of which are:

▷ The process is voluntary.
▷ The process is to be used for developmental purposes only.
▷ The data are owned by the individuals (apart from a group report of a minimum of four participants which is available to all participants).

Later Alimo-Metcalfe (1998, p. 41) comments:

> Clarify the reason why the organization wishes to introduce the process. Is it for assessment purposes, for example, for selection, promotion, or for pay for perfor-

mance, for example? Or is it for purely developmental purposes? I believe passionately that it should only be used for the latter, and am encouraged that at recent conferences in the US, this point was made by all, bar one presenter. Its value in personal, team and organizational development can be considerable, but associating it with administrative purposes, such as selection or performance-related pay for example, could create considerable damage, as has been evidenced in the area of appraisal.

Edwards and Ewen (1996, p. 52) believe that 360° feedback can be used for more than development. They present the pros and cons for using it in assessment (Table 7.6).

Table 7.6 Arguments for and against using 360° feedback for appraisal and pay

Argument against	Solution
Ruins development	Provide a non-performance affecting section
Inflates ratings	Use intelligent scoring and respondent accountability
Users manipulate the system	Use intelligent scoring and respondent accountability
Arguments for	**Explanation**
Already being used	Many organizations are already using the information
Market-driven	Users spontaneously are developing home-grown systems
Credibility and validity	Experience and research show process validity
Employee-driven	Employees are asking for the use of 360° feedback systems

Edwards and Ewen (1996, p. 59) present some guidelines for organizations already using an existing 360° feedback system for development to extend its use to pay/appraisal methods:

▷ *User surveys:* Users support from satisfaction surveys should exceed 75 percent.

▷ *Anonymity:* Users must have confidence that their individual ratings will be absolutely confidential.

▷ *Distinction:* The spread of scores should clearly differentiate high, medium, and low performance.

▷ *Valid difference:* The distinctions must represent truly high, medium, and low performance.

▷ *Response rates:* Responses from those who provide feedback should be above 75 percent.

▷ *Administrative overhead:* The time required for respondents and for process administration must be minimised and reasonable.

▷ *Invalid respondents:* Respondents must be accountable for honest ratings; invalid responses – those 40 percent different from the consensus of others – should be below 5 percent.

▷ *Diversity fairness:* Respondent do not systematically discriminate unfairly against protected status groups, and members of such groups should receive performance scores similar to others.

▷ *Training:* Users should be trained in both providing and receiving behavior feedback.

▷ *Safeguards:* Safeguards to process fairness, such as intelligent scoring which minimises known sources of bias, are understood and supported by users.

The discussion is likely to run for some time yet. Those who caution against using a 360° assessment for appraisal or pay performance have genuine and well-founded concerns. But the number of organizations who are using MRF for appraisal is growing and without deleterious results.

7.13.3 Does it work?

Few address the most fundamental question of all: How to measure the impact of 360° assessment? Smither and Walker (2001, p. 285) point out the well-known problems of measuring change after interventions. Their review of the literature led them to the following conclusion:

> Measuring change can be complicated by a host of problems: response-shift bias, regression to the mean, the ceiling effect, and difficulties associated with difference scores. The use of alternative methods, such as retrospective degree-of-change ratings and polynomial regression analysis, can help overcome some of these problems. To date, longitudinal studies indicate that managers generally improve their performance after receiving upward feedback; score improvement is greatest among managers who initially receive the most negative feedback or who initially overrate themselves, and among managers who follow up with raters to discuss and clarify the feedback. Still, we need additional research that focuses on the personal or organisational factors that facilitate (or detract from) changes following multi-source feedback, the specific goals set by individual managers after receiving it, and the causal linkages between MSF interventions and key measures of organizational results.

Seifert et al. (2003) asked two simple but important questions. Does feedback facilitate management improvement? Does it matter how the feedback is received? First, they reviewed 14 studies, all of which measured change over time in performance (from 3 to 48 months). Five showed yes (an improvement), four no (none) and five inconclusive results. Because of the problems with these studies, the authors did their own study. There were three conditions: No feedback control group; a feedback report; a feedback workshop.

Managers in the feedback workshop increased their use of some core influence tactics with subordinates, whereas there was no change in behavior for the control group or the comparison group. The feedback was perceived to be more useful by managers who received it in a workshop with a facilitator than by managers who received only a printed feedback report.

Seifert et al. (2003, p. 568) note:

> In summary, we found that a multisource feedback workshop can improve managerial behaviour even when there is little skill training, a non-supportive climate, and no extrinsic inducements. Increasing the effectiveness of the feedback beyond the level achieved in our study would probably require more of the facilitating conditions. Learning how to create these conditions should be a primary objective of future research on behavioural feedback programmes.

In an important study, London and Smither (1995) started by doing an interview of 20 American organizations using multi-sourced feedback. They concluded:

> In summary, multi-source ratings can be valuable in improving self-understanding, and suggesting directions for development and performance improvement. Agreement between self- and co-workers' ratings and among co-workers may provide diagnostic information about the extent of self-awareness. Variables that affect agreement levels suggest the need to calibrate the meaning of agreement data in relation to individual and organisational factors. Overall, agreement between and among sources has implications for self-evaluations of goal accomplishment. (p. 810)

7.13.4 The role of the feedback giver

360° assessment will continue to feature as a significant element of management and leadership development. The evidence is already strong enough to suggest that applied properly and facilitated well it can have a positive effect on most recipients. As its credibility grows this can only increase.

The burden then falls on the deliverer of the feedback to get it right and help the recipient to interpret the responses correctly. Even in this brief overview, some of the problems of interpretation have been identified. The process of feedback demands knowledge of the 360° instruments, and how to give feedback and sensitivity to the individual concerned who may be hearing some uncomfortable but true facts that he or she has not heard before.

Case study: a controversial question

Peter, a senior civil servant, knew he had to set an example and be one of the first to receive a 360° assessment. He was quite looking forward to it. He was retiring soon and, while he would do his best to respond to any critical comments, he knew that he was popular and he would not need to put much effort into changing.

Laurie had prepared hard for the session when he would give the feedback to Peter. In general, the report was complimentary but he knew there was a sting in the tail.

Peter accepted those points which were critical as fair, but felt the report was in general rather positive, until he read the response to the last question:

"Would you like to work with this person again?"

Two out of eight had answered in the negative. Peter took a deep breath, admitted that this was serious and asked if they could go through the report again. He thought that he had a strong team around him and he worked well with them and they with him. It hurt that two people would not want to work with him again. He was not angry, nor did he try to work out who had given him the negative responses. But he was determined to change some of his ways even in the few months left in the office.

Conclusion

The inclusion of that question at the end of the 360° questionnaire was controversial when designing the questionnaire. Some, including Laurie, were against it because it did not relate to a specific competence and therefore would be hard to manage if there were many negatives on a report. In fact, there were few people who received negative responses to the question and whenever they did occur, it made the assessed person think much harder about what was going wrong in their team.

Feedback stimulated the person concerned to attempt to change his ways.

7.14 Beware the Barnum Effect

It was Phineas T. Barnum, the famous circus act producer, who said "There is a sucker born every minute". His formula for success was "A little something for everybody". The Barnum effect refers to the phenomenon whereby people accept personality feedback about themselves, whether it is universally valid or trivial, because it is supposedly based on personality assessment procedures. In other words, people believe in completely bogus feedback because they accept the generalized, trite bogus descriptions, which are true of nearly everybody, to be specifically true of themselves.

A psychological study illustrates this point. Ross Stagner, an American psychologist from Wayne State University, gave a group of personnel managers a well-established personality test. But instead of scoring it and giving them the actual results, he gave each of them bogus feedback in the form of 13 statements based on horoscopes, graphology analyses and so on. Each manager was then asked to read over the feedback (a supposedly personal one, based on the "scientific" test) and decide how accurate the assessment was by making each sentence on a scale (a) amazingly accurate; (b) rather good; (c) about half and half; (d) more wrong than right; (e) almost entirely wrong.

Over half felt their profile amazingly accurate, while 40% thought it was rather good. Hardly any considered it to be very wrong. The more positive the more accurate and the two considered *least accurate* ("Your sexual adjustment has presented problems for you", and "Some of your aspirations tend to be pretty unrealistic") were negative. You see the importance of positive general feedback. People naturally have a penchant for the positive.

Research on the Barnum effect has, however, shown that belief in this bogus feedback is influenced by a number of important factors. Some of these concern the client and the consultant (their personality, naiveté and so on) and some concern the nature of the test. Curiously, factors related to the client and consultant have shown comparatively weak results. Women are not more susceptible than men, although of course in general the gullible are more susceptible. The status and prestige of the consultant is only marginally important – which is good news for the more bogus people in this field.

However, some factors are crucial. The first of these is the "personal" factor. The more detailed the question the better. In one study, an American researcher gave all his subjects the same horoscope. He found that those who were told that the interpretation was based on the year, month, and day of birth judged it to be more accurate than those who were led to believe that it was based only on the year and month. Again and again studies show that after people receive general statements that they think concern only them, their faith in the procedure and the diagnostician increases.

The second factor is that the feedback must be favorable. It need not be entirely, utterly positive; but if it is largely positive, with the occasional mildly negative comment, people will believe it.

The moral is: people will believe in, agree with and even like feedback from questionnaires if the information it gives is positive, bland and general. They won't necessarily recognize that it is bogus. So we can't trust their judgement in determining whether the test is valid.

7.15 Conclusion

There are many reasons why a trainer, coach or consultant may choose to use psychological tests. They may want to assess cognitive ability to determine the level and type of training that is most appropriate, that is, tests could be used for streaming. Next, they could be used to make judgements about how the training occurs. Neurotic introverts learn best under different conditions than stable extraverts. Many trainers use tests to improve self-awareness and provide consistent psychological or behavioral language to discuss personal and other behaviors at work.

Choosing the right test for the right purpose involves or should involve training on the part of trainers. They need to be educated in basic psychometric concepts so that they can make judicious decisions and carry out testing competently.

Alas, poorly educated trainers can be at the mercy of aggressive test publishers who quite naturally push tests of limited psychometric or theoretical quality. It means that they are often out of date, clinging onto old, long-discarded tests proven to be of little merit.

Once again, this illustrates how much information, skill and training trainers need in order to keep up to date and deliver to their clients the best possible training.

8 Assessing the Providers

8.1 Introduction

Trainers and coaches do not have a simple reaction to the concept of evaluation. On the one hand, they recognize its importance in the cycle of assessing learning needs and delivery. On the other hand, assessing their performance is never comfortable and has some of the awkwardness of the dreaded annual appraisal. Some embrace it both to prove and improve their performance. Others seem hesitant about the whole procedure, especially the validity of assessment and its impact on teaching and training.

If done properly, the assessment should be rigorous and helpful. It goes beyond the immediate reaction of the learners and is usually completely outside their control. The success of the learning objectives is tested two or three more times. If they are external, they may not even see the results.

All trainers will have experienced the first of Kirkpatrick's four levels of evaluation (see over), the post-course feedback questionnaire (or "happy sheet" as it is often described). But few will have had their work more closely scrutinized either through Kirkpatrick's remaining three levels or other more direct methods, but they know that their work ought to be evaluated more closely. Few encourage their employers to carry out these further levels. Coaches and mentors have their work scrutinized much less frequently and for the providers of e-learning, the subject is barely touched.

Evaluation is not easy, or at least calculating the benefits of training is not easy. Accountants do not take long to provide figures on the costs of training. HR professionals have a harder task identifying in such clear terms the benefits. A board faced with the firm's figures, which directly affect the bottom line profitability or potential productivity of the organization, will find the training budget a tempting area for cuts.

Even when a skill or knowledge gap has been identified and some kind of development need recognized, how does the training manager or board assess the effectiveness of what is offered by internal or external providers? Evaluation is essentially a backward-looking process; what is often needed is something which looks forward, and for the longer term project looks at what is happening now. That is the need to plan how, where, why and by whom courses are evaluated and assessed before they actually take place.

> *ROI can be predictive or historical. The best predictive ROI will draw on historical ROI data.*
>
> Don Morrison 2004, *E-Learning Strategies*

This chapter looks first at evaluation, assessing the effectiveness of past training. It will then look at how judgements can be made about prospective learning.

8.2 The Four Levels of Evaluation

The traditional method for evaluating training dates back to the 1960's following the publication of four articles by Kirkpatrick (1959). Four levels of evaluation were described by Bee and Bee (1994, p. 176):

1 *Reaction level:* measures what the delegates *think* or *feel* about the training
2 *Immediate level:* measures what the delegates *learned* on the course
3 *Intermediate level:* measures the effect of the training on *job performance*
4 *Ultimate level:* measures the effect on *organizational performance*.

8.2.1 The reaction level

Did participants like the program? The questionnaire or "happy sheet" is the most common method of evaluating training. The participant is more likely to be objective on a written questionnaire that guarantees anonymity than in a face-to-face interview. To be useful, a questionnaire should follow several criteria:

▷ Word questions carefully. Pre-test all questions by administering them to a group other than the group that will be evaluated.
▷ Measure only one aspect of the training at a time.
▷ Make the responses to each item on the questionnaire mutually exclusive and exhaustive.
▷ Leave room for additional written comments.

Some trainers prefer to focus on the trainer's performance and questions about them tend to dominate the questionnaires; learning takes second place. This is often the surest place for positive feedback. At the end of a course, participants are usually in a good mood and are likely to give positive comments (hence the term "happy sheet"). The questionnaire should, however, focus on the learning. Participants should be given sufficient time to fill it in and there should be time afterwards for discussion. Figure 8.1 gives an example of an evaluation questionnaire on a Training for Trainers course run by a British trainer overseas to six trainees.

Training for Trainers

Evaluation

We would very much appreciate your comments on this course. Please refer to the objectives and programme and reflect on the whole course. Your answers to the following questions will help us develop this and other similar courses. Please feel you can make critical comments. We can only improve if we know where we have gone wrong.

Objectives

By the end of the course participants will be able to:

▶ Describe how adults learn best
▶ Design courses which meet the training needs of the organisation
▶ Design courses which enable participants to maximize their learning
▶ Introduce to their training programmes a variety of training and learning methods, including exercises, case histories, hypothetical exercises, syndicates and ice breakers
▶ Write exercises which support the training objectives and introduce these exercises at the appropriate point of the course

As well as making a written comment you may also give a mark from 1 (good) to 5 (bad). Please put a circle around the appropriate number.

1. *General comment*
a. Please make a general comment on the value of this course to you.

                                        Good – 1 2 3 4 5 – bad

b. How might it have been improved?

                                        Good – 1 2 3 4 5 – bad

2. *Objectives*
a. Are the objectives relevant?

                                        Good – 1 2 3 4 5 – bad

b. Which objective(s) was *least* relevant to you?
c. To what extent has the course succeeded in achieving the objectives?

                                        Good – 1 2 3 4 5 – bad

Please comment on where the course failed and how it might have achieved full success

d. To what extent has the course succeeded in helping you achieve your own objectives?

                                        Good – 1 2 3 4 5 – bad

3. *Programme*
a. Was the programme properly balanced between lecture, discussion and exercise?

                                        Good – 1 2 3 4 5 – bad

b. Have you any other comments on the programme and its structure?

4. *Training skills*
Please comment critically on the quality of training:
a. Delivery of lectures

                                        Good – 1 2 3 4 5 – bad

b. Use of visual aids including hand outs

                                        Good – 1 2 3 4 5 – bad

c. How might the training be improved?

5. *Administration*
Please let us have any comments which concern the administration of the course:
a. Room
c. Other

If you have any other comments please feel free to make them here:

                            Signed by the Trainer

Figure 8.1 **Example evaluation questionnaire**
Source: JT Associates

These measurements are valuable for analysing positive and negative feedback on, or directly after, the program. But they cannot say how much a participant has learnt or the skills they acquired. They are also sensitive to many rating errors.

8.2.2 Immediate level

Did participants learn the skills? A job or task simulation is an excellent way of validating training results. An alternative is to have the participants watch each other. For example, in role plays, which are appropriate if verbal skills are being taught, one person can play the supervisor, another the employee, and a third can observe the skill being measured. To ensure that skills are measured accurately, standardized procedures and forms must be used. Skills must be measured both before and after training and a comparison made.

Naturally, there are important issues here. First, who does the pre- and post-course rating: the candidate, the trainer, or the peers of the candidate back at the workplace? Then there is the issue of what skills, knowledge, techniques are rated and at what level.

Equally important is the equivalence of the before and after test. If the "before" is much easier than the "after", it may appear as if considerable learning has occurred which is untrue. Equally if the "after" test is much more difficult than the "before" training measure, it could appear as if no training has occurred at all.

It is also important to measure observable behavior, not inferences about behavior.

8.2.3 Intermediate level

Did participants use the skills on the job? This validation attempts to prove actual skill use. To ensure that on-the-job improvements derive from training rather than from external factors, set up a control group of people within the organization who have not had training. The following guidelines tend to achieve accurate test results:

▷ To ensure consistency, the same or a proven equivalent instrument (for example questionnaire) needs to be used before and after training.
▷ To obtain objective measures, managers, subordinates and a random cross-section of all subordinates need to be selected for training.
▷ Measurements for the control group (the group who did not undergo training) and training groups must be made simultaneously to minimize the chances of measuring changes that occur over time and in the work environment.
▷ Pre-training measurements 30–90 days in advance need to be made. People sometimes behave in an "unnatural" manner if they know they are scheduled for a training program. Equally, post-training measurements should be done 30–90 days after the program.

▷ Confidentiality must be maintained, as subordinates may be worried about the repercussions of poor ratings.
▷ The assessment instrument must be valid and deliver consistent results.
▷ Measurement must be done only on what is actually taught and measure *all* the skills taught, not just a few.

8.2.4 Ultimate level

Did the program affect the bottom line? This validation demands observable, quantifiable, tangible and verifiable facts that show specific profit or performance results. Although hard data are preferable, soft data can be used if they can be verified. In other words, a statement that departmental efficiency increased by 5% is an acceptable measure of success, but only if it can be proven by a source outside the group or department. Most importantly, it must be crystal clear that it was the training as opposed to some other factor that directly caused the measured output increase. A control group is difficult to use in validation because of the wide range of internal and external variables that affect bottom line performance other than the training itself. If it is difficult to match the control group's and training group's functions and experience through random selection, match pairs of supervisors and then assign them randomly to the training or control group.

If it is not possible to create a control group, one can compare results to an earlier period. For example, you might compare production rates for the October before and after training. But you must carefully examine all external factors that might have affected the results. Although these results are not a rigorous validation, they are useful.

Kraiger (2003) has pointed out some recent critiques of the Kirkpatrick approach. They are critical for four reasons:

1 It is theoretical and outdated, based on an old-fashioned behavioral rather than modern cognitive approach.
2 There are unsubstantiated assumptions about the relationship between outcomes (that is, people cannot learn if they don't like the program).
3 It treats both trainee reactions and learning itself as if it were unidimensional, whereas we know this is not the case.
4 Evaluation has different purposes: decision making, feedback and marketing. Thus what is measured must fit the purpose.

8.3 Evaluating Coaching

Kirkpatrick's four levels are usually applied to training, and although many of the principles are the same, are there different issues for coaching? What is the evidence that coaching works? Is there absence of evidence or evidence of absence (of effectiveness)? Scientific evidence that coaching does what it says it does, that is, deliver its impressive promises, is hard to come by.

Table 8.1 Four critical training questions

What we want to know	What to look at / What might be measured	Alternative data	Measurement dimensions (source of data)	Gathering methodology
I. Are the trainees happy? If not, why not? a. Concepts not relevant b. Workshop design c. Trainees not properly positioned	Trainee reaction during workshop	Relevance Threat Ease of learning	Trainees' comments Questions about exercises "Approach behavior"	Observation Interview Questionnaire
	Trainee reaction after workshop	Perceived "worth" or relevance – learning energy	"Approach behavior" to project. Questions about project, concepts	Observation Interview Questionnaire
II. Do the materials teach the concepts? If not, why not? a. Workshop structure	Trainee performance during workshop	Understanding Application	Learning time Performance on exercises Presentations	Observation Document review
b. Lessons – Presentation – Exercise – Trainers	Trainee performance at end of workshop	Understanding Application Facility Articulation	Action plan for project Use of tools on exercises Presentation	Observation Document review Interview Questionnaire
III. Are the concepts used? If not, why not? a. Concepts – Not relevant – Too complex – Too sophisticated/simple	Performance improvement projects*	Analysis Action plan Results	Discussions Documentation Actual results	Observation Interview Document review Questionnaire
	Problem-solving technique	Questions asked Action proposed Action taken	Discussion Documentation Results	Observation Interview Document review Questionnaire
b. Inadequate tools c. Environment not supportive d. Skills/concepts not required yet	On-going management approach*	Dissemination effort Language People management process	Discussions Meetings Documentation	Observation Interview Document review Questionnaire
IV. Does application of the concepts positively affect the organization? If not, why not?	Problem-solving*	Problem identification Analysis Action Results	Discussions Documentation Results	Interview Document review Questionnaire
	Problem prediction and prevention*	Potential problem identification Analysis Action	Discussion	Interview
	Performance measures*	Output measures Diagnostic measures	Documentation Results Performance data	Document review Questionnaire Document review

* Specific to a particular workshop. *Source:* Kirkpatrick (1976) Evaluation of training. In *Training and Development Handbook*, R. Craig and L. Sittel (eds), pp. 261–70. New York: McGraw-Hill. Reproduced by permission of the McGraw-Hill Companies. All rights reserved.

One answer may be to look at how scientists try to ask a similar question, namely "Does alternative medicine work?" Scientific evaluations have a "gold standard" to evaluate the claims – random, controlled trials (RCTs). Better still, there are "blind" trials. There are essentially three features to the scientific method, all of which are important to determine whether coaching really works. The first is *randomization*. This means that people (read patients or managers) are randomly assigned to different therapists, coaches or the control group.

Randomization is important because it controls for the *volunteer effect*. We know that all sorts of factors in the doctor–patient, coach–manager relationship can affect the outcome. It may be the age, education or physical good looks of either party that affects the outcome, rather than the process itself. It is the therapist effect not the therapy effect, or in this case, the coach's not the coaching effect. It is not what is done but who does it that is important.

If coaching works, should it work for all managers? It should work for all (trained) coaches who follow the process. If it only works for certain types of people with certain coaches, then we need to know why and whether some specific factor (other than the coaching process) is having an effect.

A manager has to be (randomly) assigned to their coach. Neither party likes this much but that is too bad, at least for an experimental investigation of efficacy. We know that some psychologists have a selection interview to decide whether both parties feel they "can do business with each other". The scientific question is why the treatments only works for certain combinations of giver and receiver. If it does, this needs to be in the small (or indeed big) print.

The second feature of the scientific approach is the concept of a *control group* or indeed control groups. This means is that some managers are allotted to a real management coach, and another group may be allotted to a physical coach or another manager, acting as a guide, mentor or simply a friend. There are essentially two types of control groups: one in which the manager does nothing at all and sees if the coach experience is better than nothing. The other is where the manager does some other activity quite different from coaching.

Control groups tell the evaluator whether changes in the managers' performance would have happened naturally over time. In the business it's called "spontaneous remission". The body (perhaps the mind) heals itself. Nothing needs to be done for this to happen. Time heals. But it could be that what is having the beneficial effect is simply talking to someone else (about anything) or getting out of the office or being made to feel important. Control groups really tell us about the process itself.

The third component is called *blinding*: ideally double-blinding. In medicine this means that neither the doctor/nurse nor the patients know whether they are getting the (real) drug or a sugar pill. The reason is that patient and doctor knowledge powerfully influences the outcome via the "placebo" effect.

With therapy, you can't "blind" the parties involved. However, you can blind the assessor, in the sense that the person does not know what treatment the patient/manager has had. So after, say, six months of "something" (executive coaching, exercise, nothing), the subordinates of the managers in the trial are required to rate them on their performance. Better still, some hard behavioral data are used to see which group changes most and in what direction. Managers' self-reports may be produced, but they may be completely delusional.

Does coaching work? Maybe. How do you know? First find, say, 100 managers. Randomly send 33 to a real manager coach, 33 to a PT instructor, and 34 to listening to music for a two-hour session every three weeks for six months. After this time, measure the managers' performance, self-esteem, satisfaction and so on. Better still, ask the managers' staff to measure the managers (upward measurement) without them knowing whether they were in the coaching, PT or music group.

If, and only if, the coached manager has statistically different and better evaluations than the other groups, then we can really say coaching works for everybody. If not, the questions of for whom, when and how coaching works, if it can be demonstrated to work at all, will have only just begun.

8.3.1 Pitfalls of training

There are many reasons why training fails. These reasons help to explain poor performance or assessment. One of the aims of assessment/evaluation is to pinpoint exactly when and why courses fail or succeed in their aims. Lambert (1993, p. 244) supplies 18 reasons, many of which occur all too frequently:

1 Inaccurate or incomplete needs identification. That is, the need for training of a particular type was misdiagnosed in the first place.
2 Failure to predetermine outcomes relevant to business needs of the organisation. Unless one sets out a realistic and specific goal or outcome of training, it is very difficult to know if it has succeeded or failed.
3 Lack of objectives, or objectives expressed as "will be able to" rather than "will". There is a difference between can do and will do, often ignored by evaluators.
4 Training seen by management and participants as having little or no relationship to real life. It is seen as a break and an alternative to work, rather than as a means to improve.
5 Excessive dependence by trainers on theory and chalk-and-talk training sessions. This method is least effective for the learning of specific skills.
6 Trainers untrained or under-trained. It is far too easy to call yourself a trainer with little personal training in the skills required. Some courses have "train-the-trainer" sessions, but these are all too rare.
7 Training programmes too short to enable deep learning to take place or

skills to be practiced. The longer and more spaced out the programme, the more participants learn and the more it is retained.

8 Use of inappropriate resources and training methods which have to be considered beforehand, particularly the fit between the trainer and the trainees' style.

9 Trainer self-indulgence, leading to all sessions being fun sessions, rather than actual learning experiences.

10 Failure to pre-position the participants in terms of the company's expectation(s) of them after training. This means having a realistic expectation, per person, of what they should know, or should be able to do after the training.

11 Failure to de-brief participants effectively after training, particularly as how best to practice and thus retain the skills they have acquired.

12 Dependence on dated and invalid research to justify approaches. This is a very common problem.

13 Excessive use of "good intentions" and "flavour of the month training", rather than those known to be effective.

14 Training limited to lower levels of the organisation, because it is cheaper and easier to deliver and evaluate.

15 Inability of top management team to "walk like they talk". That is, managers do not model what trainers instruct.

16 Use of training to meet social, ideological or political ends, either of trainers or senior management. That is, training is not really about skill acquisition but rather about, for instance, a fight between various departments.

17 Failure to relate to bottom-line performance. This means that training takes place without any consideration of its effect on productivity or profitability.

18 Training design developed to accentuate enjoyable experiences and games rather than the transfer of learning to the workplace.

Assessing the effectiveness of training is desirable, but it is never going to be possible to provide hard evidence of what is precisely the added value. A person's performance is the result of many factors: did the recruiters get it right in the first place; is the individual motivated to learn and achieve in any event; how much guidance does the boss provide? Such questions apply equally to coaches, mentors and providers of technology-based training.

8.4 Assessment Before the Event

One of the problems of evaluation is that it happens after the event; when arguably it is too late or, even worse, the damage has been done. The learning cycle (see p. 66) allows for modification of training between courses, but it would be good to judge the effectiveness of training beforehand.

To do this the training manager or individual learner has to decide what mode of learning to choose. Learning in a group, one to one, using technology or a combination of all three have been analysed and compared at some length in this book already. The criteria for making a decision will be based on some or all of the following factors:

▷ Costs
▷ The number of learners
▷ Time required before learners have to be ready
▷ Availability and expertise of suitable deliverers
▷ Whether to provide it in-house or outsource it
▷ Personality and preferred learning styles of individual(s) concerned
▷ Availability of technical resources
▷ Availability of physical rooms
▷ Subject and level of expertise of subject to be learnt.

Outsourcing

Outsourcing is a serious option. Of course, it has both advantages and disadvantages and these need to be considered carefully. But does HR take the idea seriously? Big HR departments often have relatively large subdepartments – law, training, benefits and compensation, even data processing. Could any of these be beneficially or profitably outsourced?

Take training, for instance, can one really justify in-house trainers? Are they actually training enough of the time to justify being kept on? How much time do they spend 'in the classroom' and what are they doing the rest of the time?

Trainers *burn out easily*. Training must be exhausting – as any good trainer will tell you. They need to be entertainers, monitors, enthusiasts and educationalists, all at the same time. They have to coerce the unwilling, amuse the sense-of-humour failures and render the charisma-bypass manager charming. They need constant refreshing.

Trainers are notoriously *difficult to manage*. This is partly due to the sort of people that drift into training. Am-dram enthusiasts, intellectual manqués, failed preachers ... all are attracted to training. They like to do their own thing, tell their own stories, go their own way.

Most trainers are not interested in, and do not understand, business issues. Yet, employee training must be integrated with the business plan. It has to be responsive to current organizational issues. Training suffers as a result.

Many trainers become *organo-centric*. Although it may be a huge advantage that they have a full understanding and knowledge of their particular organization, they tend to know less and less about other organizations. Despite talk of benchmarking, best practice and so on, they take their eye off others and become obsessed by internal issues and politics.

Source: Furnham 2000, p. 101

There are many providers of coaching and training and judging their abilities and cost-effectiveness is fraught with difficulty. It would be nice to say that the more you pay the more you get. Certainly the big players, who tend to charge most, have quality people and products. But price is a poor predictor.

The smaller companies or individuals are inevitably more difficult to judge. They tend to charge less (they have much smaller overheads to start with) and this has an immediate attraction. Some will provide a much better service than their bigger cousins. But some will provide a poor service, however charming they appear at interview.

Having chosen the form or at least reduced the options, how can the buyer assess the providers? Is it possible to front load the whole assessment process, even to the extent of reducing evaluation costs?

There are three areas to assess: the design, the deliverers and administrative support. Similar principles apply whether considering traditional training, one to one or a technology-based program.

8.4.1 The program design

There are a number of factors which influence any program. Amongst them are:

▷ Subject and objectives of the learning
▷ Time available
▷ Numbers of participant(s)
▷ Skill and knowledge base of participant(s)
▷ Expectations of participant(s)
▷ Number of trainers
▷ Room availability
▷ Facilities in the room
▷ Budget.

These all combine to make every training program different and therefore a unique challenge.

Providers have to put together a program which maximizes the opportunities for learning, that is, they have to ensure their programs follow the known principles of learning.

Alison Hardingham (1996, pp. 61–4) identifies five key concepts for designing a program:

1. *Credibility*. Training has to be seen by participants to be relevant
2. *Commitment*. Participants must be committed to the training
3. *Risk*. Participants need to push themselves in training and do or learn new things. To do so they need to feel comfortable
4. *Attention*. People's attention fluctuates. The designer needs to introduce variation
5. *Maneuverability*. The design needs to take account of and respond to the trainees' needs and desires. These may not always be obvious before the event starts.

Chapter 4 analysed how these and other design principles can be related to a draft program. Programs can therefore be assessed before the event. The questions to ask before the event are:

▷ Is the material broken down into suitable modules or chunks?
▷ Does the program allow participants to learn from all four styles: description (theory), demonstration, experience both with help and on their own?
▷ Are there opportunities for participants to influence how they are to learn and to surface any problems either in the material being learnt or in the course administration?
▷ Is there sufficient participation?
▷ Is the material related directly to the experience or background of the participants?
▷ Is there time for proper, honest and helpful feedback?
▷ Is there formal time for reviews and reinforcement of central messages and skills?
▷ Is there sufficient variation in the course?

In short, does the program demonstrate that the course designers have knowledge of how people learn and how they can transfer that learning to the workplace?

8.4.1.1 Coaches and mentors

It is rarely possible for coaches, mentors and other one-to-one helpers to provide a formal program before the first meeting with the learner. Much will depend on what he or she wants and how much time is available. Sometimes the learner may not know exactly what is required and will need time to sort out the real issues.

Availability can be resolved as well as establishing the coach/mentors' general approach. However, much of the above should be established soon after a coach has had their first one or two sessions.

In any event prospective coaches could be asked about their methodology and how their approach fits in with the theory of learning. As will be clear from Chapter 5 on one-to-one learning, some coaching approaches are too simplistic.

8.4.1.2 Design of technology-based programs

One of the benefits of technology is that you can buy it off the shelf or more likely off the internet. This cuts costs and makes products quickly available. Unfortunately, this also means that it is hard to see what is in the package before purchase. Equally unfortunately, the package is often found wanting in training design.

Some of the issues were discussed in detail in Chapter 6. There is no reason why technology-based training packages should not conform to the basic design principles described above. The problem is that purchasers have to buy the package before they can see what is inside it. It is sometimes difficult to find the objectives on the cover or opening pages on the internet. The problem is exacerbated not only by overzealous marketing but also by a natural desire by the producers to protect the copyright of their products. By saying too much on the cover it might be possible to copy the program.

Many providers do however give useful details on the cover or on their websites. This is particularly so with true interactive programs, which do aim to provide new skills or knowledge. But few offer up a program, making it difficult to judge how they "chunk" information or whether they take their learners through all four stages of learning.

It is possible to make a tentative judgement but the proof is in trying it, which is usually only possible after the product has been bought; not a problem for training departments with big budgets, but expensive for smaller organizations.

8.4.2 Administrative support

For many learning situations the administrative burden is relatively small, but it is often complicated by the external provider having to interact with the internal HR or training department and on some occasions with participants' line managers. For technology-based programs the quality and scheduling of the helpline is essential.

When support or administrative arrangements go wrong, the negative impact on learning can be quite disproportionate to the actual disturbance. Providers should be aware of this and seek clarification and provide reassurance on a number of issues. These include:

▷ Materials to be provided (handouts, bibliographies, discs for camcorders)
▷ Details of preparations required before the course
▷ Types of and how visual aids will be used
▷ Details of extent and how evaluation should be completed
▷ Finalized program and draft letter to be issued to all participants before the event starts
▷ Who owns the copyright to the material handed out
▷ Buyers of commercial technology-based courses should be reassured that:
 ▶ There is a useful helpline preferably open 24 hours and at the weekend (for intranets the periods may be less arduous)
 ▶ There is sufficient hard copy material supporting the program
 ▶ Their computers have sufficient memory and processor speed to cope with what can often be a demanding program.

8.4.3 The deliverers

What of the people who stand up in front of the class, sit down for a coach-ing session or the designers of the technology provided for a learner? This is a topic much explored by writers of training books, some no doubt stimu-lated by a little self-glorification as they describe all their own qualities.

In fact there is little empirical research which helps the decision maker to identify the essential qualities of a deliverer, human or technical. Almost every training and coaching manual provides an intimidating and highly idealistic list of qualities and skills which a trainer or coach needs.

Hackett (2003, p. 136) produces the following list for trainers, which is suggestive rather than prescriptive:

> Interpersonal skills, negotiating and persuading skills, assertiveness, empathy, communication skills, creative skills, analytical and evaluative skills, time manage-ment skills, administrative skills, commercial awareness, technical skills, personal credibility, wide knowledge of the organization, integrity, respect for authority, tolerance of ambiguity.

Even those writing about technology-based training identify such qualities:

> E-tutors need to be positive, pro-active, patient and persistent ... The effective e-tutor needs many, many qualities, not least intuition, initiative and assertive-ness. A tutor needs to have the ability to assess students' needs by picking up on hints and reading between the lines. (Shepherd 2003a, pp. 61–2)

Do these paragons exist and if they do, aren't they just a little too perfect for the average learner to identify with?

It is possible to group the subject matter of these lists into four categories:

▷ Passion, enthusiasm, even evangelism for subject matter
▷ Flexibility, knowing how to "package the brand" differently to appeal to different individuals and groups
▷ Interpersonal skills – listening, rapport building, self-awareness, spoken and written skills
▷ Knowledge of the topic, how people learn and commitment to update both subject and learning material.

8.4.3.1 Qualification

Is there a qualification which would assure employers needing a coach or trainer that those they employ have the above qualities? What kind of exper-ience should be required?

The problem is that there is no universally accepted single qualification, but there are many bodies who offer qualifications of some sort. The prob-lems are further exacerbated because helping people to learn is something that happens all the time and in every office.

Staff are often drafted into a training department to help run a course, design it or give presentations. Few have any formal training. Every staff manager has a responsibility to develop his or her staff. They do so mostly through coaching.

The CIPD training and development survey for 2004 reported that line managers are the most likely to deliver coaching, with a third of respondents reporting that they delivered a majority of coaching and a further quarter reporting that line managers deliver about half of the coaching activities (Jarvis 2004). Helping others to learn is not a skill limited to professionals who call themselves coach, mentor or trainer, nor should it be.

The skills required are familiar to anyone who has been through management training; consider again the desirable qualities of a trainer quoted from Hackett above. Supervisor, line manager and leadership courses all seek to develop people with those same skills and qualities.

Not everyone is comfortable standing in front of a class of people or constructing a coaching session, but a four- or five-day training course can turn them into competent presenters and trainers; the better ones need no more than advice (coaching) from others in the training department before running a complex training course.

This last statement and its implications will be controversial to some. There is a wholly proper concern amongst trainers and coaches to regulate the industry and introduce standards to protect their own reputation and give buyers a degree of certainty over the product. Jarvis (2004, p. 14) writes:

> In the past, the reputation of the coaching industry has been weakened by training providers who claim to produce professional coaches from five-day training courses. Coach training needs to be "fit for purpose". While there is definitely a place for short introductory courses, as with any discipline, expertise will vary depending on the length of the course, level of qualification, depth of study, practical experience and extent of supervision while studying.

The theory of learning and memory is curiously not a major feature of courses for trainers and coaches. Look at any course on coaching or training and theory receives a tiny percentage of the time and on most prospectuses or course descriptions there is no mention at all of this skill. Consider the objectives of the CIPD flagship course in Figure 8.2. The only reference to theory is in the following objective:

▷ design training that takes account of effective learning processes, learner and trainer styles and appropriate supporting technologies and resources

There may be extensive training in theory on the course, but if so, it is not considered important enough to specify in the objectives.

Of course some people are good and some are bad at helping people learn; some are better and some worse than others. Some are good at teach-

<u>On completion of the fast-track programme, you will be able to:</u>

► describe the complete training cycle from the analysis of training needs through to the evaluation of training interventions
► identify training needs at an organisational, group and individual level that support corporate strategy
► design training that takes account of effective learning processes, learner and trainer styles and appropriate supporting technologies and resources
► use your knowledge and skills to choose, construct, implement and analyse evaluation and assessment measures
► make use of the latest technological opportunities to blend e-learning strategies with more traditional methods
► display a range of participative methods including syndicate work, case studies, exercises, role-plays and management and soft skills activities.

<u>By the end of Module 1, students will be able to:</u>

► identify factors that impact on the effectiveness of the learning process
► recognise the contribution of a range of sources of information relevant to the collection of training and learning needs
► write objectives for learning sessions
► create a cohesive framework for the learning event
► consider other issues, such as copyright and licensing, diversity, legislations and codes of practice which need to be taken when designing and delivering learning events
► prepare and deliver a short sample of training
► give constructive feedback to others based on their own observations.

<u>By the end of Module 2, students will be able to:</u>

► identify the needs of the different stakeholders in the evaluation and assessment process
► identify the range and applicability of a number of different evaluation and assessment tools
► identify the factors to take into account when analysing information on evaluation and assessment
► select appropriate participative methods for given needs, taking time, cost, facilities etc into account
► prepare participative learning activities using a step-by-step approach
► run activities taking into account setting clear objectives, observation and feedback, briefing and review processes
► give constructive feedback based on their own observations

Source: http://www.cipd.co.uk/

Figure 8.2 **Objectives for the CIPD Certificate in Training Practice**

ing very particular skills to very specific types of learners. Others are more adaptable, with wide-ranging abilities. A qualification is not necessarily going to say much more than that the individuals concerned have attended a course and if the buyer has the time to do some research, discover the style and content of the course.

Trainers, coaches and those providing technology-based learning do not come cheap. It is right to ask about qualifications and they do say something. But they are never going to have the same message as, say, a lawyer, doctor, accountant, dentist, electrician or plumber producing a certificate from a college or university. Learning is universal and we all help others to do it, whether as a parent, school teacher or boss.

Amateurism and credentialism: two wrongs don't make a right

There are, particularly in the UK, two opposite and equally misleading theories about how to acquire skills in the workplace. One celebrates common-sense, experiential amateurism; the other training course credentialism. The former believes in a paucity of formal training, the latter a plethora. Both extremes in the end make for bad trainers or coaches.

The British in particular admire amateurs. Patrick Moore, the astronomer, who has no formal education, is a prototype. Some people believe that because anything can be taught, natural genius can be detected only in the untrained amateur. It is said that the four-minute miler Roger Bannister trained at night so that nobody could see him and thus had to attribute his success to ability rather than effort. It is also a received myth that before one's final exams at Oxbridge, one should be seen drunk at parties. The idea is that any fool can get a first, if they are library swots, but only really clever people can exhibit their true genius by not working at all.

There are, however, two sides to the concept of amateur. On the one hand, the word suggests an admirer, a devotee, an enthusiast who engages in a (non-paid) pursuit for the pure intrinsic joy of the activity. The word amateur has a French etymology and is linked to the concept of love. Amateur choirs or theatrical groups can "get away" with their less than perfect production by being simply very enthusiastic. The love of the activity is enough.

On the other hand, the word amateur can suggest unskillful, inexpert dabbling. To be described as amateurish is clearly an insult: it means crude, unsophisticated, even ignorant.

The school of amateurism believes that with a modicum of intelligence and common sense anyone can become a manager or trainer. There is no need for further expensive education, which is seen as a waste of time and money. What needs to be learnt, this approach asserts, is unteachable anyway. If one is able enough – that is, appropriately selected – one should be able to pick up and then refine the rudiments quite easily. Enthusiasm and some presentation and/or people skills are all one needs.

Amateurs can, of course, be very good. If they have been exposed to good models and have good systems to follow, the "uneducated" manager or trainer can do quite well. However, the chances are likely to be against them. Companies and individuals who don't believe in training are prone to the idiosyncrasies of individuals who believe their home-spun methods and theories are best.

Precisely opposed to the amateur model is the credentialist approach. Technically, a credential is a title or letter that gives evidence of status or authority to the bearer. It is a sort of paper proof of competence. Credentialists are compensatory collectors of certificates. It is not uncommon to find on a trainer or manager's card five to eight sets of letters that one has never heard of. They are members, fellows and companions of all sorts of strange management organizations, which seem to dish out awards on flimsy evidence of competence but good evidence of cash. They nearly always do not have degrees and certainly never an MBA, but believe that they can "sort of" compensate for this with a raft of other credentials.

Another sign of credentialism are coursework book-trophies. These are great binders that collect dust on office shelves but are in some sense not only proof of course attendance but of skill competence. They are never referred to after the course and may not have been examined much on it, but they somehow remain evidence of know-how in the eyes of the credentialist attendee.

The credentialist company is training obsessed. It may produce catalogues of approved in-house or specialist outside courses on everything from negotiation skills to letter writing. The assumption is that no aspect of management, however mundane or trivial, can be acquired through observation or self-learning. Everything is course worthy and there is a course for everything. Curiously, this approach believes that course attendance is sufficient in and of itself, and companies may even have elaborate charts that check off the milestones on the long and winding road of acquiring the skills.

Rarely, if ever, is it considered important by credentialists to show evidence of course efficacy, let alone relevance or cost-effectiveness. Credentialists are, however, eager to collect certificates, books and other flimflam associated with courses. And now the new universities pander to these bizarre needs by running advanced diplomas in everything from estate agency to sports management. It is easy money in the "pile them high and sell them cheap" world of credential collection.

Some courses may be extremely useful. But it is unwise to presume that any set of letters after a person's name is indicative of any particular quality. A simple MBA and PhD is worth a dozen sets of letters, but even that may be more evidence of the ability to pass particular tests and assignments than of good management.

Neither the amateur nor the credentialist is a professional. The hallmark of professionalism is conscientious workmanship. It means that people conform to the technical and ethical standard of a vocation. The army offers a good model of professional management training. Officers go through a series of courses and exercises to learn simple but important skills. There are clear systems developed to encourage the proper skills, including appraisal systems, skills and practices; because systems are followed, there is consistency over time and across different branches. The army is also less prone to following gurus" wild mood swings as they find new magic bullets in old ideas dressed up for the modern Zeitgeist. People have not fundamentally changed much over the past 500 years and if a management style and socialization process has been found that is efficient, there seems little reason to change it.

Indeed, the way in which people join professions through a lengthy and arduous apprenticeship may be a good model. An apprentice studies with, observes and learns from a master. This rather old-fashioned approach to learning seems to have been revived of late, with the very popular "master-class concept" where people literally sit at the feet of a master and learn from him or her. It suggests a great hunger for a forgotten educational method. One goes to professionals because they are well trained to deliver exacting standards. Amateurs cannot do this, however enthusiastic they may be. Nor do credentialists, who are after the certificate not the learning experience. Too much or too little of a good thing leads to equally unhappy consequences.

Source: Adapted from Furnham 2000, pp. 9–12

8.4.3.2 Experience

Experience can also say something about the deliverers, particularly those who are external to the organization. Potentially it says something more valuable than a qualification. People who have coached or trained others will bring a deeper experience and knowledge to their new client/employer. It also gives the buyer a chance to explore how well the individual has performed in similar situations.

However, a written reference is not reliable on its own. Previous clients should be interviewed, if necessary by phone. Many coaches and trainers will have worked with other coaches and trainers and they should be contacted as well. Questions probing the relevant areas mentioned above should be carefully prepared before the interviews. The answers can then be compared with those of the deliverer themselves.

How to choose consultant trainers

There are a number of important criteria to apply to the selection process.

1. Perhaps least important, but still worth considering, is the issue of *certification* and *experience*. What is the technical and general managerial knowledge base of the consultants? Are they up to date? Is it all theory and no practical experience, or all personal experience with no thinking?

2. How good are their *explanations* for their processes? Can they explain clearly and without jargon, how the intervention works and 'where the wires go?' If it is full of platitudes and hot air, or you can't understand it, it is important to challenge its nonsense. They have to explain not what they plan to do, but why they are choosing to do it.

3. You need evidence of their *evaluation studies.* How have they evaluated, and do they plan to evaluate what they do? Do they have disinterested, impartial evidence that their strategy brings about the desired effects? What is the nature of the evidence? Is it anecdotal post hoc rationalization or are there numbers involved? Who does the evaluation and can they be trusted?

4. One wants to know about the proposed *method* used. Why one rather than another? Why things in a particular order? What will these methods achieve and what are their particular drawbacks? The answers to these questions tell one quite quickly about the quality of the consultants.

5. This is perhaps the most interesting. Many clients correctly suspect that despite all the talk of uniqueness and tailoring approaches to particular and special needs (blah blah), consultants simply give the one standard, off-the-shelf answers/advice. So the trap to lure consultants into is that of *replica-*

tion. Question: how do they know the procedure will work? Answer: because it has worked in the past! But that means you are doing the same thing as you did in the past, and you promised us it would be unique!

Good consultants easily pass the five finger tests. They have the learning, can explain the process, volunteer to monitor their effectiveness, use proven methods and understand where things have really to be tailored and when not.

Once you know the answers to the questions, start haggling about price. You will be surprised how many smart, pompous, know-alls fall at the first hurdle. You won't even need to enquire about their preposterous daily rate.

Source: Adapted from Furnham 2000, p. 64

Conclusion

Training costs should be optimized; having staff that are properly skilled, have the knowledge and whose beliefs and values match those of the employers is also crucial to the success of that organization. After the event a study can be conducted to find out how effective the learning interventions have been. On the basis of that evidence, wise managers and leaders will select training programs accordingly. Kirkpatrick's four levels of evaluation remain the simplest but probably most effective way of thinking about how and what to assess.

Before the event there is much that can be done to reduce the risks of a poor intervention. A buyer of training, be it traditional classroom, coaching or technological, should consider the design of the program, the knowledge, experience and skills of the deliverer and finally the support available to the deliverer.

The issue of qualification will remain for some time. The danger is that there will be a split between those who consider themselves "professional" and who want to limit the industry to those who have specific qualifications and those who practice coaching and training inside an organization. The latter, mostly managers, do not have time or the inclination to go onto a coaching course which might take weeks out of their busy schedule. The skills needed by a good trainer and coach are similar to those needed by a good manager; the only real difference comes in the knowledge they have of learning theory and how to apply that to a learning situation. Sadly, few organizations offering training in coaching or training provide much theory.

9 Learning in a Diverse Workforce

9.1 Introduction

That people learn in different ways, have different preferences and choices is both self-evident and well established. The coach, trainer or other facilitator will hopefully have a number of processes to choose from and adapt to the needs of the learner. Those styles and processes have been discussed in detail in this book, but are they sufficient for the wide cultural mix which exists in many workplaces?

The theory and processes have been developed almost exclusively in North America and Europe. Not only do companies and organizations operate all over the world, they employ staff of many different nationalities as well as adults with disabilities, learning difficulties or mental health difficulties and who have special needs.

Class, education, employment experience and gender influence the take-up of courses; and the gap between the well and poorly educated is apparently widening, according to a survey published by the National Institute of Adult Continuing Education in England and Wales. The report highlights some of the issues facing companies and organizations all over the world:

▷ Two out of five adults are currently in education or have followed a course within the past three years.
▷ But 59% of them are from upper and middle socioeconomic groups while only 25% are from the working class.
▷ Participation by white-collar workers and skilled working-class people has remained steady since 1990, at 32% and 17% respectively.
▷ People who go into further or higher education are more likely to return to learning later. Of those who left school at 16, only a quarter are current or recent learners, compared with half of those who stayed on after 16 and three-fifths of those who continued after 20.
▷ The groups most likely to miss out on learning are ethnic minority and part-time employees.
▷ Although almost as many women as men have been involved in current and recent learning, women are reporting more difficulties in finishing courses. More women than men have to pay their own fees (35%

compared with 26%) while more men have their fees paid by their
employer (19% compared with 13%).

▷ Full-time workers are twice as likely as part-time workers to have their
learning fully or partly supported by their employer, while 37% of
women with children under four cited care of children as a barrier to
learning and more women than men reported difficulties with travel
costs (Sargeant 2000).

9.2 Physical and mental disabilities

Physical and mental disabilities are specialized areas. The purpose of including them is to flag up the issue and underline the importance of providing a
mix of learning opportunities. One of the themes of this book is that any
group of people will learn better if the medium of learning is suited to them
as individuals and to the subject to be learnt. Those who are disadvantaged
need the same considerations.

Take, for example, autism. The use of e-learning and other technology-
based learning media can be an invaluable tool for people with autism,
according to the National Autistic Society in their response to the UK
government's consultation paper *Towards a unified e-learning strategy*:

> Computers allow them to communicate in a non-verbal environment, thereby
> overcoming many of the barriers to social communication that are usually exper-
> ienced. Computers offer a context-free environment, which can help people with
> ASD who tend to focus their attention on isolated objects. ICT can be used to
> create a predictable, and therefore controllable environment. This can help the
> user to develop an awareness of self, communicate and make errors or rehearse
> problematic real life situations in a safe environment.

> "I myself have found that the internet and email facility has opened up a whole new
> world for me. I find it easier to communicate by email as I do not find it easy to
> express my feelings verbally. Also, I don't have to deal with the tone of voice and
> the body language." (person with Asperger's syndrome) (http://www.nas.org.uk)

9.3 Cultural differences

There are many sad stories of business
executives overseas misjudging how to
play a foreign audience, whether they are
negotiating, managing or socializing. The
consequences vary from losing major
deals to embarrassment.

> *We don't see things as they
> are; We see things as we are.*
>
> Anaïs Nin

In a similar way, when helping people
from different cultures to learn, the challenge is to recognize the differences
and respond to them early enough to do something about the style and

approach. The general principles of training stand good, starting with the training/learning cycle (see Figure 4.1).

Selecting trainees is not just about choosing which people need training, it is also about finding about them and their cultural, social, career, educational and development background. Trainers, TBL designers and coaches would do that with any new student or client. Working with different nationalities brings special challenges, most importantly anticipating what they might be expecting from the experience. The emphasis is on the word "might". Every one is an individual. This process should not replace what happens at the beginning of every session and that is to spend time with the people concerned and find out about them face to face.

Trompenaars and Hampden-Turner (1997) analyse the basis of cultural differences under three headings, with the first having five subheadings:

▷ Relationships with people
  ▶ Universalism v particularism
  ▶ Individualism v communitarianism
  ▶ Neutral v emotional
  ▶ Specific v diffuse
  ▶ Achievement v ascription
▷ Attitude to time
▷ Attitude to the environment

They analyse these headings in the context of businesspeople. How well do they work for those in the business of learning?

9.3.1 Universalism v particularism

Do people follow the rule of law or do they apply their own particular analysis and do what they think is best? Universalism tends to dominate in developed countries where the law is well established. It is therefore no accident that the US, where people tend to have a highly developed sense of universalism, has the largest concentration of lawyers than any other country in the world.

Running an exercise in a country where the rule of law is not so deeply engrained can present trainers with a new kind of problem. Participants may choose to interpret the "rules" of the exercise rather more liberally than a western trainer would want.

An Afghan on an interviewing skills course (run in Afghanistan) was asked to interview a role player as a candidate for a job. Both the Afghan and the role player had to assume roles in the context of filling a post in the new Afghan government (post 2001). One of the objectives of the exercise was to discover the skills and qualities of the role player candidate. They had specifically been advised against recruiting on the basis of someone's background or tribal origins. The student and the role player still could not resist discussing tribal origins and the mutual friends they had, which apparently were quite extensive. This was not part of the "warm up" stage of the interview but in the substantive part.

When challenged, the student said that he had asked about the skills and qualities, which he had, but he considered that the background and origins were still relevant and, yes, he did remember what had been said in the lectures but this was Afghanistan.

In this particular case, it may have been the poor training which had failed to convince, but the trainers were experienced and had a good record; they reported that this was not an isolated incident. It will be some time before people in Afghanistan stop taking tribal origins into consideration. For the student he knew better than the guidelines offered by the trainer. A similar course run in Norway had no problem understanding the rules of the role play.

Those belonging to a universalist group, a North American, British, Norwegian or German, take much less time to reach decisions than those in a particularist group, who feel suspicious when hurried. Reaching decisions such as when next to meet or how long a session should be might take much more time out of the program in a particularist than in a universalist society.

A group of Afghans were asked to identify a café where they should all meet mid-morning in Kabul. They had been asked to do this the previous day and had indeed discussed the issue. In the classroom they still took 20 minutes to agree which café and precisely how to describe it for the British trainer. This was not just an isolated incident. On a second course exactly the same thing happened. The British army officer was mildly exasperated!

Finally in this section it is worth mentioning the importance that particularist societies place on relationships. An American coach or trainer might find the first few meetings with a Venezuelan hard going, but gradually the relationship will warm up. If the coach has to move on and his employers want to replace him, they may well find the coachee breaks the contract. The Venezuelan is much more likely to feel contracted to the individual than the company.

9.3.2 Individualism v communitarianism

Is it more important to focus on individuals so that they can contribute to the community as and if they wish, or is it more important to consider the community first since that is shared by many individuals? The issues here are similar but here Trompenaars and Hampden-Turner are referring to those cultures which value competition (individualistic) or cooperation (communalism).

A trainer or coach from an Anglo-Saxon culture would expect an interpreter to be no more than a vessel through which words pass and in the
process renders the words passed to him or her in one language to be rendered
accurately into another. Not so in a communitarian culture. Here the interpreter will engage with the group and the speaker to mediate understanding.

Similarly, participants coming on a course in an individualist culture will
expect to be judged by their unique contributions and abilities. In communitarian cultures, their position in society is important. In a classroom the
most important people will sit at the front and will tend to ask the questions,
while those of lower status may be at the back of the classroom.

9.3.3 Neutral v emotional

Of all the dimensions this is probably the one most easily recognized. The
Scandinavians are typically believed to be unemotional and undemonstra-
tive; those from a Latin culture flamboyant and very expressive in their
body language.

For someone helping a learner from an opposing side of this particular
dimension, adjusting can be a problem. A neutral person does not reveal
what they are thinking or feeling; an emotional person will reveal thoughts
and feelings. Neutral people tend to avoid physical contact, gesturing or
facial expression; an emotive person will touch, gesture and use strong facial
expressions. A neutral person will often read out a lecture in a monotone; an
emotive person will speak fluidly and dramatically and even if they do have a
script will depart from it regularly.

For those delivering learning, it is worth bearing in mind that learners
from a neutral culture will tend to put much more emphasis on the words
used; they will appreciate handouts with plenty of accompanying notes; they
will focus on the proposition and not the deliverer of the message. They may
look uninterested, but that is their way and not necessarily the case.

Learners from an emotional culture will show enthusiasm, will often
openly express goodwill and will expect a warm response. Their readiness to
agree or disagree with an argument, sometimes with a little histrionics, does
not mean that they have made up their mind. They tend to focus on the
presenter as a person and less on the words used.

9.3.4 Specific v diffuse

To what extent do trainers and coaches become involved with the learners?
Those from specific cultures will tend to treat their training or coaching as
relating only to the work in question. They may be standoffish, with a clear
sense of boundaries. They will deliver the course or discuss specific issues and
not move into other areas or engage people on other matters. If overseas they
will tend to go back to the hotel and not try to create a social relationship.

Those from more diffuse societies will be willing to engage on a much wider scale. They will allow the conversation to move into more personal areas or those which at work might not have been included in the agreed objectives of the course or sessions beforehand.

> In Singapore a trainer was running a Training for Trainers course which lasted a week. His students and hosts took him out every night. The same happened in Brunei a few months later. Conversation was wide-ranging and husbands and wives were introduced. The same course run in Scandinavia produced only one evening invitation and that was a formal dinner at the end of the course to say thank you.

9.3.5 Achievement v ascription

Are people judged according to what they have accomplished or by their age, kinsmen, gender or connections? Are people more interested in what someone is qualified in or where they qualified? If asked about another's education, will they respond by saying they went, for example, to Oxford or by saying they read mechanical engineering?

This has a number of implications for those in the learning business. An achievement-oriented society will be impressed by the coaching company whose staff have a long list of qualifications, whereas those coming from ascriptive societies will want to know about other clients and any references.

In some countries, the award of a certificate is an important part of the course and a ceremony is expected at the end of the course when the certificates are handed out. Those from an achievement culture will prefer a certificate which gives details of the course content and what they did; the ascriptive learners would prefer the emphasis to be on who gave the course and where they came from.

An aspect of this status issue is the attitude that learners have in different societies to their teachers, be they lecturers, trainers, coaches or mentors. In many countries the teacher has considerable status and children and university students are expected to treat them with respect. This can be disconcerting for some trainers and coaches who expect to have to work for this respect and not be given it automatically at the first meeting.

> A trainer from the UK went to Bangladesh to give a Training for Trainers course and arrived some 40 minutes early for the first day of his course (this was later than he would have wanted but he was dependent on his hosts for transport and they assured him that 40 minutes was more than enough). The director of the training institute greeted him at the door and took him to his office. They took his CD-ROM and loaded it up on the PC without the trainer being there. Shortly after 9am, the official start of the course, the trainer was taken to the classroom to find his students at their desks and sitting in rows. They stood up immediately on his entrance and politely greeted him with a chorus of good morning.

This was radically different from his normal start, where he would have been in the classroom early enough to set up his own equipment and greet the students as they arrived. He did manage to reject the rather heavy mahogany lectern but it took some hours before he was able to get them comfortable with the idea that they should not be in rows.

As the course was about training, these issues were raised during the week. All the students could see the learning advantages of a closer and more informal relationship between learners and trainer, but they explained this was what their students, who would not be from such a high intellectual level, would expect. They would take advantage of a less structured regime.

9.3.6 Attitude to time

There are many ways to judge people's attitudes to time in different cultures. A dinner party in Sweden starts at 7pm and guests arrive at two minutes to seven; in the UK dinner is usually an hour later and guests arrive between ten and 20 minutes past the hour. Closer to the Mediterranean, dinner is even later and guests can be up to 45 minutes late. In India guests can arrive anytime up to 11pm for dinner but as soon as it is eaten they leave. Some say that in Latin America guests may even arrive the following day, but this is perhaps apocryphal!

Trainers and coaches do not usually have the same problems with the start of their courses, but the tendencies are there. A course run in Sweden starts at the appointed time and sessions are expected to last as indicated in the program. In Namibia the program provides only a rough guide to what might happen. If the coach or trainer wants to move items around, the learners will not be in the least concerned; much less so in Northern Europe.

There are other and perhaps more significant implications for how different peoples consider aspects of time. Trompenaars and Hampden-Turner (1997) consider cultural views of time on two scales: how cultures see the relative importance of the past, present and future and whether activities are carried out sequentially or synchronically.

If a culture values the past and tends to see events and business in the light of what has happened before, a trainer or coach would be wise to relate the learning to the history not only of the country concerned but the trainer's own cultural antecedents. When the future is more significant, such retrospective linking will not be helpful, indeed it may be seen as irrelevant. Links should then be to events which have a future or potential.

Countries such as France, Russia and Venezuela have a strong sense of the past and a presentation with references to the FrenchRevolution, Tolstoy or Bolivar, as appropriate, would be well received. Japan, Malaysia, Germany and the US do not rate their history so significantly. For citizens of these countries, a presentation with links and anecdotes from the world of modern technology, industrial and manufacturing excellence and the future potential of their economies would be better.

Trompenaars and Hampden-Turner illustrate this by using circles to represent the past, present and future, basing the results on the work of Tom Cottle. Candidates were asked to think of the past, present and future as circles and then to draw three circles representing past, present and future using different size circles and if they wished the circles could interlink. The results were as shown in Figure 9.1.

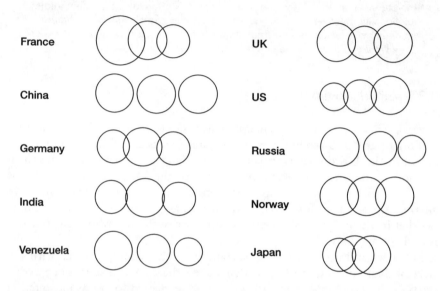

Figure 9.1 **Past, present and future**
Source: Adapted from Trompenaas and Hampden-Turner 1997, based on Cottle 1967

For those cultures which appreciate a sequential time line, learners are more likely to respond well to doing one thing at a time, and having mastered that skill or piece of knowledge they will then tackle the next. Appointments are scheduled in advance and kept to. Those more inclined to a synchronic approach are happy doing more than one activity at a time. Appointments are approximate, the relationship with people is more important.

9.3.7 Attitude to the environment

Some cultures see the major focus affecting their lives and the origins of vice and virtue as residing within the person. Here motivations and values are derived from within. Other cultures see the world as more powerful than individuals. They see nature as something to be feared or emulated. (Trompenaars and Hampden-Turner 1997, p. 10)

Learners who feel they are in control of their own destiny will make their own minds up. They will want to see evidence before they are convinced. Those who feel that fate determines their future are often more flexible, willing to accept compromise and accept the views of other more senior, experienced people. A trainer needs to be patient with this cultural group, to be gently persistent and maintain the relationship if they are to make any headway.

Other writers use slightly different analytical tools. Philip Rosinski (2003) uses a "cultural orientations framework" which has 17 dimensions:

▷ Control/harmony/humility
▷ Scarce/plentiful
▷ Monochromic/polychromic
▷ Past/present/future
▷ Being/doing
▷ Individualistic/collectivistic
▷ Hierarchy/equality
▷ Universalist/particularist
▷ Stability/change
▷ Competitive/collaborative
▷ Protective/sharing
▷ High context/low context
▷ Direct/indirect
▷ Affective/neutral
▷ Formal/informal
▷ Deductive/inductive
▷ Analytical/systemic.

Hofstede (1991) produced some influential research on cultures and developed the concept of a power distance index, based on a study of the multinational employees in IBM. The study does not lend itself so well to understanding how learners might behave in the classroom or with a coach, but it does give a stimulating insight into the minds of those nationalities and how to work with them.

Those in the learning business spend some time thinking about their learners before they plan a course or a session. Whichever tools they choose to use to help them, the starting point for all should be to think about their own cultural background. By knowing their own preferences, they will better understand how to respond in the face of others. Trompenaars and Hampden-Turner's seven headings are a good place to start the process of analysing their own culture.

9.4 Language

The English-speaking world and the English in particular feel that they have a great advantage because it is the dominant language of the internet, science and to a large extent international business. There should, however, be a large health warning notice around the neck of anyone entering into a world where the mother tongue of others is different. This applies to trainers, TBL designers and coaches in particular.

The nuances of all languages are almost infinite and while listeners might get the drift of what is being said in a foreign language, the subtleties may well be lost. Furthermore, people are reluctant to admit that they have missed big chunks of the spoken word. The chances for misunderstanding are much greater than believed.

Trainers, who are used to the transmit mode more than most in the learning business, can forget their audience is not as proficient in their language as they would like to admit. Coaches and trainers might think they have understood what a learner was saying but may miss the point.

There are a number of things a learning provider operating in their own language with learners speaking another language can do to minimize misunderstandings. All the skills of an active listener are needed.

In brief, interpret all the signals: observe the eyes, the body language and listen to the tone of voice. Look for any signs of discomfort, indications they have not quite understood what has been said or that they are losing concentration.

Secondly, demonstrate that the learner is being listened to. Encourage him or her to speak and give them time to express their views or questions. Of all the listening skills the one which is probably most helpful is to paraphrase what the other has just said. This gives them time to think whether this is really what they want to say and it does ensure that the listener has really understood the point. This applies to people who appear to have a high standard in the foreign language. Complacency is a real threat when people think they or the other is "bilingual" – very few are, but many sound as if they are.

When speaking, deliverers also have to take care. The most common faults are:

▷ *Speaking too quickly.* There is the danger of appearing patronizing, speaking very slowly can be infuriating, particularly if the speaker follows the caricature of the English abroad and speaks loudly as well! When using our own language with others with the same native tongue, people tend to speak quickly. By using sensitive listening skills, it should be possible to judge when the speed of speech is about right.
▷ *Complex sentence structure and overuse of subjunctives and conditionals.* Keep sentences short and simple. This applies to the ideas as well. Presenters should be skilled at breaking down their ideas and this will be reflected in the language used.
▷ *The words themselves.* The fact that the same word in English can have different meanings in other parts of the English-speaking world is well known and the subject of many cartoons and joke books. It is just as important to recognize that some words have a cultural baggage. "Respect", for example, has a different connotation in cultures where status is important as opposed to achievement.

In addition, there are the usual caveats about using difficult words and jargon.

9.4.1 Translation and interpretation

Using an interpreter is often avoided, wherever possible. This is wrong. Of course there are bad interpreters, but most are good and with a little preparation they can be a godsend and even add to the quality of the presentation. There are a number of advantages:

▷ As the interpreter is speaking, the speaker has a few seconds to think about what they are going to say next. This should mean that the next sentence is shorter, pithier and slang or difficult words can be avoided.
▷ While the speaker is speaking, the audience, not able to understand what he is saying, will be able to think about the previous intervention and if they wish take notes.

(These do not apply when the interpretation is simultaneous.)

Providing learners with time is a bonus. They are more likely to absorb what is being said and the speaker can concentrate more easily on packaging what they have to say in small, easily understood parcels. The chances are that they will learn more.

Time spent with the interpreter before a meeting or session is valuable. This enables the interpreter to get used to the presenter's language and way of speaking. It is also possible to talk through the ideas and objectives. This is particularly important in cultures with a strong "communitarian" bias where interpreters are likely to want to go beyond the strict mechanics of interpreting.

Handouts and visuals should, whenever possible, be translated into the language of the learner. At the least they should be shown to and discussed with the interpreter beforehand.

Gained in translation

The impressive skills of the simultaneous translator are ever in demand; partly as a function of the remorseless growth of the EC and world trade in general. So we need people to translate Czech into Dutch, Finnish into Portuguese and Polish into Greek. How long will we have to wait before there are demands for Catalan into Welsh or Irish into the musical language of the Laps (Saumi).

Written translation is one thing; simultaneous interpretation quite another. It won't be long before we will have good computer-generated translations from one text to another. Until then, scholarly language students scrupulously translate dreary policy documents searching for synonyms for "subsidiarity" or "set aside".

Written translators are often scholars, but interpreters need to be actors as well. They have various tasks. Sometimes they shadow their (literally) Great Leader. So, in the old days when we had more than one superpower it was not uncommon to see the American and Russian translators just behind their bosses, subtly, sotto voce and almost ventriloquently informing their man what the other said. Interestingly, the leaders did not look at their co-linguist informant. They smiled, nodded and non-verbally looked at their opposite number directly – and for good reason.

There are also conference (press announcement, business/educational seminar) translators. Many sit in glass-faced boxes like porta-confessionals, so that they can see the speaker and his/her slides but not necessarily (certainly not the faces of) the audience. And in this soundproof cabin, they endeavour to faithfully repeat what was said.

The other type appear "on stage" with the speaker, who stops at the end of every sentence or major clause to hear the words translated. The former is monologue, often monotone, the latter staccato. No doubt audiences and individuals have strong preferences for either type, according to their linguistic ability and the topic of the address.

Few speakers enjoy the experience of interpretation, as much for what is gained as what is lost. Everyone is aware of how written notices in different languages can take up quite different amounts of words/space. Some languages seem better for certain functions: hence George III purportedly spoke to his horse in German, his cook in French and his lover in Italian.

The simultaneous translator has to find the right phrase, simile or metaphor immediately. It might not even exist but you can't hang about so a substitute has to be found. And as for jokes – many know they are often unwise and backfire, but can't resist it to liven up the speech.

Good speakers often do puns, asides and glory in the possibilities of the language. Alliteration can be a very powerful mnemonic device as can onomatopoeia. Some words simply taste and sound better than others. Somehow "lugubrious" sounds faintly ridiculous and "vicissitude" pretentious.

But more than *what* is said, it is *how* it is said. Timing, timbre and pitch are all important. Watch a dubbed favorite movie with a known star. The dubbing actor may do timings well but quality of voice is crucial. The chuckle, the sardonic laugh, characteristic patterns get changed and it makes a difference.

Paralinguistic features of communication are so important that some people believe it is as easy to detect a liar on the phone as face to face. Latency of response (speed in answering), pitch raises at the end, linguistic distancing (not using "me"), holding silences, umm-ing and err-ing all create a powerful impression.

In this sense simultaneous translation does not exist. Translation has a precise meaning and a precise process. Psychologists do back translations to ensure nothing is lost or gained. The questionnaire is translated from language A to B by a fluent cross-cultural traveller. A different person from a similar background translates from B to A. The scientist compares the two versions of A.

Interpreters, at best, get the gist of what is being said. But they can't do how it is said. Can they get mocking irony and if so how is it translated? Americans can't understand British irony, understatement or humor. How would a translator convey these? Audiences look at the translator and speaker if both are on stage. They resemble centre court spectators at Wimbledon, heads swivelling in unison from left to right and back again. But it is the interpreter's vocals and non-verbals that convey subtle and extra meaning. On stage speakers have to be taught about gesturing. Translators may have also been taught but many gesticulate in order to emphasize concepts.

No wonder that presidents look at each other while translators whisper in their ears. What is being said is as important as how and when it is said. And for most it is less worrying that things are lost in translation than what they do not want, understand or intend is gained.

9.5 Social differences

As organizations, companies and governments seek greater productivity, they will increasingly turn to every element of society to maximize their potential. There are other drivers as well. Pensions are becoming increasingly expensive. The demographics of the world's population presents a challenging picture. In 2002, 7% of the world's 6.2 billion population were over the age of 65; in 2050 it is estimated that 17% of a world population of 9.1 billion will be over 65 (Marie-Therese Claes, taken from a speech to SIETAR Europe, Berlin, 2 April 2004).

Age, educational, social, gender and ethnic diversity are going to present the deliverer of learning with new challenges in the coming decades. All have something to offer and the rewards are potentially great for all concerned. The principles are the same: the deliverer has to get to know their audience and relate the learning to their experience.

9.6 Conclusion

Delivering learning overseas or to people with a different background and culture is usually rewarding and challenging; it can also be very frustrating. Deliverers have to accept this new dimension.

A cross-cultural study of management development

Sparrow (personal communication 1995) contrasted the attitudes to management development of companies in different countries.

USA

▶ Management is considered something separate, definable, generalizable, teachable.

▶ The climate is of expansion, oversupply of space, undersupply of resources and time.

▶ Drive, entrepreneurialism, versatility, adaptability and opportunism favored.

▶ Empirical thinking, numerical skills, personal experience (not society's codified wisdom) are valued.

▶ Man-management skills, social and political skills, and leadership are considered important.

▶ Training and thinking focusses on basic character: personality and behavior are thought to underlie most skills.

▶ Trial period of 5–7 years before being assessed for management.

▶ Vertical moves through functional hierarchies – career anchor jobs are usual.

► Formal assessment of general management potential through assessment centers, and so on.

► Mobility within internal labor market; skills believed transferable.

► 80/20 internal/external resourcing rule.

► High potential elites of around 10% of management population.

► Age 40 make or break for advancement.

FRANCE

► Only 13% take part in dual in–out house training courses.

► Strong central government control over education curriculum (school and university).

► Companies spend 1.5% of payroll on training by law.

► Mainly in-company training, company-specific contingencies, no more than needed for the job.

► Training does not improve external mobility for most managers.

► Little training for manual workers; resources biased towards off-the-job management training.

► Elite political model: tall hierarchy, intricate careers, patronage, mobility.

► Legally defined "cadres": five years' study at grande ecoles after baccalaureat.

► Preparatory test for grandes ecoles final selection.

► Headquarters in Paris.

► Pantouflage – movement from civil service to private industry.

► Management is a position from which it is legitimate to hold authority.

► Management is an intellectual task, not interpersonally demanding educated cleverness.

► Advertisements for managerial jobs stress reasoning ability, analysis, synthesis, evaluation, articulation.

GERMANY

► Sophisticated system of vocational education and training.

► Dual system of school/company experience.

► Triple stakeholders in training: company, trade unions, government.

► School leavers selected for company programs.

► Broad competences values: managers and manual workers have common exposure.

► Low supervision mentality, greater control of quality, that is, supervision is found in early stages in any process.

► Blurred divisions between supervisors, technical staff, manual workers.

▶ Employees rotate through two or more jobs usually.

▶ Promotion dependent on starting qualifications, nature of work, access to training.

▶ Management development function neither company-specific nor strategic.

▶ No MBA educational philosophy.

▶ Job grades have more validity than skills or competences.

▶ Two-year part-time course for managers who are "late age" graduates.

▶ Highest proportion of PhDs in the world in management.

▶ Functional career model – move in same sector, contiguous functions.

▶ Managers must manage something – select on functional and technical knowledge.

▶ Career development coincides with increased skill specialization.

JAPAN

▶ Tradition which links education level with business success.

▶ Education is seen as a means of self-improvement.

▶ Senior members required to "take care of" younger members.

▶ Propensity to learn anything of value to the group, that is, share learned information, and knowledge for perceived corporate good.

▶ Exclusive "outside shunning" corporate culture – stronger internal bonding.

▶ Planning and organization of development activities over long term and on grand scale with other Japanese participants.

10 Conclusion

10.1 Four maxims

The introduction to the book posed questions about whether those involved in helping others to learn were delivering a quality product. The intervening chapters have examined the state of the learning industry. The methods and techniques of trainers, coaches, mentors, consultants and the providers of technology-based learning have been reviewed and the issue of value for money has been addressed. What conclusions can we draw from this examination and what of the future of learning?

There are many excellent learning products of all varieties in the market and in training departments in big and small companies. What do they provide which others should aspire to? There are four maxims, which when practiced will turn providers of learning into legends of the learning business.

10.1.1 Maxim 1: Excellent practice from best theory

There is a scientific basis to the understanding of memory and learning. The mysteries of the brain are gradually being unraveled. Learning may be instinctive when we are young but instinct does not have much influence in the institutions of the workplace. By the time we are adult, self-esteem, fear of failure, cognitive ability and the whole aging

> *He who learns but does not think is lost. He who thinks but does not learn is in great danger.*
>
> Confucius (551–479 BC)

process affect our approach to learning. Learning ability is also affected by the motivation to learn. If people want to learn, they will do so however poor the material provided or delivered to them. If they see no reason why they should learn, they will not.

The challenge today is maximizing the learning potential of the whole workforce. There is not much place in the training world for the gifted amateur, for the consultant who can only deliver a good-looking package, for an e-learning product that sings and dances but has no practical learning value at all.

Unfortunately, neither big names nor major qualifications guarantee knowledge of, or good practice in, training. There is little evidence if any that the big companies involved in training, coaching or consultancy pay much attention to *how* people learn. They rely on existing programs and a well-packaged product. Their courses are tried and tested and produce results, but are rarely evaluated, let alone benchmarked against known theory. The course and training objectives tend to be about the end product, the presentation and the process.

Courses on coaching put considerable emphasis on such issues as non-directional methods or about how to build rapport with the learner; important subjects but they leave the student with little flexibility. The non-directive style of coaching is paradoxically promoted in a very directive manner.

Much technical training is in a highly limited straitjacket because of the nature of technology. It often looks initially attractive because it is well designed and responds directly to the learner and no one else. The product is appealing to like-minded technocrats but less so to those not so sympathetic to the digital age.

It is possible to look good as a trainer or coach or produce a neat package of technical training and help people to learn, without knowing learning theory. There are inspirational speakers and role models who people will follow to the ends of the earth. They have an important place in any organization's learning structure.

Learning inevitably involves many people. They might not quite constitute a team but they are bound by one objective – to promote the maximum development of employees. The learner has some important issues to explain, the employer, the boss, the training manager and, in the case of technology, the designers all have a role to play. Among this group someone has to know the business of learning.

10.1.2 Maxim 2: Adopt a flexible approach to learners' abilities and circumstances

One of the attractions of being a trainer or coach is that every course is different; it is the people on the courses or the clients who make it so. The group dynamic is different every time.

As we saw in Chapter 9, audiences are becoming increasingly varied. Retirement age is increasing, learners come from a rich mix of cultures and social backgrounds. The challenge for trainers is to respond to the

> *The illiterate of the year 2000 will not be the individual who cannot read and write, but the one who cannot learn, unlearn and relearn.*
>
> Alvin Toffler
> US social commentator

mix and the needs of the individuals. Training has to be fit for purpose; knowledge of the learner's skills and preferences is an essential prerequisite.

But it is not just the learner. There are other customers. Those who pay, HR, the manager all have a role to play in influencing the nature of learning. The delivery will increasingly be scrutinized and trainers will have to respond.

10.1.3 Maxim 3: Develop relevant personal qualities

Writers in the training and coaching business provide long lists of the ulti-mate qualities of a trainer or coach. Their picture of such a supertrainer is not always an attractive one. Paragons of virtue are difficult to relate to. Eccentricity and quirkiness can be attractive even if they do occasionally stray away from political correctness.

Personal qualities are important for a good trainer. Not everyone can be inspirational, but all good trainers should be enthusiastic, know or care about the subject and provide up-to-date material. They set high standards. They do not have to be the best in their subject but they have to bring some-thing special to the subject (consider, for example, some of the greatest sports coaches).

10.1.4 Maxim 4: Giving value for money

There are two parts to the equation; the easy part is the cost or the price charged by the consultant, trainer or coach. The hard part is ensuring that there are results and that trainers encourage proper evaluation of their work. Only then can they learn how to improve and stay at the top of the tree and become a legend of the learning business. Consultants and coaches can be "reassuringly expensive", but above all they have to ensure that learning happens.

The issue is how to evaluate training. Trainers must confront return on investment questions explicitly and sensibly; after all everything that exists, exists in some quantity and can therefore be measured.

10.2 Transfer of Learning

For training to be most effective, what is learnt during training must be applied to the job. In fact, the more closely a training program matches the demands of the job, the more effective the training will be (Baldwin and Ford 1988). By using sophisticated computer-based techniques to simulate real flight conditions carefully, airline pilot trainees can learn what it is like to manipulate their craft safely, without actually risking their lives and expen-sive equipment. Naturally, training that is any less elaborate in the degree to which it simulates the actual work environment is less effective (for example, a home computer flight-simulation game).

Porteous (1997) has argued that transfer of training is improved if five steps are put in place:

1. *Overlearning of skills:* All skills should be practiced until completely profi-cient.
2. *Principles:* Workers should fully understand *why* something is done or works, not merely *how* to do it.

3. *Realistic simulations:* Training is best done with real equipment, real customers and in real situations.
4. *Adaptive:* Training should include ambiguous, tricky or unusual situations so that trainees find their own solutions outside regular procedures.
5. *Monitoring:* Newly trained staff need monitoring and updating, showing when and whether they are practicing new skills.

The success of transfer from the training to the work setting depends on various things. For instance, successful transfer is a function of:

▷ *Time:* the amount of positive transfer decreases as a function of time.
▷ *Task similarity:* having to learn a new response to an "old" stimulus leads to negative transfer.
▷ *Amount of initial learning:* the more (and better) the learning on the initial task, the better the transfer.
▷ *Task difficulty:* there is greater transfer from a difficult task to an easier task than vice versa.
▷ *Knowledge of results:* feedback affects performance but not learning.

Transfer of learning ensures generalizability of training over time, skills and place. It is a fundamentally important issue.

10.3 The Future Challenge

That learning in the workplace has a future is not an issue. Companies have to stay on top and to do so they need their employees to be knowledgeable, skilful, creative and committed. The test will be whether trainers and their associated organizations can raise their standards to meet the challenges of modern business. Training departments should be seen as indispensable and leading the way. They are rarely in such a position.

Three conditions are necessary to change:

1. Those in the learning business have to be well suited to the job and themselves eager to learn
2. Companies and organizations should provide a variety of learning options that make a difference to employees
3. Trainers should think strategically about the whole business.

The one follows from the other. Only when the profession attracts high-quality people will they be able to sit comfortably and be welcome at the top table (that is, the board). It is not just about employers appointing good people to their training departments. Trainers have to work hard to gain the respect of their peers. Like other successful workers, they need to be innovative, keep abreast of new learning techniques and provide the best products for the job.

Governing bodies also have to play their part and raise their game. The ASTD and the CIPD have to set high standards. That is not just about best practice and ethics but about intellectual standards and rigor. HR and training in particular, has too comfortable an image. There are too many tree huggers and not enough minds that are focussed and business-like.

> *An MBA's first shock could be the realization that companies require experience before they hire a chief executive officer.*
>
> Robert Half, American personnel agency executive

Quality does not come from qualifications alone. Examinations and certificates play their part but it is how people apply their knowledge and whether they genuinely seek to keep up with developments in their profession. Do they set the example as lifelong learners? Those representing the profession have to be at the cutting edge of the learning business, intellectually and in practice.

Training departments should really welcome innovation. The concept of "blended learning" is not new; the Open University has adopted such an approach for decades. The debate over what blended learning has to offer is, however, welcome. Technology has much to offer, but so does a good coach or mentor, as does a trainer with a group of people interacting efficiently to stimulate learning.

> *Who dares to teach must never cease to learn.*
>
> John Cotton Dana (1856–1929)

When there are excellent people in the business, learning will naturally rise to the top of the agenda and trainers will take their place on the board. Indeed, a recent study showed that the single best predictor of being a business high flyer was whether a person constantly sought out new learning opportunities. If those in the learning business want a more influential position, they need to earn it. If companies care about maximizing the full potential of employees, they need to appoint excellent people to training positions.

Bibliography

Adams, J., Hayes, J. and Hopson, B. (1976) *Understanding and Managing Personal Change*, London, Martin Robinson

Alimo-Metcalfe, B. (1998) 360-degree feedback and leadership development, *International Journal of Selection and Assessment*, 6: 35–44

Armstrong, M. (2001) *Human Resource Management Practice*, London, Kogan Page

Atkinson, R.C. and Shiffrin, R.M. (1968) Human memory: a proposed system and its control processes. In Spence, K.W. (ed.) *The Psychology of Learning and Motivation: Advances in Research Theory*, New York, Academic Press

Atkins, P. and Wood, R. (2002) Self versus others ratings as predictors of assessment center ratings: validation evidence for 360-degree feedback programs, *Personnel Psychology*, 55: 871–901

Baddeley, A. (2003) *Essentials of Human Memory*, (2nd edn) Hove, East Sussex, Psychology Press

Baldwin, T. and Ford, K. (1998) Transfer of Training, *Personnel Psychology* 41: 63–101

Bandura, A. (1977) Self-efficacy: toward a unifying theory of behavioural change, *Psychological Review*, 84: 191–215

Bartlett, F. (1932) *Remembering*, Cambridge, Cambridge University Press

Bee, F. and Bee, R. (1994) *Training Needs Analysis and Evaluation*, London, CIPD

Boud, D. and Garrick, J. (1999) *Understanding Learning at Work*, London, Routledge

Boyd, R. (1980) *Redefining the Discipline of Adult Education*, San Francisco, Adult Education Association of the USA

Buzan, T. (1995) *Use your Memory*, London, BBC Books

Buzan, T. (2004) *Mind Maps at Work: How to Be the Best at Work and Still Have Time to Play*, London, HarperCollins

Cattell, R. (1986) The 16PF personality structure and Dr Eysenck, *Journal of Social Behaviour and Personality*, 1, 153–60

Chapman, T., Best, B. and van Casteren, P. (2003) *Executive Coaching: Exploding the Myths*, Basingstoke, Palgrave Macmillan

Chatman, J.A., Caldwell, D.F. and O'Reilly, C.A. (1999) Managerial personality and performance: a semi-idiographic approach, *Journal of Research in Psychology*, 33: 514–45

CIPD (2003) *E-Learning: The Learning Curve*, London, CIPD

CIPD (2004) *Training and Development 2004, Survey Report*, London, CIPD

Clutterbuck, D. (2001) *Everyone Needs a Mentor*, London, CIPD

Cook, M. (2004) *Personnel Selection*, Chichester, Wiley

Cottel, T. (1967) The circles test: an investigation of perception of temporal relatedness and dominance, *Journal of Projective Techniques and Personality Assessments*, (131): 58–71

Covey, S.R. (2004) *Habits of Highly Effective People*, London, Simon & Schuster

Cox, R.H. (1990) *Sport Psychology: Concepts and Applications*, 2nd edn, Dubuque, Wm. C. Brown

Craig, R. and Sittel, L. *Training and Development Issues*, New York, McGraw-Hill

Cranwell-Ward, J., Bossons, P. and Gover, S. (2004) *Mentoring: A Henley Review of Best Practice*, Basingstoke, Palgrave Macmillan

Davies, D. (1989) *Psychological Factors in Competitive Sport*, Lewes, Falmer Press

Demming, W.E. (2000) *Out of the Crisis*, Cambridge, MA, MIT Press

Department for Education and Skills (2003) *Towards a unified e-learning strategy*, Nottingham, DfES Publications

Downey, M. (2003) *Effective Coaching*, New York, Texere

Dublin, L. (2004) *The Nine Myths of E-Learning Implementation: Ensuring Your Real Return on Your E-Learning Investment*, ASTD, www.astd.org/astd/Conferences/ICE/NineMyths.htm

Dweck, C. (2000) *Self Theories: Their role in Motivation, Personality, and Development*, Philadelphia, Psychology Press

Edwards, M. and Ewen, A. (1996) 360-degree assessment: royal fail or "holy grail", *Career Development International*, 1: 28–31

Egan, G. (1986) *The Skilled Helper: Systematic Approach to Effective Helping*, Belmont, Wadsworth

Elliott, B. (1999) *Training in Sport: Applying Sport Science*, Chichester, John Wiley

Ellis, R. (2004) *E-learning Trends 2004*, Alexandria, VA, Learning Circuits

Eriksson, S.-G. (2003) *Sven-Göran Erikkson on Football*, London, Carlton Books

Eysenck, M. (1981) Learning, Memory and Personality. In Eysenck, H.J. *A Model of Personality*, Berlin, Sponger

Eysenck, H. (1985) Can personality study ever be scientific? *Journal of Social Behaviour and Personality*, 1: 3–19

Federal Consulting Group (2002) *FCG Coaching Guide*, http://www.fcg.gov/exec

Ferguson, F. (2002) *The Rise of Management Consultancy in Britain*, Aldershot, Ashgate

Fleming, I. and Taylor, A.J.D. (2003) *Coaching Pocket Book*, Alresford, Management Pocketbooks

Folkard, S., Monk, T.H., Bradbury, R. and Rosenthall, J. (1977) Time of day effects in school children's immediate and delayed recall of meaningful material, *British Journal of Psychology*

Furnham, A. (1992) *Personality at Work*, London, Routledge

Furnham, A. (1996) *The Myths of Management*, London, Whurr

Furnham, A. (1999) *The Psychology of Behaviour at Work*, Hove, Psychology Press

Furnham, A. (2000) *The Hopeless, Hapless and Helpless Manager*, London, Whurr

Furnham, A. and Stringfield, P. (1994) Congruence of self and ratings of managerial practices as a correlate of supervisors' evaluation, *Journal of Occupational and Organisational Psychology*, 67: 57–67

Furnham, A. and Stringfield, P. (1998) Congruence in job-performance ratings: A study of 360-degree feedback. Examining self, managers, peers and consultant ratings, *Human Relations*, 51: 517–30

Furnham, A. and Taylor, J. (2004) *The Dark Side of Behaviour at Work*, Basingstoke, Palgrave Macmillan

Gallwey, W.T. (2000) *The Inner Game of Work*, New York, Random House

Gardner, H. (1983) *Frames of Mind: the Theory of Multiple Intelligences,* New York, Basic Books

Goleman, D. (1996) *Emotional Intelligence,* London, Bloomsbury

Goleman, D. (1998) *Working with Emotional Intelligence,* London, Bloomsbury

Gould, D. (1998) *Mental Skills Training in Sport.* In Elliott, B. (ed.) *Training in Sport: Applying Sport Science,* Chichester, John Wiley

Gower, Sir E. (1987) *The Complete Plain Words,* London, Penguin Books

Hackett, P. (2000) *Introduction to Learning,* London, CIPD

Hackett, P. (2003) *Training Practice,* London, CIPD

Handy, C., Gordon, C., Gow, I. and Randlesome, C. (1988) *Making Managers,* Financial Times/Prentice Hall

Hardingham, A. (1996) *Designing Training,* London, CIPD

Hardingham, A. (1998) *Psychology for Trainers,* London, CIPD

Harrold, F. (2001) *Be Your Own Life Coach,* London, Hodder & Stoughton

Hofstede, G. (1991) *Cultures and Organizations: Software of the Mind,* London, McGraw-Hill

Honey, P. and Mumford, A. (1992) *The Manual of Learning Styles,* Peter Honey Publications

Hudson, F.M. (1999) *The Handbook of Coaching,* San Francisco, Jossey-Bass

Institute of Management (1999) *People Management,* London, Hodder & Stoughton

Jarvis, J. (2004) *Coaching and Buying Coaching Services,* London, CIPD

Jones, S. (1993) *Psychological Testing for Managers,* London, Judy Piatkus

Jowett, S. and Cockerill, I. (2002) Incompatibility in the coach–athlete relationship. In Cockerill, I. (ed.) *Solutions in Sport Psychology,* London, Thomson

Jung, C.G. (1923) *Psychology of Types,* London, Routledge & Kegan Paul

Kilburg, R.R. (2002) *Executive Coaching,* Washington, American Psychological Association

Kirkpatrick, D.L. (1959) Techniques for Evaluating Training Programs, *Training and Development, Journal of ASTD*

Kirkpatrick, D.L. (1998) *Evaluating Training Programs,* San Francisco, Berrett-Koehler

Klasen, N. (2002) *Implementing Mentoring Schemes,* Oxford, Butterworth Heinemann

Kline, P. (1993) *Handbook of Psychological Testing,* London, Routledge

Kline, P. (2000) *A Psychometric Primer,* London, Free Association Books

Knowles, M. (1998) *The Adult Learner,* Woburn, Butterworth Heinemann

Kolb, D.A. (1984) *Experiential Learning,* New Jersey, Prentice Hall

Korman, A. (1970) Toward a hypothesis of work behaviour, *Journal of Applied Psychology,* **54**: 31–41

Kraiger, K. (2003) Training in Organisations. In Borman, W., Ilgen, D. and Klimoski, R. (eds) *Comprehensive Handbook of Psychology,* New York, Wiley

Kremmer, J. and Scully, D. (1994) *Psychology in Sport,* London, Taylor & Francis

Lambert, A. (2001) *Obtaining Value from Executive Coaching and Mentoring,* London, Careers Research Forum

Lambert, T. (1993) *Key Management Tools,* London, Pitman

Landsberg, M. (1997) *The Tao of Coaching,* London, HarperCollins

Lenhardt, V. (2004) *Coaching for Meaning,* Basingstoke, Palgrave Macmillan

London, M. and Smither, J. (1995) Can multi-source feedback change perceptions of good accomplishment, self–evaluation and performance?, *Personnel Psychologist,* **48**: 579–88

Luft, J. (1969) Of Human Interaction: Johari Model, New York, Mayfield

Mager, R.F. (1962) Preparing Instructional Objectives, Belmont, CA, Fearon Publishers

Malone, S. (2003) *Learning about Learning,* London, CIPD

Martin, C. (2004) *The Life Coaching Handbook,* Carmarthen, Crown House

McAdam, S. (2005) *Executive Coaching,* London, Thorogood

McMurrer, D.P., Van Buren, M.E. and Woodwell, W.H. Jr. (2000) *The ASTD 2000 State of Industry Report,* Alexandria, VA, ASTD

Maslow, A. (1970) *Motivation and Personality,* New York, Longman

More, C. (1980) *Skill and the English Working Class 1870–1914,* London, Croom Helm

Morrison, D. (2003) *The Search for the Holy Recipe,* http://www.
learningcircuits.org

Morrison, D. (2004) *E-Learning Strategies,* Chichester, John Wiley

Murray, H. (1938) *Explorations in Personality,* New York, Oxford
University Press

O'Brien, D. (2000) *Learn to Remember,* London, Duncan Baird

Parslow, E. (1999) *The Manager as Coach and Mentor,* London, CIPD

Peltier, B. (2001) *Psychology of Executive Coaching, Theory and Practice,*
New York, Brunner-Routledge

Petrides, K.V. and Furnham, A. (2001) Trait emotional intelligence:
psychometric investigation with reference to established trait
taxonomies. *European Journal of Personality,* **15**: 425–48

Porteous, M. (1997) *Occupational Psycholgy,* London, Harvester
Wheatsheaf

Quinn, J.B. (1992) *Intelligent Enterprise,* New York, Free Press
Reynolds, J., Caley, L. and Mason, R. (2002) *How do People Learn?*
London, CIPD

Robertson, I.T., Baron, H., Gibbons, P., MacIver, R. and Nyfield, G.
(2000) Conscientiousness and managerial performance, *Journal of
Occupational and Organizational Psychology,* **73**: 171–80

Roddick, A. and Miller, R. (1991) *Body and Soul: How to Succeed in
Business and Change the World,* London, Ebury Press

Rosinski, P. (2003) *Coaching Across Cultures,* London, Nicholas Brealey

Rossett, A. (ed.) (2002) *The ASTD E-Learning Handbook,* New York,
McGraw-Hill

Rotella, B. (2001) *Putting Out of Your Mind,* New York, Simon &
Schuster

Salovey, P. and Mayer, J.D. (1990) Emotional Intelligence, *Imagination,
Cognition and Personality,* **9**: 185–211

Sargeant, N. (2000) *The Learning Divide Revisited,* Leicester, National
Institute for Adult Continuing Education (NIACE)

Seifert, C., Yukl, G. and McDonald, R. (2003) Effects of multi-source
feedback, *Journal of Applied Psychology* **88**: 561–5

Sheldrake, J. and Vickerstaff, S.A. (1987) *The History of Industrial
Training in Britain,* Aldershot, Avebury

Shepherd, C. (2003a) *E-learning's Greatest Hits,* Brighton, Above and
Beyond

Shepherd, C. (2003b) *Learning Object Design Assistant*, Brighton, Above and Beyond

Sloman, M. (2001) *The e-Learning Revolution*, London, CIPD

Sloman, M. (2003) *Training in the Age of the Learner*, London, CIPD

Sloman, M. (2004) Helping people learn. In Philpott, J., Thomson, I., Parsloe, E., Wolf, A. and Sloman, M. (eds) *Reflections, New Trends in Training and Development*, London, CIPD

Smither, J. and Walker, A. (2001) Measuring the impact of multi-source feedback. In Bracken, D., Timmreck, C. and Church, A. (eds) *The Handbook of Multi-source Feedback*, San Francisco, Jossey-Bass, pp. 275–88

Statt, D.A. (1994) *Psychology and the World of Work*, London, Macmillan – now Palgrave Macmillan

Starr, J. (2003) *The Coaching Manual*, Harlow, Pearson Education

Sternberg, R. (1990) *Metaphors of Mind*, Cambridge, Cambridge University Press

Stoddart, C. (2004) *Blended Learning: a Case Study*, London, CIPD, (http://www.cipd.co.uk/subjects/lrnanddev/blendlrng/blendlearn.htm?IsSrchRes=1)

Sugrue, B. and Kyung-Hyun, K. (2004) *2004 State of the Industry: Annual Review of Trends in Workplace Learning*, Alexandria, VA, ASTD

Thomas, H. and Lilley, R. (1995) *If They Haven't Heard It, You Haven't Said It! A Guide to Better Communication*, Potters Bar, Progress Press

Thorndike, E.L. (1920) Intelligence and its uses, *Harper's*, **140**: 227–35

Townsend, J. (1996) *The Trainer's Pocketbook*, London, Melrose

Trompenaars, F. and Hampden-Turner, C. (1997) *Riding the Waves of Culture*, London, Nicholas Brealey

Truss, L. (2003) *Eats, Shoots and Leaves*, London, Profile Books

Tuckman, B. (1965) Development sequences in small groups, *Psychological Bulletin*, **63**: 384–99

Von Raalte, J. and Brewer, B.W. (eds) (2002) *Explaining Sport and Exercise Psychology*, (2nd edn), Washington, American Psychology Association

Warr, P. (2000) Job Performance and the Aging Workforce. In Chmiel, N. (ed.) *Introduction to Work and Organisational Psychology*, Oxford, Blackwell

Warr, P. (2002) *Psychology at Work*, London, Penguin Books

West, L. and Milan, M. (2001) *The Reflecting Glass*, Basingstoke, Palgrave Macmillan

Whitmore, J. (2002) *Coaching for Performance*, London, Nicholas Brealey

Williams, J.M. and Krane, V. (1993) *Training in Sport*, Chichester, John Wiley

Woodward, C. (2004) *Winning!*, London, Hodder & Stoughton

Wright, J. (1980) Community Learning: A Frontier for Adult Education. In Boyd, R. (1980) *Redefining the Discipline of Adult Education*, San Francisco, Adult Education Association of the USA

Zeus, P. and Skiffington, S. (2002) *The Complete Guide to Coaching at Work*, Roseville, McGraw-Hill Australia

Useful References

Aiken, L. (1985) *Psychological Testing and Assessment*, New York, Allyn & Bacon

Anastasi, A. (1988) *Psychological Testing*, New York, Macmillan

Cohen, R., Montague, P., Nathanson, L. and Swerdlike, M. (1988) *Psychological Testing: An Introduction to Tests and Measurement*, California, Mayfield

Cook, M. (1988) *Personal Selection and Productivity*, Chichester, Wiley

Cronbach, L. (1984) *Essentials of Psychological Testing*, New York, Harper International

Groth-Marnat, G. (1984) *Handbook of Psychological Assessment*, New York, Van Nostrand Reinhold

Kline, P. (1983) *Personality: Measurement and Theory*, London, Hutchison

Taplis, J., Dulewicz, V. and Fletcher, C. (1988) *Psychological Testing: A Practical Guide*, London, Institute of Personnel Management

Index